HUMAN GEOGRAPHY
A History for the 21st Century

Edited by Georges **Benko** and Ulf **Strohmayer**

HUMAN GEOGRAPHY
A History for the 21st Century

A MEMBER OF THE HODDER HEADLINE GROUP
LONDON
Distributed in the United States of America
by Oxford University Press Inc., New York

First published in Great Britain in 2004 by
Arnold, a member of the Hodder Headline Group,
338 Euston Road, London NW1 3BH

http://www.arnoldpublishers.com

Distributed in the United States of America by
Oxford University Press Inc.
198 Madison Avenue, New York, NY10016

The advice and information in this book are believed to be true and
accurate at the date of going to press, but neither the author[s] nor the publisher
can accept any legal responsibility or liability for any errors or omissions.

British Library Cataloguing in Publication Data
A catalogue record for this book is available from the British Library

Library of Congress Cataloging-in-Publication Data
A catalog record for this book is available from the Library of Congress

ISBN 0 340 75932 1

1 2 3 4 5 6 7 8 9 10

Typeset in 10/13pt Caslon by Phoenix Photosetting, Chatham, Kent
Printed and bound in Malta

What do you think about this book? Or any other Arnold title?
Please send your comments to feedback.arnold@hodder.co.uk

CONTENTS

LIST OF CONTRIBUTORS

Mark Bassin is Reader in Geography at University College, London. His research focuses on the geography of identity and nationalism, as well as political theory and the history of geopolitics. He has held research fellowships at the Kennan Institute, New York University, the American Academy, Berlin and the Institut für Europäische Geschichte, Mainz and has received grants from the Fulbright Foundation, the British Academy and DAAD. His *Imperial Visions: nationalist imagination and geographical expansion in the Russian Far East 1840–1865* was published by Cambridge University Press in 1999.
Address: Department of Geography, UCL, 26 Bedford Way, London WC1H 0AP, United Kingdom, m.bassin@geog.ucl.ac.uk

Georges Benko is a Professor at the University Panthéon-Sorbonne and Researcher at CEMI (Centre d'Études des Modes d'Industrialisation) and EHESS (École des Hautes Études en Sciences Sociales), Paris. He is the founding editor of *Géographie, économie, société* (Paris) and a member of the editorial boards of more than 16 journals, including *Economic Geography* and *L'Année de la régulation*. His work covers economic geography, planning, French regulation theory and social theory. He is the author of over 200 articles and numerous books, and has edited, with Ulf Strohmayer, *Space and Social Theory* (1997, Oxford: Blackwell) and *Geography, History, and Social Sciences* (1995, Dordrecht: Klüwer).
Address: Université Panthéon-Sorbonne, 191, rue Saint-Jacques, 75005 Paris, France, gb@univ-paris1.fr

Vincent Berdoulay is a Professor at the University of Pau, Chair of a CNRS research centre (Laboratoire Société-Environnement-Territoire) and Chair of the IGU Commission on the History of Geographical Thought. He studied in Bordeaux, France and the United States, where he received his Ph.D. from the University of California, Berkeley. He also held a position in Canada (University of Ottawa) before moving back to France. His interests are grounded in epistemology and the history of ideas, and they range from historical cultural geography to environmental planning. His books include *La Formation de l'école française de géographie (1870–1914)* (1995, 2nd edn., Paris: Editions du CTHS), *Des Mots et des lieux* (1988, Paris: Editions du CNRS) and (with O. Soubeyran) *L'Écologie urbaine et l'urbanisme* (2002, Paris: La Découverte).
Address: Laboratoire SET–CNRS, Domaine Universitaire, 64000 Pau, France, vincent.berdoulay@univ-pau.fr

Paul Claval is Professor Emeritus of Geography at the Université de Paris IV (Paris-Sorbonne). For the last 40 years his interest has focused mainly on the history of geographical thought and its relation to other social sciences: economics in the 1960s, sociology and political sciences in the 1970s and ethnology from the early 1980s

onwards. He has also stressed the role of communication in the spatial processes and
defined cities as forms of spatial organization which minimize the costs of commuting
between partners. He used this approach for analysing the relationship between
globalization and the growth of big metropolises.

Address: 29 rue de Soisy, 95600 Eaubonne, France, p.claval@wanadoo.fr

J. Nicholas Entrikin is Professor of Geography and former Chair of the UCLA
(University of California Los Angeles) Geography Department. He is also a founding
member of the UCLA Institute of the Environment. His research interests are in
cultural geography, especially modern ideas of place and landscape. The intellectual
framework for these studies was set forth in *The Betweenness of Place: towards a geography
of modernity* (1991, Baltimore and Basingstoke: Johns Hopkins University Press and
Macmillan). More recent work, such as 'Democratic Place-Making and
Multiculturalism', in *Geografiska Annaler* (2002) and other articles in both English and
French journals and books, explores the geography of democratic theory.

Address: Department of Geography, Box 951524, University of California Los Angeles,
CA, 90095-1524, USA, entrikin@geog.ucla.edu

Peter Gould was the Evan Pugh Professor of Geography at the Pennsylvania State
University until his untimely death in 2000. A leading figure in the advancement of
spatial science, Gould was a prolific writer, a frequently honoured member of the
geographic community and an admired teacher. The best known among his many
publications are (with Rodney White) *Mental Maps* (1974, London: Penguin),
The Geographer at Work (1985, Oxford: Blackwell) and *Becoming a Geographer*
(1999, Syracuse, NY: Syracuse University Press).

Chris Philo is Professor of Geography and Head of the Department of Geography and
Topographic Science, University of Glasgow. His research interests include social and
historical geography, with particular reference to the socio-spatial 'exclusion' of people
with mental health problems, past and present. A forthcoming book, *The Space Reserved
for Insanity: An historical geography of the 'mad-business' in England and Wales to the 1860s*
(Edwin Mellen Press), tackles this theme in detail. He is also interested in the history
and theory of geographical thought, and is a co-author (with Paul Cloke and David
Sadler) of *Approaching Human Geography: an introduction to contemporary theoretical
debates* (1981, London: Paul Chapman).

Address: Department of Geography and Topographic Science, University of Glasgow,
Glasgow G12 8QQ, United Kingdom, cphilo@geog.gla.ac.uk

Allan J. Scott is Professor of Regional Planning at UCLA (University of California
Los Angeles). The recipient of the Vautrin Lud International Geography Prize in 2003,
his research and teaching interests fall into three distinct areas: the cultural economy of
cities, industrial organization and location and regional development. He has published
numerous books and articles, including *Regions and the World Economy* (1998, Oxford:
Oxford University Press) and *Technopolis: high-technology industry and regional*

development in southern California (1993, Berkeley and Los Angeles: University of California Press).

Address: Department of Geography, University of California Los Angeles, Los Angeles, CA 90095, USA, ajscott@geog.ucla.edu

Ola Söderström is Professor of Geography at the University of Neuchâtel, Switzerland. He has taught at different universities in Switzerland and as a visiting professor at the Department of Geography, UCLA (University of California Los Angeles). His research interests are in the social and cultural geography of the city, the history and theory of human geography, visual studies and the social studies of science. He has recently published *Des Images pour agir. Le visuel en urbanisme* (2000, Lausanne: Payot) and co-edited (with Elena Cogato Lanza, Roderick J. Lawrence and Gilles Barbey) *L'Usage du projet. Analyser les pratiques sociales et concevoir le projet urbain* (2000, Lausanne: Payot).

Address: Université de Neuchâtel, Faculté des Lettres et Sciences humaines, Institut de géographie, Espace Louis-Agassiz 1, 2001 Neuchâtel, Switzerland, ola.soderstrom@unine.ch

Ulf Strohmayer is Professor of Geography at the National University of Ireland, Galway. Educated in Germany, Sweden, the USA and France, he previously taught at the University of Wales, Lampeter. His interest in social theory and philosophy is matched by his curiosity about the conditions and consequences of historical processes of modernization in Western Europe. Currently he is completing a book on 'Modernity and the Urban Geography of Paris, 1550–2000' for Cambridge University Press.

Address: Department of Geography, National University of Ireland, Galway, Eire, ulf.strohmayer@nuigalway.ie

Peter J. Taylor is Professor of Geography at the University of Loughborough and Research Professor at the Metropolitan Institute, Virginia Polytechnic, USA. Founding editor of *Political Geography* and *Review of International Political Economy*, he is a world-systems analyst who specializes in political geography and world cities (he is the founder of the Globalization and World Cities (GaWC) study group and network). Among his more than 250 publications are (co-edited with P. L. Knox) *World Cities in a World-System* (1995, New York: Cambridge University Press), *The Way the Modern World Works: from world hegemony to world impasse* (1996, New York: Wiley), *Modernities* (1999, Cambridge: Polity Press), (co-edited with C. Flint) *Political Geography: world-economy, nation-state and locality* (2000, 4th edn., Harlow: Pearson Education), (co-edited with R. J. Johnston and M. J. Watts) *Geographies of Global Change* (2000, 2nd edn., Oxford: Blackwell) and *World City Network: a global urban analysis* (2004, London and New York: Routledge).

Address: Department of Geography, Loughborough University, Loughborough, LE11 3TU, UK, p.j.taylor@lboro.ac.uk

Herman van der Wusten retired from the University of Amsterdam in 2001 where he was Professor of Political Geography (1984–2001) and Dean of the Faculty of Social and Behavioural Sciences (1997–2001). He has written extensively on the geography of international relations and of parties and movements. He co-authored (with Ben de Pater) a book on the history of geographical thinking in Dutch, *Het geografisch huis* (1991, 1996, Coutinhol Place: Muiderberg) and edited a book on academic institutions and their social environment, *The Urban University and its Identity. Roots, location, roles* (1998, Dordrecht: Kluwer Academic Publishers). He is currently working on a comparative study of European capital cities.
Address: Faculty of Social and Behavioural Sciences – Afdeling Geografie en Planologie, Nieuwe Prinsengracht 130, 1018 VZ Amsterdam, Netherlands, wusten-gritsai@planet.nl

Introduction
Ulf Strohmayer and Georges Benko

Wherever we live, our lives are shaped by events about which we have little choice or control. As students, teachers or citizens, we are all born at a time in history that is not of our own making and into specific places, cultures and classes which predate our existence. The colour of our skin is still not an option, and only a few choose their own gender. Together, these and many other aspects constitute the social conditions of individual human existence: being 'situated' within, or 'thrown' into, a world with others, our action and practices in turn recreate a world for others. Interestingly, however, humankind today no longer considers its own conditioning context immutable or god-given; instead we seek actively to influence and steer people towards individual or communal improvement. Many have labelled the ensuing process 'Modernity'; one of its key accompanying tools is science: the science that was born out of an Enlightenment no longer content with accepting things as they are.

Human geography is part of this enlightened endeavour. It takes its initial cues from the fact that conditions of human existence vary geographically at each and every given time in history. It is this difference that we as human geographers try to understand, hoping to derive from this a better comprehension of human existence in general. Whether this latter is held to be a goal in and of itself or is validated within a more teleological framework (be that progressive or conservative in orientation) matters little at this point; the editors take it to be crucial, however, that human geography originates in a recognition of both differences *and* identity. But why do conditions of human possibility such as culture, economic organization or the role of gender (just to mention three of the themes discussed in this book) differ across space? The answers that human geography has offered in the course of its short history are themselves varied and often contradictory, but traditionally have been focused within more or less clearly identifiable areas of discourse: social, historical, economic, cultural and political in nature, these discourses attempted to circumscribe causes of difference, which, when reassembled, could illuminate the human condition. The reasons that have governed the formation of what are effectively major subheadings within human geography are mostly pragmatic: the 'whole' of human geography has proven to be simply too extensive a terrain to be studied, let alone mastered, by any one individual. Hence the designation of 'specialty' areas in most geographical associations, as well as the naming of areas of interest in job advertisements for geographers. True, the welding together of these separate 'spotlights' has proven to be a problem waiting to be resolved in practice as well as in theory, just as there has never been more than a temporary consensus within each of these geographic sub-disciplines. Yet the task is seen generally to be an important one and presumably will occupy the wider geographic community for some time to come.

This book is an attempt to inform undergraduate and new postgraduate students and their teachers about the wealth of debates, positions and knowledges adopted throughout the last century, with occasional forays into the nineteenth century, where a broadening in scope was felt to be beneficial for the overall project. The topic is not accidental, for although many readings now exist of the debates and contexts that have shaped the early, discipline-forming decades of the nineteenth century, comprehensive surveys of the twentieth century are few and far between. And yet, for anyone involved in the shaping and creation of human geographies, the twentieth century was an exciting time to be alive and working. Far from being a threat to the intellectual state of the discipline, the absence of consensus has fostered a culture of debate within human geography that the editors take to be second to none in the wider world of academia. The different conceptual, methodological and theoretical propositions that are discussed and analysed in the individual chapters of this book have all, in their individual ways, contributed to the general sense of excitement that has accompanied human geography into the twenty-first century. Looking back at the twentieth century, we find not a linear trajectory, no gently flowing stream of geographical knowledge, but an often disrupted river with parallel branches, rapids and dead ends. The resulting highly contested territory of human geography, with its real and imagined (r)evolutions, is the subject of this book.

While everyone involved in writing this book is very much aware of the limitations that any project like the present one is bound by, we are confident that enough voices have been captured to convey to the reader many of the elements that together make human geography a thriving and worthwhile intellectual enterprise. Although often overlooked or neglected, geographically different traditions are themselves contributing to this healthy state of the discipline. It is with this in mind that *Human Geography: a history for the 21st century* has made an attempt to combine different practices and discourses into one narrative. Naturally, given the limits of individual experience and knowledge and the boundaries imposed by any book, the best that this attempt can produce is to present traces of different traditions. Still, it is better to open up what all too often remains effectively a retelling of Anglocentric histories than to be intimidated by one's inability to master traditions beyond one's orbit. Regrettable as the exclusion of Japanese, Indian, Latin-American or African geographies is from the resulting narratives, we hope that the combined efforts of an Anglo-Saxon and a Continental European geographer in each of the critical surveys that follow will enlarge the scope of any future reference to the ongoing development of human geography. The editors see the moulding together of different traditions accomplished in each of the subsequent chapters not in the tradition of all-inclusive survey articles, but as invoking and contextualizing both differences and similarities for the sake of opening up alternative possibilities.

We chose the sub-disciplines included in this book in recognition of their contribution to the overall debates within human geography over the course of the twentieth century. For reasons of analytical clarity and accessibility, the book is restricted to systematic sub-fields of inquiry, a choice that effectively sidelines the more contextual or thematic concerns, especially of the 'urban' and 'rural' variants. The editors decided to include historical and cultural axes of inquiry alongside the three classical axes – social, economic and political. This was done to allow for the broadest coverage and to provide as complete a vision of geographical debates as was possible given the customary limitations.

None of this is to imply that the sub-fields chosen were all equally present or important as sub-disciplines throughout the century, but rather to insist that concepts and terminologies which have found a home within them have shaped discourses across the field. We are aware that, to some extent, such a choice marginalizes highly welcome and indeed productive recent developments, especially within cultural ecology and other concerns that fit less well into the traditional form of approaching human geography. We wish to express our hope that future surveys will have to include these discourses by sheer force of their longevity and the powerful illuminations of the human condition they have produced.

At this point, a word about the structure of the volume might be in order. Given the collective nature of the enterprise, the editors felt it necessary to impose a rather stringent sense of external homogeneity, while leaving individual contributors to shape their own argument and place emphasis where they saw fit. The resulting development of an implicit dialogue between chapters was one of the most interesting facets to emerge from the project as a whole. Furthermore the editors invited the contributors to present critical assessments of their respective sub-disciplines. This, it was felt, would allow readers to appreciate the ongoing nature of the debates in hand and to immerse themselves – whatever their individual positions – in the individual narratives.

The chapters have been ordered in alphabetical fashion, with the exception of the epistemological survey, which we decided to use as an opening lens through which to approach 100 years of human geography. Common to all chapters is a sense of change that can be located historically in the late 1960s. Some of the chapters characterize this shift as a 'break', others present it as an 'enlargement', but common to both approaches is the recognition of the 'discursive' nature of the discipline. Quite obviously, the present volume stands squarely in the tradition of this change – indeed, how could it not? In the volume as whole, readers will thus encounter linguistically conscious reflections on the changing nature of concepts within the discipline as well as adaptations of the discipline to the changing geographies that have shaped our planet in the twentieth century. Together, ideology and adaptability both shape the ways in which we interpret and create human geographies on a variety of different scales.

It is in this context that we wish to locate the discipline of geography as a whole. Judged from a distance, the twentieth century has not been the kindest to the discipline. A tale of relative decline, the history of geography in the last century has been marked by increased marginalization within the human, social and natural sciences. Itself positioned at a crossroads, geography was not necessarily present on any of the main axes of scientific discovery – and often had to pay dearly for its 'misplacement'. It is only during the last two decades of the twentieth century that the various crossroads that define geography as a 'synthesizing' discipline have been recognized by a wider public, both within academia and beyond. We will address this change in our concluding 'outlook'. Overall, we hope that the book will speak to geographers and non-geographers alike, reminding the former of the astonishing diversity that is our discipline and informing the latter of ways to integrate a spatial point of view into the social and human sciences.

The editors owe a great deal of recognition to many individuals who have helped in shaping the present volume. In particular, we should like to thank the contributors for their cooperation and openness, Ronald Abler, Tim Cresswell, Anthony Gatrell, Jo Gould, Matthew Hannah, Ron Johnston, Geoffrey Martin, John Morrissey and Gunnar Olsson for their help when help was needed. At Arnold, we profited from the wisdom and encouragement of Luciana O'Flaherty, Colin Goodlad, Liz Gooster, Emma Heyworth-Dunn, Lesley Riddle and Abigail Woodman. We would like to thank you all.

More than most other projects, the writing and editing of *Human Geography: a history for the 21st century* was beset by delays due to illness and events beyond the control of anyone involved in the undertaking. With the rest of the geographic community, we share the deep sense of loss that was brought about by the untimely death of Peter Gould early in the project. With an inspiring sense of duty, Peter worked on his promised contribution to the opening chapter, despite knowing that he would not see its realization. Our gratitude to him – for his work and friendship – is beyond words.

Galway and Paris, summer 2004

1 Geographical visions: the evolution of human geographic thought in the twentieth century

Peter Gould and Ulf Strohmayer

My utmost ambition is to lodge a few poems
where they will be hard to get rid of.

—Robert Frost

The poet's ambition speaks to other realms. Throughout the twentieth century, and particularly in the latter half, it has been the ambition of successive generations of geographers 'to lodge a few poems where they will be hard to get rid of' – in other words, to set the professional discipline of geography on such a sound conceptual and methodological footing that it will be hard to dislodge it from the true and rightful path revealed. Have any groups succeeded? The general answer, in this eclectic discipline, must be no. And yet, as each phase has appeared and disappeared, it has left a residue, a kernel of insight that has given geographers much enhanced methodological competence, as well as deeper conceptual perspectives viewed from positions of greater sensitivity, which have developed as a result of more critical and reflective traditions (Abler 1999).

In this first chapter, we seek to present critically some of the key positions and voices that have shaped (or attempted to shape) the discipline as a whole. Needless to say this cannot but be a highly selective attempt and one that is influenced by the interests and generational affiliation of its authors. These limitations, among others, will become apparent in the relative space allocated to pre- and post-Second World War developments within the discipline. As such, this essay will provide a context for the chapters to follow, as it concentrates on the philosophical positions and theoretical issues that surround the more topical debates within human geography. In the interest of the volume as a whole, we have made every effort to reduce repetitive overlaps with subsequent chapters. The overall aim of this introductory chapter is to provide a context for what is to follow rather than to give its readers a definitive account of theoretical considerations. Given the scope of the present undertaking, any pretence of comprehensiveness would be dwarfed by the sheer number of traditions and voices that demand to be heard. The relative neglect of many important voices from this chapter –

Harold Mackinder, Vidal de la Blache and Carl Sauer, to name but a few – is thus in no way intended as a negation of their importance for twentieth-century human geography.

Throughout, we have attempted to give weight to individual practitioners contributing to change within the discipline just as we have sought to do justice to the power of structural conditions shaping geographical discourses. Clearly, the precise mechanisms through which individual creativity and persistence contribute to (and are in turn shaped by) networks of power, technologies and institutions within a discipline and beyond constitute one of the more hotly contested subject domains within the social and human sciences today. The following pages will not attempt to resolve the issue; they will, however, be quite content to provide some material for future discussions.

STANDING IN THE NINETEENTH-CENTURY HERITAGE

The roots of geography, considered broadly as a sense of place and space, go back a long way in human history. It is not our intention here to imply in any way that geography 'started in the nineteenth century', even though these were the years that saw many geography departments emerge in universities in Europe. In an essay looking back on the changes in twentieth-century geography, we can only tip our hats to Herodotus, and many other Greek writers, who wrote thoughtfully about the conjunctions of the physical and human worlds (Staszak 1995). And the same polite but cursory acknowledgment must be given to the geographers, cartographers, navigators and explorers who opened their own worlds to other peoples, places and civilizations, all the while introducing other worlds to the often one-sided power of mercantile and later industrial forms of capital (Livingstone 1992; Wallerstein 1974, 1980).

But centuries are arbitrary demarcations, and justice demands that we point to a few geographers of the eighteenth century who laid a thoughtful foundation of teasing questions, not least of which was the notion that the natures and characteristics of human beings were largely a product of physical environmental conditions and thus differed across space. The theme of environmental determinism would provide a powerful organizing concept right up through the first quarter of the twentieth century, a concept that received full expression in Montesquieu's concern for the effects of soil and climate on human nature. Thus a broad theme of spatial variation took its place in human geography.

This was soon challenged by Johann Herder, who, perhaps more than any other of his time, extolled a sense of *Bodenständigkeit*, a sense of being at home, of rootedness or a sense of place. This still made room for pleasure in the great spatial variety of places and people throughout the world and, more importantly, for respect for indigenous cultures that in turn informed the revival of cultural relativism in ethnography and anthropology characteristic of those working in the non-imperialistic tradition of the twentieth century (Boaz 1928; Herskovits 1962). Further dissent with the position of environmental determinism came from Immanuel Kant, who was prepared, on occasion, to elevate geography to the status of a universal science. His dissent was shared by Alexander von Humboldt, even as he acknowledged the intimate relationships between plant life and soil variations in micro-climatological conditions. Indeed, so powerful were the voices antagonistic to environmental determinism in human affairs, that we remain astonished that it maintained its strong, eventually almost ideological, position in geography through the nineteenth and early twentieth centuries. The students of empire may be less amazed, but the longevity of this seventeenth-century doctrine remains a puzzle nevertheless.

So although there are ancient roots to geographical curiosity and inquiry, the heritage of the past hundred years stems from the mid- to late-nineteenth century. While von Humboldt's *Kosmos* (1845) and Elisée Reclus' *Nouvelle Géographie universelle* (1876–94) may have been prominent in the homes of educated Europeans, it is difficult to characterize the overall inheritance as 'rich' in any genuine intellectual sense. In the USA, most geographies were texts for schoolchildren (one or two were required reading for freshmen in a few colleges and universities), and all tended to be strongly oriented towards physical geography, with some facts thrown in about the human world – although generally these were presented in list form only. The physical emphasis would continue to dominate through to the 1920s. Human geography was largely presented as environmental determinism, despite George Perkins Marsh's splendid, and deterministically inverting, *Man and Nature, or Physical Geography as Modified by Human Action*, published in 1864, and *The Earth as Modified by Human Action*, which appeared in 1874. The gradual softening of the environmental deterministic paradigm may be seen in the language of Ellen Churchill Semple, as 'determinism' becomes 'control', which elides into 'influence' and finally 'adjustment' (Martin 1998: 10).

Some European influences were felt in the USA during this period – a pertinent example would be the writings of Arnold Guyot from Switzerland, introducing the writings of Carl Ritter – but the stronger, though still highly ephemeral, influences from France, such as Jean Bruhnes, Paul Vidal de la Blache and the annual lectures of Raol Blanchard of Grenoble at Harvard, would not arrive until the late 1920s. Geoffrey Martin (1998: 11) has described geography's development as a university subject as 'punctiform', a most appropriate adjective capturing the 'on again, off again' nature of geography's representation at major universities. In the USA in particular, the 'off again' would continue to characterize the fate of a number of departments, such as those at Harvard, Yale, California (Santa Barbara), Michigan and Chicago, well into the 1970s.

In Europe itself, geography became reasonably securely established, frequently as an arm of imperial conquest and colonization. An early and quite singular chair of geography had been held by Carl Ritter at Berlin since 1820, but it was not renewed upon his death. In German-speaking Europe generally, Vienna (1851) and Giessen (1864) were the first genuine departments (Taylor 1985a), but over the next half-century, virtually every university formally founded departments of geography. Like many departments, their purpose was twofold: to train teachers for the growing state school system and to be useful to the worlds of expanding commerce and imperialism. These aims were not viewed by other scholars as reasons for university status, and the nineteenth-century need for constant justification would be felt well into the twentieth century.

A CRITICAL TRADITION

What geography lacked in the first half of the twentieth century was a general critical tradition, in contrast to the second half, in which a critical tradition slowly emerged, although still occasionally focusing on the person or the ideological base rather than the ideas (Symanski and Agnew 1981). As a small, emerging discipline, in which many professional geographers were acquainted with one another through national and international meetings, many felt that criticism would be taken personally, misinterpreted or simply provide fuel for those perceived to be antagonistic to geography's presence in the university. Much time and effort was spent defining and redefining 'geography' – time which, with hindsight, might have been better spent in geographical inquiries with some intellectual depth, commanding the respect of others.

Such a background of intellectual insecurity informed two important events in the USA. The first was the founding of the Association of American Geographers (AAG) in 1904. It rapidly led to an exclusive club, in which further memberships were formally proposed and voted upon. Only real, professional and research-oriented geographers were to pass such exacting standards. This led to a revolt, a renegade group calling themselves the American Society of Professional Geographers, advocating a larger, much more public and involved membership, including students who would form the future of the profession. Differences would be resolved in 1948, when the two groups joined again as the AAG at the annual meeting in Madison, Wisconsin, but the mark of division can still be discerned in the two publications, the *Annals of the AAG* and *The Professional Geographer*. In Europe, the teaching of geography had a firmer foundation, and geography's emergence as a university discipline, although not without its difficulties, had an easier time, not least because of the long and splendid tradition of scientific exploration and the cosy ties to the rampant imperialism so characteristic of the late nineteenth century.

The second event was the publication of Richard Hartshorne's *The Nature of Geography* (1939), a text through which a whole generation would wade in order to learn the true chorographical path of the discipline. Written in Germany and Austria in 1937–8, it claimed that geographical inquiry should focus exclusively on spatial distributions and their possible juxtapositions, and that geographers had no business dealing with time, process and the emergence of change in such geographical distributions, which would be a 'poem' dislodged. Alfred Hettner (1927) was frequently invoked as a source of authority for the chorographical path to geographic enlightenment, and he was not averse to using what was essentially his own journal, the *Geographische Zeitschrift*, to excoriate young upstarts like Hans Spethmann (1928, 1936), who dared to think in dynamic terms and had the temerity to write a three-volume work on the development of the Ruhr. Yet Hettner, strongly influenced, like many educated Germans of the time, in Kantian and neo-Kantian philosophy, was himself equivocal. And as Lukermann points out (1983, 1989), Kant never separated what were for him fundamental dimensions of the human world – space and time.

What strikes us, looking back, is the total lack of any critical appraisal of a work that was to have such an intellectually dominating effect upon a whole generation of geographers, many of whom, in eastern and midwestern universities, were forced to write as the first chapter of their dissertations a justification of why they were constraining their research to the chorographic tradition. Critical dissent did exist, although it was so muted it was never heard in public. Carl Sauer, writing to John Leighly, was scathing about *The Nature of Geography* and its excision of time from space (Bancroft Library Archives, Berkeley), but we have no public evaluation. Jacques May's (1970) mild, diffident, but deeply informed appraisal was essentially dismissed out of hand (May 1972). Elsewhere, *The Nature of Geography* appeared to make little impact, receiving only one review by John Wright in 1941 in *Isis*, a history of science journal. These were the war years in Europe, and other matters became more important. In Sweden, as Stefan Helmfrid (1999: 27) has noted, '. . . the Hettnerian anathema of time series in geographical analysis was never really understood or accepted . . .'. An older, strongly intellectual tradition of landscape evolution and historical geography would inform a later emphasis on spatial dynamics and change, invoked in new and highly imaginative ways.

In many ways, however, the climate contextualizing the reception of Hartshorne's *magnum opus* was indicative of the 'taken for granted' positions within geography in many countries. Often referred to as the idiographic tradition, it was characterized not merely by its overt emphasis on descriptive methods and techniques, but also lent credence to a cumulative, conflict-free vision of geography as a science, with a unique but largely homogeneous point of view. Despite different national traditions, it was this rendition of geography that reigned supreme throughout the first half of the twentieth century; in fact, the existence of different national traditions made the persistent lack of critique and alternative visions all the more easy to maintain within national boundaries.

POST-WAR DEVELOPMENTS AND CHALLENGES

It is as dangerous to assign strict boundaries to time periods as it is to draw strict lines on a map separating regions. Nevertheless, the years immediately following the Second World War saw a definite sea change in the way geography, as a teaching and research enterprise, began to be conducted. One question, easily posed but difficult to answer, was what the influence was of wartime experiences upon those returning to teach and learn (Balchin 1987). For those who held university teaching positions before the war, the answer appears to be very little. Many in Britain spent much of their energy compiling factual handbooks about the various theatres of war (Tuan 2001) or marshalling cartographic evidence about the physical conditions of potential invasion sites – neither task particularly helpful for post-war teaching or research.

   In the USA, a number of American geographers served in the Office of Strategic
Services (OSS), the forerunner of the Central Intelligence Agency (CIA). A few have
made much of this 'nefarious' connection, but only in the light of subsequent cold-war
developments and particular ideological stances that became prominent in the late
1960s. While there appears to be no intrinsic reason to condemn geographers and other
scholars for their involvement in the OSS, the link that was thus re-established between
the state as a recognized source of power on the one hand and science on the other
proved to be one of the points of most heated debate in the late 1960s. True, many
scientists served their country in the best way they could and in a cause they saw as just.
In the case of German geographers, however, this 'service' in the years leading up to and
throughout the Second World War was anything but a neutral and benevolent
involvement of science with power, as the slowly unravelling history of geography's
complicity in the justification and maintenance of the Nazi state makes abundantly
clear (Sandner and Rösler 1994).
   In the sphere of theory, wartime activities of factual compilation and the production of
handbooks reinforced the 'checklist approach', discussed frequently at the time for the
pertinence of the items to be included. Whether geography saw itself as *Landeskunde*
(the knowledge of countries or places) or regionalism (*géographie régionale*) matters little
in this context; what is important is a persistent deficiency, the almost complete erasure
of temporal aspects from the realm of geography, facilitated by a widespread 'collector's
ethos' prevailing within the discipline in most countries. But in this business-as-usual
tradition, there is a small caveat to be made. In the USA in particular, several future
professional geographers entered graduate schools after serving as meteorological
officers in the European and Pacific theatres of war, namely John Borchert, Edward
Taaffe, William Garrison and William Warntz. The first three would go on to become
presidents of the AAG, while William Warntz would produce one of the most
remarkable macro-perspectives on the discipline, including a prescient work drawing a
direct analogy between the advance of weather fronts and what he would call 'income
fronts' (Warntz 1965). John Borchert (1961) essentially opened up the dynamic study of
cities, while Edward Taaffe's studies of airline passenger traffic were grounded in the
dynamics of central place structures and their interactions. All four men had spent past
years with questions of spatial dynamics, process and time inherent in weather maps
and forecasts, so to return to an atemporal chorographic tradition must have seemed
bizarre. As for William Garrison, whose applied research always looked to the future
effects of transportation development, he simply noted: 'The Hartshornian world never
bothered me because I thought it was just dumb' (Garrison 1999).
   Unfortunately, the unchallenged authority of the chorographic imperative still
moulded thinking in most eastern and midwestern universities of the USA, although
the intellectual connections between checklist compilations and deeply informing
regional syntheses were too shallow for a number of universities with high standards of
scholarship. Although particular local conditions were clearly influential, geography
departments were dismissed at Harvard, Yale and Stanford and were never appointed at
many other universities with strong liberal arts traditions. Sometimes even the popular
press got wind of a particularly egregious case of 'gut courses' and banal instruction

(*Time Magazine* 1963) and such adverse, but generally well-deserved, publicity generally hastened the case for dismissal – for example, at Yale.

With the intensification of the cold war, feelings of anti-communism reached fever pitch in the USA, exacerbated by the notorious hearings of the House of Un-American Activities Committee (HUAC) and the accusations liberally broadcast by Senator Joseph McCarthy and his aides, such as Richard Nixon. It is difficult, two generations later, to invoke the fearful feelings of the time, when prominent people from the State Department and other branches of the government, major foundations – especially those with an Asian (particularly Chinese) connection – and even Hollywood actors, directors and writers were pulled up before the bullying HUAC questioners. Nor were academics immune, particularly those whose writings had expressed sympathy for the ordinary people of Asia and criticized the corruptions of the Chang Kai-Chek regime, which had received the support of the USA since before the war.

The case of Owen Lattimore is particularly, and quite deservedly, notorious, for it involved not only a scholar of Johns Hopkins who was an acknowledged world authority on Mongolia and China, but a man denounced on the flimsiest of grounds: snatches of conversation at a picnic overheard by a fellow geographer, George Carter. 'One must understand the pathology of that decade', wrote Robert Newman in a definitive study of the Lattimore case (Newman 1992), and that may be precisely the problem for those who come later. The academic world, too, was marked by fear, and few were courageous enough at the time to stand up in support of those under suspicion.

The feelings of the time also permeated attempts to honour prominent scholars from abroad. In the early 1960s, for example, the Association of American Geographers (AAG) attempted to honour the theoretical contributions of central place theory by Walter Christaller, then living a penurious existence in his native Germany. Unfortunately, as a young man, and during the despairing years of the 1920s, Walter Christaller had joined the Communist Party for a few months. This was enough to condemn two successive visa applications in 1964 to visit the USA to receive a prestigious award at the AAG annual meeting, and it was left to Sweden to publicly honour this theoretical pioneer with a gold medal a few years later.

LATER POST-WAR DEVELOPMENTS AND CHALLENGES

It was against this backdrop that the most momentous of breaks in the theoretical orientation of human geography took place. Initiated from within key university locations, mostly on the west coast of the USA, and against considerable resistance, a new orientation gradually moulded human geographic practice according to its premises and ideals. Nowadays mostly recast as the 'quantitative revolution', this revolt actually had a much wider spectrum and broader set of goals than such a designation would have us believe. At stake was little short of the status of geography as a rigorous science. With a new wave of graduate students entering expanding, not to say explosive, university systems, voices of discontent began to be heard that were unnerving to an older generation grounded in traditional and authoritarian ways (Lukermann 1983, 1989; Butzer 2001). Any 'narrative of revolt' is difficult to pen in a simple linear fashion, because signs of moving forward to more intellectually demanding topics and methodologies developed at many places (Billinge, Gregory and Martin 1984), but there appear to be three fairly consistent themes of influence common to most attempts to rethink the future directions of geographic inquiry and, therefore, teaching.

The first of these was the courageous though difficult to define influence of Walter Isard at the University of Pennsylvania. Isard had become dissatisfied with the totally aspatial aspects of traditional economics. In his first book (Isard 1956), the initial publication of which he had to pay for himself (subsequent editions and later volumes were paid for by MIT Press), he brought attention to the works of earlier economists and geographers, including Heinrich von Thünen (1826), the extraordinary and pioneering work of August Lösch (1954) and the theoretical geometries of central place systems proposed by Walter Christaller (1966). These works, never previously offered to graduate students, provided not simply a body of informing spatial theory, but also a realization that there were more intellectually demanding ways of approaching and describing geographical phenomena (Haggett 1965). Hartshorne could dismiss von Thünen with a one-liner, but those in daily contact with Third World agricultural students (Chisholm 1982) or those trying to elucidate almost identical patterns of development in America's older cities (Bunge 1962) had very different, empirically informed views.

With a growing awareness of theoretical issues came a realization that appropriate methodologies were badly needed. It is this relation between theory and methodology that marks the second theme of influence: the extraordinary conjunction of students working under William Garrison at the University of Washington in the late 1950s and the similar, but somewhat less innovative, stirrings at Iowa and Northwestern Universities. Those in the Washington group, later to be nicknamed the Space Cadets, clearly had a catalytic effect upon each other, exploring and then sharing methodologies and topics, virtually all of which were empirically grounded. It must be noted that those who took part in this quantitative revolution had all received thoroughly traditional undergraduate educations in geography, but went on to graduate school with a sense that there was a higher level to achieve. Brian Berry (1966, 1967) quickly became known for his pioneering work in central place studies; William Bunge's concern for spatial theory became well-known when his *Theoretical Geography* (1962) was finally published in Sweden, after being excoriated by traditional American reviewers; Waldo Tobler (1962, 1993), perhaps the only true analytical cartographer of the twentieth century, led pioneering work in map projections, transformations, 'winds of influence' and many other areas of cartographic analysis and expression; while Richard Morrill (1970b) was the first to use optimization techniques (linear programming) for such topics as physician care and patient services.

This was also the time that the computer, utterly archaic by today's standards, emerged as a practical way to undertake the computations for advanced multivariate methods and optimization procedures. Duane Marble, another of the Washington group, became highly adept at writing 'pre-language' computer instructions and was instrumental in furthering a number of methodological breakthroughs. It was the sheer practicality of computing, combined with Richard Morrill's astuteness in recognizing the expanding conditions of possibility for asking geographic questions that previously had been unthinkable, which introduces the third theme informing the quantitative sea change then taking place.

Sweden, with a traditionally strong concern for landscape evolution, appears to have taken for granted the dynamic possibilities of geographic research. There seems to have been an openness to new approaches combining space and time, at least in a few, highly innovative geographers at the University of Lund. The full story is complex and cannot be explained here; suffice to say that a childhood friend of Torsten Hägerstrand, Karl Erik Fröberg, a physicist who had built Lund's first and very primitive computer SMIL, returned from a visit to the USA, where he had come across a mimeographed copy of a paper presented by the mathematicians John von Neuman and Stanislav Ulam, on the Monte Carlo methods used to compute the thickness of concrete shielding around some of the first atomic reactors. Given the heterogeneous nature of concrete, classical mathematical approaches were intractable. At the time, Hägerstrand had moved on from a series of detailed studies of out-migration (1949) and was focusing on the spread of ideas and innovation in Swedish farming. His subsequent research on the diffusion of innovations (Hägerstrand 1952, 1953) using Monte Carlo methods stands as the first use of this methodology in the social sciences as a whole. In 1959, he spent a semester at the University of Washington, where Richard Morrill was quick to realize the potential of these methods, subsequently spending a post-doctoral year at Lund, where he conducted studies in the dynamics of central place systems (Morrill 1965a) and then applied this same approach to 'blockbusting', and all its ugly ramifications, in highly segregated neighbourhoods in the USA (Morrill 1965b).

The second 'Lund voice' was that of Sven Godlund, whose innovative studies of changes in transportation and central place structures were outstanding for their time (Godlund 1956). Yet two other 'Baltic voices' must be acknowledged. The first is that of Edgar Kant, formerly of the University of Dorpat in Estonia, who escaped to Sweden ahead of the advancing Russian armies. Holding a personal chair, his encouraging influence is acknowledged by all those who were postgraduate students at the time, not least for his ability to recall innovative ideas published up to a century before in the eight different languages that were familiar to him (Hägerstrand 1983). The second is that of Reino Ajo in Finland. Rejected by the 'folklorists' of his day for a permanent university post, he supported himself and his family as an inspector of automobiles in Turku, while conducting highly innovative studies (Ajo 1953, 1955). These were often hard times for innovators in a highly conservative discipline.

THE REACTION OF THE TRADITIONALISTS

But no science ever progresses in a uniform manner. Instead, shifts in emphasis, aim and methodology – in short, shifts in 'paradigms' (Kuhn 1962) – compete with older theories and practices for some time before new hegemonies emerge, if they emerge at all. In the case of the displacement under investigation, it is extremely difficult, at the beginning of this century, to give an account of the degree of vituperation and vindictiveness often contained in the reactions of traditionalists and be believed (Gould 1979; Warntz 1984). Most of the evidence that could document the vehemence of the reaction consists of highly ephemeral material – letters, reviews, etc. – some of which were circulated at the time, only to be thrown out as people cleared out old files as they reached retirement. After all, it occurred a long time ago. Yet Carl Sauer (1956), with geomorphologists and climatologists in his department at Berkeley, could write with a sneer: 'Enumeration we can leave to the census takers', while Richard Hartshorne (1939), warning neophytes of the dangers of bringing time into geographic studies, wrote: 'the purpose of such dips in the past is not to trace developments', thus dismissing one of the strongest intellectual traditions of the time in historical geography. In Britain, we have the now amusing, but then deadly serious, confrontation of Professor Steers of Cambridge with a young Peter Haggett, whom he accused of 'bringing the discipline into disrepute' (Chorley 1995), after a presentation at the Royal Geographic Society using trend surface analysis in an innovative way (Taylor 1976).

With the reactions came a high degree of 'gatekeeping' by traditional editors. Joseph Spencer, editor of the *Annals*, became notorious for the sarcasm in his letters of rejection, many of which were circulated, while the then editor of *Economic Geography* reluctantly wrote that no paper submitted for review would be sent out if it contained mathematical notation. An exception was Wilma Fairchild, editor of *Geographical Review*, who was much more open to new ideas clearly expressed. And so, parallel to the gatekeeping, came the first 'discussion papers' in geography, produced on shoestring budgets by individual departments such as Washington, Iowa, Ohio State, Pennsylvania State and the consortium of Michigan, Michigan State and Wayne State Universities known as the Michigan Inter-University Community of Mathematical Geographers (MICMOG). Such attempts to bypass the traditional journals and circulate freely new ideas for comment and criticism were a harbinger of new geographical journals to come in the 1970s (chief among them *Progress in Human Geography*, possibly the first geographic journal aimed at a general audience that acknowledged a growing alienation between physical and human geographers), a development which was to continue sporadically as new fields of specialization and new challenges came into view, along with the necessities of publication for promotion and tenure which become more and more intense over the next few decades.

INCREASING THE METHODOLOGICAL CONDITIONS OF POSSIBILITY

In these days of readily available software and powerful personal computers, it is difficult to recall that these are relatively recent developments of the last two decades of the twentieth century. Many software packages allow ready access to highly sophisticated, multivariate and optimization techniques, some so sophisticated that users may easily become misusers. Sometimes, for example, canonical correlation may only expose canonical ignorance, for an interpretation of empirical analysis depends on knowing exactly what is going on between data input and output. Early users formulating field theory, examining relations between traditional concepts of homogeneous and functional regions (Berry and Garrison 1958a and c) or the effects of lag and lead on infrastructure investment and regional growth (Gauthier 1968), grounded themselves thoroughly in a highly complex and sophisticated approach that only became practical with the growth of computing power. Too often taxonomic algorithms were 'taken off the shelf' – they came in many varieties producing somewhat different results – and used without much thought about the set of things being partitioned by an equivalence relation (Gould 1999). Users of multivariate techniques often invoked standard tests of significance, unaware that a fundamental assumption underlying them was almost certainly broken in any problem of the slightest geographic interest.

Yet one must be aware that question posing and methodological advances may be two sides of the same coin. While traditionalists decried (sometimes quite rightly, albeit for the wrong reasons) methodological applications for their own sake, we must realize that new approaches opened up thinking and questioning that were literally unthinkable before. Good examples would be linear programming, which raised seriously and for the first time in geography whole questions of normative possibilities based on practical optimization procedures. And in Leslie Curry's conceptual thinking based on queuing theory (1966, 1998), the whole notion of random processes and a random spatial economy appeared for the first time. What is thinkable, and therefore what is approachable from an entirely new perspective, becomes a new 'condition of possibility' for geographic inquiry.

As for testing theory – using the word in the traditional sense recognizable by all the physical sciences, where a statement, a positing of how things are, may be accepted conditionally but may be refutable in the Popperian sense (Popper 1959) – the new methods often made significant contributions. Unfortunately, the meaning of 'theory' has become so general, often used as little more than a cachet of intellectual respectability, that it now stands as a general term for almost any body of speculation, testable or not (Strohmayer 1993). Nevertheless, the term invokes one of the most remarkable, if generally unremarked upon, developments of geography in the latter half of the twentieth century: namely, the confrontation of the sheer spatiality and specificity of place inherent in geography with bodies of 'theory' in other overlapping or osculating fields.

CONFRONTING THEORY WITH GEOGRAPHY'S CONCERN FOR SPACE AND PLACE

Largely implicit in our rendition of the turn towards more challenging and mature theories in the wake of the quantitative revolution is a specific relationship between genuinely geographic theories and those imported from other disciplines. The shift away from idiographically confined regional concerns and the incorporation of time into geographic analyses was felt at the time by many as a development of the latter at the expense of the former. Those critical of change professed a wistful nostalgia for bygone days, with clearer boundaries and a more pronounced academic division of labour. But a real concern remained – and remains to this very day: is it possible simply to 'spatialize' theoretical constructions or methods developed in other contexts, for different goals and by dissimilar disciplines?

We acknowledge at once here the influence and perspicacity of David Harvey. He was the first to note explicitly the way in which the aspatial theoretical constructs in adjacent disciplines began to disintegrate when confronted with space and place, often to the point where theoretical concern had to be rethought, radically modified or abandoned altogether. Working from a Marxist perspective, he insisted that the dominance of nineteenth-century temporal and historical thinking was inadequate, and that for any attempt to ground research in Marxian theory, the theory itself had to be modified and rethought to include the geographic fundamentals of the specificity of place and the generality of space (Harvey 1982). Today, after the turn of the millennium, with a marvellous variety of local cultures under fire from 'Coca-Colarization', and with small nations being constantly hammered by the multinational corporations hunting for the next 'spatial fix', we can see how extraordinarily perceptive he was.

But a number of other examples of confrontation are available. Perhaps the earliest stems from the research of Tjallings Koopmans and Martin Beckmann (1957), as they tried to maintain price – the Holy Grail, not to say fetish, of economics – as the mechanism capable of producing equilibrium in locational assignment problems, while accounting simultaneously for agglomerative effects. Yet as soon as transportation costs were introduced, neo-economic theory fell apart. So disquieting was this development that the authors delayed publication 'for several years' (Koopmans and Beckmann 1957: 71) and they pleaded with their fellow econometricians to come to the rescue.

A third example of a discipline confronting the spatiality of geography was the collision of spatial analytical methods with the assumptions of what was then classical statistical theory. After a number of inappropriate invocations of tests of significance, including the temporal and spatial independence of observations, both geographers and statisticians realized that crucial assumptions underlying both parametric and non-parametric tests of significance seldom, if ever, held in problems of the slightest geographical interest (Gould 1970). In both spatial and temporal problems, true independence of observation would simply produce the 'white noise' of a time series, or the oxymoronic random pattern of the map – neither, by definition, containing information of the faintest interest to the geographer. It is true that Ronald Fisher, working on early experiments at the Rothamsted Agricultural Experiment Station, recognized the effects of spatial heterogeneity in field trials (Fisher 1958) and devised elaborate block designs to overcome some effects (Fisher and Mackenzie 1922; Fisher and Eden 1929; Fisher and Wishart 1930). But such concerns appear to have been confined to experimental design in the analysis of variance, and the related problem of spatial autocorrelation does not appear to have been involved or invoked (Cliff and Ord 1973).

Closely related is aetiology's and epidemiology's virtual abandonment of the nineteenth-century heritage of mapping disease occurrences and their subsequent spatial developments. Here we have a distressing case of techniques – mainly time series analysis and related approaches – becoming so prominent that they shape the thinking of a whole discipline. For most modern epidemiologists, time is dominant, made all the more attractive by canned programs of differential equations which extrapolate often sensible initial assumptions into banal and generally useless conclusions. The notion that there might be a geography as well as a history to an epidemic, that valuable scientific information might be contained in spatial series, appears to have been forgotten. Yet at a time when 13 million people fly between Los Angeles, Houston, Chicago, New York and Miami each year, one would expect some sense of the spatial to penetrate epidemiological thinking concerned with the intervention and control of new diseases. There is some evidence that spatial series are beginning to emerge once again as data of interest. A concern for the geographic clustering of cases never entirely disappeared (Mantel 1967), and many recent advances in this most difficult area of marshalling evidence have been led by geographers (Bailey and Gatrell 1995), often in collaboration with challenged and concerned statisticians.

The confrontation of geography's spatiality with adjacent fields continues; in the case of the new-found interest in cosmopolitanism by political scientists, it continues in a real sense, since the concern goes back to the publication of Kant's essay 'Perpetual Peace' (Habermas 1998). Kant, aware of difference in a world literally opening up, and never quite comfortable with it, recognized the 'contrast between the universality of [his] cosmopolitanism and [his] ethics and the awkward and intractable particularities of his geography . . .' (Harvey 2000: 535). Harvey continues: '. . . Kant's geography is heterotopic. Cosmopolitanism cast upon that terrain shatters into fragments. Geography undermines cosmopolitan sense' (2000: 536). This particular confrontation constitutes an insertion of space and place in yet another attempt to formulate social theory as a universal framework within which *all* human life is viewed. Only theoretical constructs which take into account the spatiality of the world from the very initiation of their development will stand as pertinent constructs to knowledge that may be pleased to call themselves genuinely useful and illuminating.

LATER REACTIONS TO QUANTIFICATION AND SPATIAL SCIENCE

Every reaction produces a counter-reaction as new perspectives make ever greater claims, which begin to receive increasingly hostile criticism (Hanson 1999). Perhaps the classic case is Romanticism's rise in the early nineteenth century contra the sometimes excessive claims of the Enlightenment (Berlin 1999), although sweeping statements such as these tend to obscure the subtleties and complexities of important eddies forming in mainstreams. Yet there is no question that opposition emerged to the essential mechanism that lay behind much of the quantified sea change of the 1950s and 1960s.

The first was a challenge less to the methodological orientation of the evolving landscape of spatial science than to its behaviourist underpinnings. Where much of the early quantitative work was constructed around largely implicit models of what caused and influenced human behaviour, these models gradually took on a life of their own and began to mature into fully fledged psychological approaches to the analytical problems caused by the acceptance of sub-optimal spatial distributions or patterns, or outright irrational human behaviour (Lowenthal 1961; Wolpert 1964; Saarinen 1966). The best known development of the resulting interest in the spatiality of human perception is probably the evolution of 'mental maps' as a distinct area of geographical knowledge (Gould and White 1974).

In hindsight, the turn towards environmental perception clearly paved the way for a second challenge that is customarily summarized as the rise of 'humanistic geography'. This movement owed its designation to its attempt to bring back human beings to centre stage in human geography, a position from which a number of geographers thought they had been displaced by the functional mathematics and 'geometricizing' of the spatial turn. The fundamental concern was woven from a number of strands, prominent among which were wide-ranging Christian influences, from Catholicism to Welsh Evangelical Protestantism, and more philosophical approaches that attempted to incorporate phenomenological insights into geographical research (Seamon 1979). Basic human (read western) values were often ignored (Buttimer 1974), both in approaches and topics chosen, and a desire to bring out the truly human element within a more general analysis began to be exemplified in research programmes (Ley 1974). There was a sense that much of the world, both nationally and internationally (Webber and Rigby 1996), was a miserable and unjust place for many human beings, and that geography's business-as-usual approach to research too frequently resembled those who walked by on the other side in the New Testament parable of the good Samaritan.

It was also a sense of justice, sharing Marx's horror and outrage in the mid-nineteenth century's traumatic years of the Industrial Revolution, which mobilized the highly influential turn to the Marxian perspective and its economically grounded analysis. Few would deny that David Harvey's *Social Justice and the City* (1973) was a major catalyst. Applications of rent surfaces might account for similarities in some locations within the land use patterns of America's cities, and topological inversions might account for the *favelas* of Latin America and the growing rings of slums in some European cities, but what about the plight of the real human beings living in such conditions? The search for deeper explanations occurred during the rise of other, then radical movements (the vehement protests against the war in Vietnam, etc.), and confrontations between 'quantitativists' – who came to be viewed as the Old Guard – and those who saw enlightenment in Marxian analysis became increasingly bitter. So bitter, in fact, that some who had made the running in the late 1950s and early 1960s now appeared to be little more than technologically motivated practitioners. Many, who may not have been persuaded entirely by the Marxist turn, were markedly sensitized by the underlying current of concern for a more decent and just world. It is difficult to document such an increase in social sensitivity, but many chose research topics trying to illuminate injustice at home or turned their attention to relationships of power between north and south, centre and periphery. Many subsequent developments in, or incorporations into, geographic theory from the late 1970s onwards – including feminism, the rise of ecological concerns, postcolonialism and the study of hitherto underrepresented groups in society at large – find their roots and take their motivation from such a perception of injustice.

If the idea of justice was shaping and continues to shape the passions of many engaged in the Marxist turn, its importance derives equally from its advocacy of a new and different conceptualization of theory within human geography (Peet 1977). Put briefly, this emerged as a direct challenge to the linearity of the causal relations that were at the heart of the quantitative revolution. 'Scientific Marxism', in particular, insisted on the importance of treating geographical relations as the outcome of processes rather than as spatial patterns. Since all such processes were historical, they could, in effect, be changed, a fact customarily rendered invisible by pattern-orientated, 'positivist' pursuits of geographic knowledge (Smith 1979a). As a particular form of practice, Marxist geography derived much of its force from the ensuing claim for the necessity of socially useful forms of geographic knowledge (Lacoste 1977; Harvey 1984). But it is the insistence of Marxists on the link between theory and the procedural character of social reality that was of lasting influence: it was through this crucial nexus that 'social theory' gained widespread acceptance within the discipline at large (Gregory 1978a). What is more, the most intellectually challenging outgrowths in recent geographic theory, such as the rise in postmodern (Dear 1988; Hannah and Strohmayer 1992, 1995) or post-structural thinking (Doel 1999) and the turn towards network-oriented modes of analyses (Bingham 1996; Hinchliffe 1996), all emerged in a manner reminiscent of the emergence of Marxist geography in the early 1970s: from critical analyses of the perceived general failures of homogeneous theoretical assumptions or epistemological foundations (Claval 1980). In the context of the 1980s, and as we might expect in this narrative of reaction and counter-reaction, the Marxist perspective was to receive challenges in its turn, not least of which was the charge that it was a nefarious 'meganarrative', ignoring a number of 'constituencies' – although it was sometimes difficult to see anything particularly geographic in these otherwise perfectly legitimate concerns.

Predicting future developments is a hazardous occupation, and even as various confrontations were being played out in the 1970s and 1980s, a development of enormous geographical importance was beginning. Few had the prescience to recognize the rise and impact of geographical information systems (GIS), and even the most astute seers could not have imagined the developments and ramifications based on modern satellite and other technologies. Such an important emergence requires an interlude in this narrative before returning to the latest challenges and developments, but an interlude with great import for geographic inquiry and the infusion of spatial thinking into many other areas of modern life.

GEOGRAPHICAL INFORMATION SYSTEMS (GIS)

So rapid was the emergence of geographical information systems (GIS) in the last 20 years of the twentieth century, and so swift was their impact on many applied sciences and areas of practical affairs, that it might be tempting to consider them as a separate and distinct field. This would be a mistake, however, ignoring the roots in more traditional forms of cartography and geographical analysis and their strengthening relationships to GIS (Brewer 1999; Brewer and McMaster 1999). Five main strands can be discerned in the rise of GIS, the beginnings of which owe much to David Simonett's (1964) vision in the 1960s of the then seemingly futuristic potential of combining satellite sensing and the orders of magnitude increases expected in the speed and capacities of computers (Simonett and Brown 1965; NASA 1966). It was he who persuaded the National Aeronautics and Space Administration (NASA) to sponsor a conference on what was then the distant future at the end of the century, a future that was to arrive with breathtaking speed. John Pickles (1999), quoting Stephen Hall (1993), notes that the rise of GIS is '. . . arguably the greatest explosion in mapping, and perhaps the greatest consideration of "space" (in every sense of the word) since the times of Babylon'.

The first strand is represented by the sheer technological advances in remote sensing, advances that were made possible by the colossal investments in instrumentation and satellite launching systems by government agencies, particularly NASA and its branches, such as the Jet Propulsion Lab (JPL), but also by its European equivalent, the European Space Agency (ESA). Hyperspectral cameras, the result of NASA and JPL developments, now record up to 224 bands for 1 m pixels and, quite apart from planetary sensing, they are used increasingly for earthbound ecosystem management, agriculture, mining, hazardous waste clean-up and many other applied uses (Robbins 1999). Terabyte capacities are required to run the software, and one Environmental Protection Agency (EPA) project cleaning up Leadville, Colorado gathered the data in 45 seconds, but required 10 months to analyse it!

The second strand lies in traditional cartography and its age-old concern to represent human and earth phenomena at various scales. Since such concern must be shared by those wishing to transform electronic impulses into useable and useful forms, it is hardly surprising that relationships between cartography and GIS today sometimes make certain strands in both virtually indistinguishable.

The third informing strand is the quantitative analytical tradition that arrived in the late 1950s and early 1960s with the quantitative revolution. From its inception, the analytical tradition was entwined with the map as a source of data, an effective medium of presentation and a possibility for visually effective spatial transformations. Harold Moellering (1991) has noted: 'Analytical cartography . . . has become the core of modern GIS'. The early developments are closely associated with, if not inspired by, the research of Waldo Tobler (1966), who pioneered work on effective data compression, map projections and transformations, and many other analytical approaches.

The fourth strand is essentially political; it is the desire of government agencies (in the US context, particularly NASA and the Defense Mapping Agency) to demonstrate the way in which military and planetary research contains great potential benefits for civilian use. Such practical applications make good fodder for congressional sympathies for increased funding. Those in the academic world, whose research can demonstrate its usefulness in problem-solving within a clearly defined context, are generally welcomed by such agencies, which show their appreciation in the form of generous research and institutional grants. As ever, the relationship between empirical geographic research and power, which is expressed in the approval or disapproval of research funds, is a highly complex one; suffice it to point to the discrepancy between the official – and often industry-backed – total funding provided for GIS-based projects and the lack of funds made available to other, seemingly less relevant, projects.

Finally, the fifth strand consists of a growing concern across many applied scientific fields for the question of visualization (MacEachren 1994; MacEachren and Kraak 1997), particularly the animation of sequential data to disclose dynamic phenomena that sometimes would never be suspected, let alone seen (Fisher 1993). As a result of the workings of all five strands, it is difficult to think of a greater contrast in geographical research than 'the map writ large' in 1900 and 2000. While other areas of important research – one such being the History of Cartography Project inspired by Brian Harley and David Woodward (1992–4) – still have discernible roots in the nineteenth century *fin-de-siècle*, the overwhelming technological advances of the past 30 years have literally revolutionized cartography by its association with GIS and the concomitant developments opening out into the twenty-first century.

Almost as an aside, and despite the emphasis placed on remote sensing as the major provider of GIS data, it must be noted specifically that GIS is a development allowing entirely new analytical approaches, as opposed to simply carrying out older, and now traditional, approaches more quickly. It is in this context that a progressive use of new technologies manifests itself most rigorously. A prime example is Stan Openshaw's Geographical Analytical Machine (GAM), first used to establish scale-examined clusters of leukaemic children around the atomic reprocessing plant at Sellafield in northern England (Openshaw *et al*. 1988). By organizing the data in a GIS format, he was able to examine 9 million hypotheses of clustering at many scales to establish the fact – initially criticized heavily (to no avail) by conventional statisticians hired by the atomic industry – that there was indeed the strongest of evidence that high densities of leukaemic children were associated with spatial proximity to the reprocessing plant. This, along with other highly imaginative data-dredging and exploratory approaches to huge data sets, makes GIS a methodological development undreamt of 30 years ago.

In fact, so rapidly have GIS methods and perspectives penetrated many civilian and academic areas of concern, that a new Center for Spatially Integrated Social Science has received large-scale funding at Santa Barbara. At least part of the difficult dream of bringing the social sciences back together may be realized by the growing recognition of the spatiality inherent in all human phenomena. Geography and space appear to be taking their rightful place alongside history and time after a century of neglect, as well as the realization of new opportunities and perspectives opening into the next century.

The developments have not been without their critics, as some involved in the developments of GIS appear either unaware, unreflective or oblivious to its social implications and the way in which such taken-for-granted developments can create a 'world' of thinking that goes unexamined (Schuurman 2000). The first signal that a critical stance should be taken came from Brian Harley (1990), who pointed to the subtexts of traditional maps (typically within national, not to say nationalistic, atlases). His penchant for 'Deconstructing the map' (1989) was taken up in a GIS context by John Pickles (1995), who was concerned that the social implications of the exploding geographical information systems were not being examined and thought through. In particular, he was concerned that those extolling the possibilities for the democratization of GIS – and all that meant in terms of providing 'everyone' (that is to say, the relatively rich with personal computers) with vastly increased access to spatial information – seemed to be ignoring the simple fact that many important developments and databases were within often secretive businesses, government agencies and centres of military planning. Another disturbing aspect of the GIS revolution, increasingly loaded with its virtual reality paraphernalia, is that it may resemble all too closely '. . . the display technologies of panorama, arcade, world exhibition, and shop-window of end-of-century Imperial Paris' (Pickles 1999). At the beginning of the twenty-first century, we face greatly increased possibilities for re-presentation. One can only hope that they are used wisely, thoughtfully and with a sense of justice by those practising these skills and embedded within institutional frameworks that develop representational techniques for non-propagandistic ends.

THE NON-QUANTITATIVE TRADITION

As we suggested earlier in this chapter, broadly conceived quantitative methods and approaches were not alone in shaping the overall picture of the discipline in the second half of the twentieth century. The last quarter of the century, in particular, witnessed the emergence and gradual solidification of a number of alternative visions and practices within human geography, three of which we should like to discuss in this penultimate section. Instrumental in the rise of critique to an unprecedented status within human geography was beyond doubt the changed perception of politics that originated in the late 1960s in general and in the worldwide civil unrest during the summer of 1968 in particular (Wallerstein 1991). The most important of outcomes of this watershed, from a scientific point of view, was the critique of the boundary separating science from politics. If before 1968 most social and human scientists held on to the belief that their scientific activities could be described as 'neutral' practices contributing to some greater good, after 1968 this belief gradually became a minority position. What most geographers today would accept as the 'social construction' of science in general takes its roots in this politicization of human geography in the 1970s.

This, then, was not a critique that sought to contrast an alleged 'objective' form of human geography with more 'subjective' approaches. While such a response had been instrumental in the 'humanist' reply to the quantitative revolution, it was now seen increasingly as a mere sidestep where a more radical approach was needed. Aided by the eventual proliferation of new journals like *Antipode* and *Society and Space* in the United States, *Hérodote*, *Espaces et sociétés* and *EspacesTemps* in France, new forms of social theory began to transform the landscape of geographic epistemology. We have already mentioned the Marxist turn earlier in this chapter. The 1970s witnessed a gradual refinement of Marxist approaches in geography, culminating in its convergence with humanistic concerns in the appraisal of 'structuration theory' in the 1980s (Thrift 1983). This refinement is all the more remarkable since it incorporated a strand of genuine geographic theory that had originated in Scandinavian geography. 'Time geography' was seen by many at the time as a solution to the problem of how to render theoretical claims about society more geographic in kind (Carlstein, Parks and Thrift 1978; Pred 1981); what is more, its two-dimensional weaving together of space and time appeared to hold the key to moving human geography beyond the chorological impasse (Hannah 1997). A similar motif may well have been the driving force behind a second strand of refinement in Marxist geography: the enormous interest sparked by work of Henri Lefebvre and his notion of the 'production of space' (Merrifield 1993; Unwin 2000).

But Marxist geography was not alone in responding to the call for a 'progressive' and 'engaged' form of geographic inquiry; feminist approaches, in particular, heeded the call and developed their own brand of geographical theory. Influential at first as a call for inclusiveness and as a critique of concrete practices within a host of sub-disciplines (Monk and Hanson 1982), feminist geography gradually developed a theoretical agenda of its own. This included, among other issues and topics, a reinterpretation of the uses and structures of specific places (Massey 1984; England 1993), a reappraisal of wider methodological issues in human geography and a critique of underlying assumptions within geographical theory as such (Rose 1993).

Implicit in many of the theoretical advances and propositions of this time was a turn towards 'everyday' forms of geography. This was most apparent in the reappraisal of 'culture' as a broad theme in much geographic writing during the 1980s and 1990s, but it also left a mark in the ongoing development of many other theoretical positions. For example, the eventual convergence of many of the theoretical strands mentioned earlier in this chapter into ever smaller and more refined elements of social reality – be they called 'daily' or 'life paths' (time geography; Dyck 1990), 'performances' (humanistic geography; Crang 1994), designated by specific sexual preferences (Valentine 1993) or the 'body' (feminist geography; McDowell and Court 1994) – is indicative of this desire to 'ground' empirically theoretical claims in concrete experiences. It should thus come as no surprise that this *de facto* reduction in analytical scale in geographic analyses quite effortlessly incorporated an emerging focus on language that took place elsewhere in the social and human sciences (Pred 1990). This 'linguistic turn', and the simultaneous elevation of 'discourse' to centre stage, highlighted both the textual nature of knowledge (Curry 1996; Barnett 1998a) and the importance of representation in human geography (Barnes and Duncan 1992; Duncan and Sharp 1993; Grant and Agnew 1996).

A similar change affected geographic thinking and visions of nature and the environment. Where a previous century saw fit to hypothesize 'nature' in the form of a largely constant context, the turn towards cultural modes of explanation increasingly constructed environmental factors through discourse and contestation. 'Nature' here emerges both as a social construct and as shaped through particular manners of representation (Henderson 1994; Willems-Braun 1997a), resulting in a certain historicizing of the conceptual apparatus sustaining particular notions of 'nature' (Fitzsimmons 1989; Demeritt 1994), which can be contrasted with the notion of environmental determinism in order to gauge the distance separating human geography at the end of the twentieth century from its earlier predecessors, thus introducing a useful notion of difference and critique into environmental discourses in general (Harvey 1996a).

These changes may well have resulted in a loss of causalities across a host of contexts, but in our view they represent a clear gain in topological breadth in general and focused analyses of geographical realities in particular. Here, as elsewhere, the importance of the kind of 'spatial thinking' that is embedded in human geography appears best promoted not through grandiose theoretical claims, but by attempts to illuminate concrete conditions of existence everywhere. From Harvey's writing about the plight of workers in the meat industries of the American South (Harvey 1996b) to the works of Sibley and Cresswell on spatial means of exclusion within modern democracies (Sibley 1995; Cresswell 1996), from analyses of the implications of legal constructs on people's everyday lives (Chouinard 1989; Blomley 1994; Peters 1997) to historical studies of systemic features of imperialism (Gregory 1995a) – just to mention a number of remarkable geographical projects of recent origin – the discipline appears to be in a healthy state indeed. A state, we hasten to add, that is further enriched by the sheer explosion of methodological possibilities within the discipline. The old dichotomy between qualitative and quantitative forms of research – which had been implicit in many of the debates surrounding the quantitative revolution – has been shattered for good: just as GIS multiplied the different possibilities available to anyone with a knack for numbers, so the non-numerical canon has been opened up with the help of largely ethnographic insights and practices (Katz 1992; Cook and Crang 1995), which has lead to a multiplication in choices for anyone interested in 'alternative' scientific practices (Rocheleau 1995; Sharp 2000). Here again, the recognition of 'language' is at the forefront of developments (Tuan 1991).

POSTMODERNISM AND THE RELATIVISTIC TURN

The forms of critique we have portrayed in the previous section of this chapter all share, to some extent, a concern for neglects and injustices brought forth by (an increasingly globalized) society at large. Whether this is represented as 'capitalism', 'patriarchy' or 'colonialism', or some complex intertwining of the three, matters little at this juncture; what is important is that these considerations obey a certain normative imperative to produce knowledge that is both critical and useful. Yet there is another strand of geographical theory that attempted to shed some light on this connection between critique and usefulness that has become known as a postmodern form of geographic inquiry. Questioning common assumptions about the accessibility of reality and the desirability of stable theoretical constructs, postmodern ideas erupted with some fanfare in human geography in the early 1980s (Dear 1988; Claval 1992b) and have since led to a broad field of inquiry (Harvey 1989) that remains ill defined and somewhat fuzzy around the edges (Benko 1997). Dreaded by some because of an alleged inability to make clear distinctions and an 'anything goes' attitude, postmodern geography has nonetheless initiated a set of radical new practices within human geography. The best known of these are probably those attempts to redefine parts of social reality as postmodern in one way or another. Urban areas appear to be the main focus of this kind of analysis, with Edward Soja in particular proclaiming and analysing the intrinsically postmodern metropolis, Los Angeles, where new forms of urbanism are explored and contrasted with older, 'modern' forms of planning (Soja 1989, 2000; Dear and Flusty 1998).

Different in kind from these considerations are those 'postmodern geographies' that do not make claims about a new and postmodern era and its alleged characteristics, but attempt to mount a critique of 'modern' scientific approaches to social reality as such. Where paired with a creative licence and wit, the latter can produce often startling insights about language and its role in the creation of geographic knowledge and practice (Olsson 1991; Doel 1999). What unites both strands is a concern for the heterogeneity of human existence and a perceived failure of traditional geographic inquiry to do justice to such differences. Yet the most obvious consequence of the geographic flirtation with postmodernity has certainly been a change in attitude within the discipline as a whole. The 'plurality' of geographic knowledge, once a byword for unresolved theoretical issues, has become the norm. This is all the more surprising given that even conflicting forms of knowledge are increasingly accepted and placed alongside one another. In short, 'geography' begot 'geographies', often within the space of a single paper.

This increase in diversity has led to a further significant influence of the postmodern on the discipline: the novel awareness of often incompatible 'positionalities' that situate knowledge within specific cultural contexts (Rose 1997). To what extent this insight circumscribes degrees of incompatibility between different forms of knowledge remains to be seen; at the very least, it forces the discipline to rethink the manner in which it has achieved some degree of consensus in the past. One of these – the strategic deployment of dualities, where stable theoretical configurations like 'numerical' and 'non-numerical' or 'public' and 'private' were used to guarantee the status of knowledge – had already been questioned by feminist geographers. Now it was to become a fruitful practice in many areas of human geographic inquiry (Demeritt 2000). The determined attempt to dislodge these (and other) 'modern strategies' is sometimes referred to as 'deconstruction' (Harley 1989; Barnes 1994) and has perhaps yielded the most promising insights in the growing field of postcolonial geographic research (Gregory 1994; Barnett 1997; Sidaway 2000); however, the extent to which this strategy can be categorized as postmodern remains a subject for debate (Doel 1999).

What unquestionably has become more difficult through these interventions is the construction of coherent bodies of geographical knowledge. Knowledge in today's rapidly changing academic world has become more akin to a socially constructed crossword puzzle, where some pieces fit while others do not and where the overall picture is not known to anyone at the beginning, rather than representing solid pieces of reality uncovered (Haack 1998; Curry 1998). Sustaining the analogy, we could further lament the continued fragmentation of geographic insights into crossword puzzles bound by specific national traditions; all too few are willing to shed light on the construction of other people's knowledge puzzles. The global hegemony of English as the prime medium through which scientific insights are communicated has to some extent helped to overcome this problem; at the same time, however, it has eliminated a wide array of practices from the fold (Beaujeu-Garnier 1983). Synthetic disciplines (such as geography), in particular, are threatened by many of these developments in that the fragmentation of concerns both within and outside the discipline proper results in ever smaller audiences (witness the explosion in the number of geographical journals during the 1990s). At the same time, however, the fragmentation of the human sciences in general has arguably led to an increased reception of geographic knowledge within such diverse fields as cultural and gender studies, regional and urban studies, or within the realm of more philosophically oriented interests like postmodernism or feminism. Whether the discipline as a whole stands to profit from this evolution remains to be seen.

CONCLUDING THOUGHTS

The often disparate image of the discipline notwithstanding, there are a number of clearly identifiable epistemological issues that run through many of the debates and theoretical positions taken up by various practitioners within human geography. It is to these that we would like to turn as we conclude this chapter. The first of these common topics or problems is a time-honoured one, centring round the idiographic–nomothetic dichotomy that separates and unites the social sciences at one and the same time. A central point of contention, especially during the early debate about 'exceptionalism' in geography (Schaefer 1953), this axis had been a dominant one in the human and social sciences at least since the *Methodenstreit* in the German *Staatswissenschaften* during the second half of the nineteenth century (Strohmayer 1997b). Is geography a science concentrating on the specific, on difference and the uniqueness of place(s)? Or is its goal to uncover law-like structures that apply under observable conditions and which can be used for planning and other socially relevant purposes? Human geography has found many different answers to these questions during the course of the twentieth century and has witnessed seemingly stable configurations vanish every so often. Take, for instance, the resurrection of a concern for particularity within the postmodern paradigm: was this a return to an earlier geographical practice or something altogether new and different? Was it a child of its time just like any other epistemological break and thus necessarily a form of 'local' knowledge (Ley 2003)?

Mention of 'particularity' should remind us not to overlook a second axis that structured geographic theories during the twentieth century. Often hidden beneath the idiographic–nomothetic divide, the difference between generality and particularity is thought by many to be synonymous with the former. However, one can well imagine a nomothetic approach to particulars, just as idiographic concerns for generalities exist. Implicit in this difference, therefore, is little less than the importance of scale (Marston 2000) or the reminder that the geographies we observe change depending on context, frame of reference and point of view.

Both axes mentioned revolve around epistemological issues in that they present us with a choice between different conceptualizations of what kind of science geography is and should be. But there is a third axis we can identify that centres around questions of causation. Centrally implicated here is the dichotomy between structure and agency. Largely implicit in the theoretical assumptions of human geography up until the 1970s, this axis provided geographers with a whole set of answers to the question of what or who was responsible for the creation and maintenance of geographic realities: was it people's preferences that shaped spaces, or was the particular context within which such choices were made responsible for the geographies we could observe empirically? For as long as geography held fast to the kind of 'checklist' mentality observed earlier in this chapter, this latter part of the question apparently did not become an issue. Things started to change, however, with the move towards more theoretically informed research agendas: here the choice between prioritizing individual actors over social structure (or vice versa) was often perceived to be fundamental.

But what about these axes? The real change in the closing decade of the twentieth century has been to view them less as essential and mutually exclusive choices and to appreciate their commonality of construction. Here, again, we need to acknowledge the importance of the debates surrounding structuration theory in the late 1970s and throughout the 1980s for the overall shape of theoretical discourse within the discipline (Harris 1991; Chouinard 1997). Together with simultaneous developments in feminist geography, it was in these debates that the connective nature of alleged opposites was first acknowledged: what had presented itself previously as a choice between mutually exclusive positions or theoretical points of origin was now increasingly viewed and theorized as a field in which mutually constructive elements acted to bring forth geographic realities (Thrift 1983; Gregory 1994). In fact, the closing years of the last century witnessed a proliferation of papers that analysed a professed instability and constructed nature of the categories that were used to manufacture (often polarized) axes in the first place (Gibson-Graham 1996; Battersbury et al. 1997; Whatmore 1999). In the emerging hybrid world of networks, a future generation of geographers may well find many of the issues and conflicts of old unresolved, perhaps even unresolvable (Thrift 2000a).

We would like to end by expressing our admittedly minimalist hope that a geography for the twenty-first century will no longer have to deny the contested nature of its categories and move towards mature and tolerant manners of dispute and discourse. The emergence of research in the years flanking the turn of the millennium that aims to integrate rather than divide positions that were previously thought to be only loosely connected, exclusive or downright opposed, might be read as a sign that such hopes are not in vain (Mattingly and Falconer-Al-Hindi 1995; Dixon and Jones 1998; Barnett 2001; Castree 2003; Jacobs and Nash 2003; England 2003). However, it might also be a sign of fatigue: only history can judge us now.

2 Cultural geography: place and landscape between continuity and change

Paul Claval and J. Nicholas Entrikin

Geography has a long history, but human geography was born only in the late nineteenth century, in Germany, with the publication in the 1880s of the first volume of Ratzel's *Anthropogeographie* (1881–91). From the outset, culture was thought to be a significant aspect of human geography, but the cultural approach to the discipline was hampered by the dominant naturalist and positivist epistemologies.

Geographers held different views of their field. For the majority of them, geography had to explain fundamentally the regional (and local) differentiation of the earth. With the growing influence of evolutionism, the relationship between man and milieu appeared as the most successful challenger of the earlier regional perspective. In order to avoid conflict between the two conceptions, the idea that geography was the science of landscapes began to flourish. It offered a major advantage: a specific field for geographic inquiry.

These three conceptions were generally combined: geographers explored the diversity of the earth and prepared maps to show it; they had an interest in the diversity of landscapes, which introduced a large-scale, local component, to their approach; they often focused – either at the global, regional or local level – on man–milieu relationships. Their ambition was to present an objective description of the earth and develop a knowledge of the laws which explained its organization. Generally, they had no interest in the geographical views or interpretations developed by the people they studied. These conceptions evolved, but their epistemological basis remained remarkably stable until the mid-twentieth century.

WHY A CULTURAL APPROACH IN GEOGRAPHY?

Culture versus nature

Human geography was born out of the evolutionist challenge: what was the role of natural constraints and the weight of the environment in shaping human societies and their distribution on the earth's surface? Environmentalism was at the root of the new discipline, but it soon appeared that in its crude form it did not offer a satisfying paradigm. Hence a simple idea: in geographical distributions, two types of factors were at work, nature and culture. In the first, culture represented whatever in human behaviour escaped physical contingencies. In some countries, map legends pointed to such a classification: they were ordered under two headings, nature and culture.

The positivist view: culture as a residual variable

Most geographers conceived their discipline as a natural science, but were well aware of the developments taking place in the social sciences. Many of them combined the naturalistic perspective convenient for earth sciences with the positivist views adopted by the social sciences. As a result, geography was conceived as a combination of sub-disciplines falling in two parts: physical geography was a natural science and dealt with topography, hydrology, climatology and biogeography; human geography analysed as objective facts the production, distribution and consumption of goods, the diversity of social relations and institutions, and the significance of power. Viewed from such a perspective, human geography was composed of economic geography, political geography and, up to a point, social geography.

Besides these two general facets, geography studied the relations between the physical environment and human societies when analysing places, regions, countries, landscapes or cities and rural areas. These approaches deciphered man–milieu relationships, which were generally thought of as constraints, albeit in a narrow, determinist sense. The success of the probabilist interpretation of geography proposed by Vidal de la Blache and the Vidalians was due to the partial relaxation of these determinist constraints (Vidal de la Blache 1921; Berdoulay 1981; Claval 1998). When using this type of approach, geographers explained an important proportion of the distributions they observed, but there was also a residual element: how to explain it. Generally, people just spoke of the cultural factor. However, was culture a real explaining variable? No. It was simply a way to recognize the weakness of existing approaches.

In an intellectual context, where the dominant scientific paradigm was either naturalistic and/or positivistic, geographers lacked elbow room to explore the cultural dimensions of geographical distributions; since they were specialists of the earth, they did not dare to explore the mental aspects of man–milieu relationships. When dealing with the religious aspects of life, for instance, they were interested in the way beliefs were expressed through the building of churches, temples, shrines, mosques and stupas, and exercised a variety of influences on cultivation, cattle raising and the types of calendar they involved. They refused to explore the beliefs themselves – the way they were experienced by people, the conception of the cosmos they provided and their translation into profane or sacred space.

Geographers' personal experience and religious or philosophical background

The ban on representations was grounded in methodology. However, it did not prevent geographers from developing personal views on the nature of societies, the role of sociability and the evolution of social forms. In France, Vidal de la Blache had certainly been influenced by the neo-Kantian philosophies that developed at that time in Germany and France. He had an interest in evolutionism and felt closer to its neo-Lamarckian form than to Darwinism (Berdoulay and Soubeyran 1991; Soubeyran 1997). His emphasis on the role of habit certainly came from Lamarckian sources, but at that time habits were also central to other interpretations of social life – Maine de Biran's, for instance. Jean Brunhes had a different background. He was more keen on positive methodology than other geographers because of the scientific orientation of his family, but was also a left-wing Roman Catholic, greatly interested in the new social orientation of the Church (Jean-Brunhes Delamarre 1975; Claval 1998). He was inspired by John Ruskin, about whom he and his wife published an essay. In Germany, Friedrich Ratzel owed much to the forms of Darwinism developed by Ernst Haeckel, whose influence was prominent in the first period of Ratzel's scientific life (Büttmann 1977). After 1876, he became increasingly interested in the role of migration as analysed by Moritz Wagner, another German Darwinist. He also worked for a time in ethnography as well as geography, and developed at this time his conception of human geography. By the end of his life, he was closer to the *Naturphilosophies* of the early nineteenth century and detected a divine creative force within the material world. Eduard Hahn was born into a Lutheran family. Trained as a zoologist, he shared the prevailing views on scientific methodology, but was exceptional in the role he gave to religious beliefs in his interpretation of the domestication of plants and animals and the origin of agriculture (West 1990). He emphasized the role of women in the invention of hoe farming. He was also very critical about the technical aspects of European civilization. Thanks to the influence of neo-Kantism, the significance of the *Methodenstreit* for all the social sciences and the development of ethnology, German scholars were more attentive than French, British or American scientists to the role of values (Strohmayer 1997).

Carl O. Sauer owed part of his formation to his family background, his youth in a German community in the midwest (Sauer 1956) and the years he spent as a student in Germany (Leighly 1978; Hooson 1981). He was well aware of social thought as it developed there from the 1880s to the 1920s (Sauer 1927). In his paper on 'The morphology of landscape', he quoted the German philosopher Keyserling, demonstrating his awareness of the early stages of modern phenomenology (Sauer 1925). As a result, he developed an original interpretation of the nature of social life and the evolution of civilization, which explained his critical view of western technology and its impact on nature (Sauer 1938).

Most geographers of the late nineteenth and early twentieth centuries were perfectly conscious of the role of spiritual forces in collective life. It was because they wished to use scientific methods that they refrained from relying on these insights when exploring human problems. The positivist or naturalist ideologies of scientific inquiries prevented them from going deeper into the cultural dimension of social life and its geographic expression. In order to deal with cultural realities, geographers had to focus on aspects of material life through which some aspects of the mental and social life of the groups they studied were expressed. Three avenues could be explored: the role of techniques, the idea of geography as a science of landscape and the idea of place.

THE FIRST VERSIONS OF THE CULTURAL APPROACH: THE SIGNIFICANCE OF TECHNIQUES

The significance of material techniques for the analysis of man–milieu relationships

Culture ceased to appear as a residual variable when geographers began to explore the technical aspects of man–milieu relationships and the mobility of men, goods and information (from the time of Ritter, Ratzel and Vidal de la Blache, the idea of circulation was thought of as complementary to the ecological approach). Techniques have evident mental dimensions: they exist as mental schemas in the minds of the workers fabricating tools or machines and of those who use them. But they are materially expressed in tools, buildings, field systems, etc. There was no taboo for geographers in this domain: they could investigate it freely.

The emphasis on techniques was particularly important in French geography. Vidal de la Blache initially sought an explanation of man–milieu relationships in the direct influence of climatic facts upon the human body and mind – the old Hippocratic connection. Thanks to the analysis of the Mediterranean climate provided by Theodore Fischer, he discovered that the Mediterranean environment was better characterized by its long summer drought and its effect on vegetation than by the purity of its light. People had to adapt to the climatic constraints: they developed specific types of agriculture and cattle raising, adapted their diet to local products and organized their life according to the types of activities they practised (Claval 1988). The *genre de vie* concept was a complex one: it stressed the means used for exploiting the environment and described its social aspects. Through the emphasis it put on habits, Vidal opened a perspective on social life and representations.

The *genre de vie* concept gave an important role to techniques, making necessary exploration in a number of areas: ploughing, cropping, transforming grains, using animal power through harnessing, transforming milk into butter and cheese, mobilizing wood, crude earth, bricks or stones to build farms and houses, relying on wheels and carts for higher mobility, etc. However, Vidal de la Blache and Vidalian geographers never succeeded in conceptualizing completely this aspect of their method. According to Jean-René Trochet (1998b), it was the main weakness of the French school of geography. Techniques were central to the *genre de vie* explanation, but they were never systematically explored.

There were different reasons for this limitation, the main one being the ban on the study of mental processes. If you wished to build typologies of tools, to understand the way they were conceived, built and transformed, you had to accept the idea that techniques existed as structural schemas in the minds of toolmakers and as gestures and practices in the minds of the people who used them. You had to know the names of the different parts of the tools since these formed part of their manufacture and use. Geographers generally refused to move so far away from the solid world which was their *raison d'être*.

Jean Brunhes was influenced by Vidal de la Blache, but developed genuine conceptions of the field. Because he had been raised in a family of physicists and hard scientists, he gave a very positivist interpretation of the bases of geography, but pleaded for the development of a second level of interpretation, in which history and ethnography played a role (Brunhes 1904, 1909). His interest in techniques was certainly keener than Vidal's. Pierre Deffontaines gave a decisive impulse to the French cultural approach in the 1930s, 1940s and 1950s, mainly through the series he directed: 'L'Homme et la montagne' (Blache 1934), 'L'Homme et l'hiver au Canada' (Deffontaines 1957) and so on. It included monographs on lifestyles and their technical bases, and explored the influence of specific tools, for example, 'L'Homme et la charrue à travers le monde' – man and plough around the world (Haudricourt and Jean-Brunhes Delamarre 1955).

French geographers gave more room to the technical dimension of geography than many of their colleagues, but the interest in technology was present everywhere, especially in Germany and the United States. In Germany, where the idea of landscape as the main object of geography became popular from the 1900s, the clearing of forests, organization of fields, presence of hedges and the form of farms increasingly appeared as significant features for the discipline (Schlüter 1952, 1954, 1958). They could not be explained without reference to the techniques known by the people who settled and exploited the area. Eduard Hahn took a step further: he stressed the central role played by domesticated plants and animals in the mastering of natural environments. He showed how different, from the start, plough and hoe agricultures were (Hahn 1896a and b, 1914). In plough agriculture, men prepared a homogenized environment for seeding one crop, while in hoe agriculture, women took advantage of a variety of ecological niches to plant a range of cuttings.

In the USA, Carl Sauer was well aware of the developments of German geography. He stressed the significance of landscape and focused the cultural approach he developed on the man-made component of landscape. He was fascinated by the way in which natural landscapes were turned into cultural ones and explored the complexes of plants and animals created by man's attempt to domesticate the landscape (Sauer 1938; 1947). As a result, his human geography was based on botanical evidence and explored the impact of man's action on the natural equilibrium. The sets of cultivated plants and domesticated animals introduced by settlers sometimes escaped control, with long-term damaging consequences for the environment. Clark's study on the transformation of the South Island in New Zealand from the eighteenth century onwards is the best of these monographs (Clark 1949).

Ideas concerning techniques of domestication were systematized, in the inter-war period, by the Russian botanist N. N. Vavilov (1951). Using the evidence provided by genetics, he showed that domesticated plants and animals originated in a few regions of the earth: the Middle East, South-East Asia, Indonesia and New Guinea, northern and central China, the north-eastern part of Africa, West Africa, the uplands of Mexico and the Andes in South America.

Geographers played a significant role in the development of the scientific approach to techniques in the first half of the twentieth century, but because of their taboo on mental processes, they ceased to be on the frontier from the 1930s. A scientific discipline developed to analyse the origin and evolution of techniques, the way they were diffused and their role in human history. In France, for instance, ethnographers developed typologies (Mauss 1947) and reflections upon the conceptions of tools (Leroi-Gourhan 1943–5). Close to geographers, but independently of them, Georges Haudricourt (a former student of Vavilov) and Mariel Jean-Brunhes Delamarre (the daughter of Jean Brunhes) produced innovative works on transport and plough techniques (Haudricourt 1987; Haudricourt and Jean-Brunhes Delamarre 1955).

The analysis of the influence of techniques on man–milieu relationships had a deep impact on the Annales school of history. Fernand Braudel owed much to the Vidalian idea of *genres de vie*. As a historian, he translated this into the idea of constraints, explaining the slow rhythm of transformation of the lower part of societies – the theme of long duration. Techniques were central for him in this history of long-term trends – hence his wonderful book on *Civilisation matérielle et capitalisme* (Braudel 1967).

The idea of social techniques

Pierre Gourou worked mainly in the tropical world, Vietnam before the Second World War and Central Africa after it. While preparing his doctoral dissertation on the rural areas of the Red River delta in North Vietnam, he was fascinated by the techniques used by the local farmers to control water levels and produce irrigated rice (Gourou 1936). They were so complex that their efficiency depended upon their coordination: the techniques that allowed the local society to master, through its *genre de vie*, its local environment were not only material, they were also social. It was because the Vietnamese village was a coherent group, with efficient forms of social control and an acute sense of the collective interest, that the irrigation system worked, even if the tools and machines it relied upon were small-scale ones, in an environment where floods, typhoons and other natural hazards involved often important corrective action from the farmers.

The idea of social techniques soon became important in French geography. Later, when working in Africa, Pierre Gourou often spoke of the determinism of cultures: in the rather homogeneous environments of savannah or rain forest, which prevail over most of Central and Western Africa, different ethnic groups used practically the same array of tools, but did not achieve the same results. The difference derived from their social organization, the domains in which they invested their work and energy, the share of men and women in the preparation of fields and the distribution of products among the population (Gourou 1970, 1973).

In such a conception, techniques are conceived as go-betweens that mediated the relation between humans and their environment; they are also analysed as mental structures, as grammars, as sets of possible social combinations at the disposal of social groups. When confronting nature, people are using, at the same time, a wide array of tools, domesticated plants and animals, and more or less efficient modes of social organization.

Techniques, communication and diffusion

When focusing on techniques, the cultural approach was necessarily conducive to reflection on the conditions of their transmission – the ways they were conceived, built and used were learnt and involved a communication process. Since they relied on experience rather than formalized knowledge, it was impossible to capitalize on perfectly rationalized modes of explanation when teaching them. Observation and the imitation of gestures were essential in this process. Techniques – material techniques at least – were part and parcel of the oral low cultures; their transmission from one generation to the next was relatively easy within a locality, but their diffusion from place to place was more difficult.

Social techniques differed from material ones in that their foundations were partly ethical: they were based on values, which meant they could be thoroughly expressed through coherent discourse, which often took written form. As a result, their diffusion over wide areas could be achieved easily.

From the 1880s, diffusion seemed to be the main research orientation concerning communication processes in the field of culture. Since this field was very significant for them, some geographers, most notably Friedrich Ratzel (1885–8), also became active in anthropology. The majority of them relied on past anthropological results. Both anthropologists and geographers drew on nineteenth-century evolutionary arguments concerning speciation, which added an aura of scientific authority to their environmentalist arguments (Campbell and Livingstone 1983; Entrikin 1988). For example, Ratzel's American student, Ellen Semple, applied the science of anthropogeography to the cultural evolution of the Mediterranean region in describing the key role played by diffusion:

> Whatever flower of culture each small region developed in its own garden plot was disseminated over the whole basin by the multitudinous paths of the sea. So varied were the local conditions of temperature, rainfall, soil, relief, area, coastline and vicinal grouping, that each district commanded some peculiar combination of natural advantages in the production of its distinctive contribution to the civilization as the whole. These cultural achievements in turn, transplanted to distant shores, took on new aspects in response to a changed environment or were remodeled by the genius of needs of new masters . . .
>
> (Semple 1931: 9–10)

Diffusion research relied on a simple hypothesis: cultures were considered as sets of independent features. Each cultural feature was born in a specific place or culture area from which it had diffused. Thus the main objective of anthropology was to locate the places where cultural features were born and map the different phases of their diffusion. The interest in diffusion was strengthened by the neo-Lamarckian bent of many of the geographers who conceived human geography around 1900 (Roger 1979; Berdoulay and Soubeyran 1991; Soubeyran 1997).

There was practically no discussion about the theoretical foundations of such a hypothesis: the idea that innovation could occur at the same time in different places was seldom considered, which impaired the value of the results. In spite of these inbuilt limitations, however, the diffusionist theory came to some interesting conclusions. In many cases, the hypothesis of a unique place of origin was coherent with observations, but something did not fit this general schema: the idea that cultural features were independent from each other. It soon became apparent that diffusion did not proceed at the same speed all the time and in all directions. In some areas, innovations were quickly adopted; in others, they were resisted. In the case of the diffusion of domesticated plants, for instance, crops which appeared as perfect substitutes for traditional ones were soon accepted: a new cereal was incorporated into the crop rotation system when it produced more abundant crops, provided the same food as the older ones and withstood more efficiently the local natural hazards. When the new crop involved new modes of consumption, the process was slower. In Europe, the standard diet was based on grain, not on roots: hence the long delay before the potato was integrated into crop systems, in spite of its high performance as a food crop.

Through the discovery of different attitudes concerning the acceptance of innovations, geographers were introduced to a new dimension of the cultural approach: the existence of mental structures which were difficult to transform. Change occurred more easily when it did not require an overall transformation of existing social and mental systems, but only of local substitutions.

THE FIRST VERSIONS OF THE CULTURAL APPROACH: THE LANDSCAPE

From a functional to an archaeological and cultural approach to landscapes

Another way to deal with culture, without delving too much into mental processes or social problems, was to focus on landscapes. Otto Schlüter was the first, in Germany, to understand the advantage of such an approach to geography (Schlüter 1899, 1906). At a time when people disagreed about the influence of nature on the human mind and social life, the landscape approach offered a way round the problem without relying on hypotheses that were too restrictive, whether deterministic or possibilist. Landscapes are made of material features: they are natural, man made or combine nature and human activity.

The human – or 'cultural' – part of the landscape was mainly made up of fields, meadows, hedges, farms and roads. The first hypothesis used in studies of this assemblage considered rural landscapes as functional expressions of human activity. Such an interpretation was conducive to the analysis of the field systems, the crop rotations they involved and the way cattle raising and grain production were combined in order to build sustainable agricultural production. Meitzen proposed to associate each type of settlement pattern and rural landscape with a particular ethnic group (Meitzen 1895). The analysis escaped from the simplifications of the ethnic interpretation between 1900 and 1930 (Vinogradoff 1905; Gray 1915; Bloch 1931).

It soon appeared, however, that all the features which could be discerned in a landscape were not functionally linked with the present forms of exploitation. Fields were organized centuries ago, at a time when ploughs and teams were different. Farmers sowed different varieties and crops, did not sell their produce to the same markets and so on. The permanency of features that were functional a few decades or centuries ago, but had ceased to harmonize with the prevailing economic and technical conditions, had important correlates for the cultural approach:

1| It introduced the idea that a landscape never perfectly reflected current conditions: it was also – and in some cases, mainly – an archaeological document. It could be used as evidence for reconstructing the land uses of the past and the societies which conceived them. In France, a good part of the Annales school of history relied on this discovery, since it provided historians with new documentary evidence and ways to explore the slow history of the commonplace components of traditional cultures and societies (Friedman 1996).

2| It was conducive to addressing questions about the reasons for the conservation of specific features: in some cases, the presence of non-functional features in extensive landscapes did not entail higher costs. In other cases, people had to accept lower productivity and less efficiency, which meant that the permanence of some landscape features could be explained only through their valorization – a new dimension was added to the cultural approach. Depending on the situation, it revealed the significance of localism, nationalism or religion.

Landscape and the idea of harmony

Landscape studies were prominent in Germany, where they often departed from the strictly functional and archaeological conception presented above. From the time of Johann Gottfried Herder, the idea of a subtle correspondence between people and the country they lived in had been popular. This correspondence could be interpreted as an influence of nature on the behaviour of people. In a romantic perspective, it could also be ascribed to a deeply rooted harmony between the different components of nature, topography, vegetal landscapes and the people who inhabited them (Bartels 1969). Thus an aesthetic dimension was introduced into the cultural landscape and played a role in the development of studies upon the regional differentiation of low cultures, as expressed in the creation of open-air museums in Sweden, Denmark and, later, across Central and Eastern Europe.

At the beginning of the twentieth century, German geographers considered themselves natural scientists. They spent much time deciphering the history of the natural components of landscapes, the deforestation process, the evolution of prairies and the ensuing erosion and accumulation processes. They were interested in the human ('cultural') landscape, but mainly in terms of its functional or archaeological aspects. They were also familiar with the harmony concept: rural landscapes were sometimes pleasant, well kept and trimmed. In other contexts, they offered the image of a disorderly society and conveyed the feeling of groups unable to create sustainable relations with their environment. In this way, aesthetic considerations introduced a moral scale for judging the relations between groups and nature. This peculiar form of cultural analysis was used by some German geographers during the Nazi period to justify the extension of German rule westwards or eastwards in Latin or Slavic-speaking countries (Eisel 1980).

Sauer, landscapes and the biological dimension of cultures

Even if Carl Sauer was aware of the different trends of German geography and open to the significance it gave to landscape, he never used a similar scale for evaluating the role of social groups as geographical agents. He was too critical towards modern forms of civilization. He considered that rural societies – for example, the German immigrant communities of Missouri in which he was raised – were in many ways superior to the forms created by modernization. He did not consider that presenting moral judgements was off-limits for geographers, but the harmony he praised was not fundamentally aesthetic – it was biological.

For Sauer, landscapes were biological realities first. Natural landscapes had been transformed by man's activity; through deforestation and cultivation, societies reshaped the biosphere. Sauer believed that cultural geography was mainly concerned with the transformation of the biological dimension of the environment through human agency. Landscapes were in a state of balance and human activity could destroy natural equilibria. Groups differed by the set of plants they cultivated and the animals they raised; parasites or pests living on their crops or herds signified a major problem.

Sauer focused on landscapes, but at the same time had a deep insight into human societies. Even if he was mainly interested in the way they modified nature and produced cultural artefacts, he knew that groups were tied by values and organized by culture. This culture was more or less sensitive to the biological realities. At a time when nobody was speaking of sustainability, Sauer's main interest was the capability of groups to organize long and stable relations with their environment.

The study of place and the early cultural approach in geography

Within the dominating paradigm of man–milieu relationships and the prevailing naturalistic and positivist epistemologies, geographers had to rely on the study of intermediaries, like techniques, or on transversal concepts, like landscape, in order to deal with cultural realities. Place was just another of these concepts. It did not play as important a role as landscape, but it was significant nevertheless, especially in French geography.

Everyone is familiar with the definition of geography Vidal de la Blache proposed: 'Geography is the science of places, not of men'. Even if the significance of this sentence should not be dissociated from the context in which it was presented, it meant that the concept of place – and, more generally, the concepts of region and country – was significant for the geographers of the early twentieth century.

There were different reasons for this:

1| The Kantian conception of geography as the science of the regional differentiation of the earth was shared by many geographers, which meant that all the differences had to be analysed, even those which were certainly more subjective than objective.

2| From the end of the eighteenth century, geographers considered that their role was to convey, through their descriptions and the documents they used to complete them, the atmosphere of places and the feelings associated with them. These efforts grew out of the significance conferred on observation as a foundation for the naturalist approaches to science.

3| When analysing a country, it is necessary to use place names. Some are associated with a specific locality. Parallel to the toponyms are choronyms (*noms de pays* in French), which are very useful for geographers, since they encapsulate complex sets of associated specificities and allow for their evocation through the utterance of a single word. In France, geologists were the first to discover the usefulness of popular or regional place names towards the end of the eighteenth century. By the end of the nineteenth century, geographers were also using them and trying to evaluate their scientific significance.

The study of place mixed these different curiosities or motivations. It introduced the lived experience of space as a category of geographical analysis, but geographers were rather reluctant to accept this theme, as was shown by the critical study of Lucien Gallois (1908).

The main impulse was rooted in the works of Jules Michelet. In his *Tableau de la France* (1833), he wrote that Britain was for him 'an Empire, Germany a race and France a person'. What did he mean by 'une personne'? Michelet's ideas became more significant later, when the French defeat against Prussia, in 1871, initiated a process of reflection on the nature of France, the French people and French identity. Because of the history of the country, it was impossible to equate French men or women with a particular race – there was in France a mixture of Celtic, Roman and German components. People were also critical of the German idea of ethnic unity as the foundation of a nation. Hence the interest given to the geographical reflection on France and the influence of Vidal de la Blache's *Le Tableau de la géographie de la France* (1903). His answer was a subtle one: because of the interweaving of southern, northern and western influences brought about by the natural distribution of relief and climate, the same themes were repeated time and again all over the country, teaching all the inhabitants how to build unity out of diversity, and conferring on the whole a specific *personnalité*.

Vidal's study was developed at the national scale, but evidently it could be transposed: the theme of geographic personality was mainly employed at regional and local levels during the first half of the twentieth century. It had a significant component of physical geography, but was mainly concerned with the way people experienced the space in which they lived and the values they attached to that space.

The limits of traditional forms of the cultural approach in geography

For geographers during the first half of the twentieth century, culture was not only a homonym for human geography or a residual category found when all the systematic approaches had been used; the cultural approaches developed at that time also opened interesting perspectives on geographical distributions and introduced the experience of space as a dimension of geographical analysis. However, these results were limited by the epistemological constraints inherent in the prevailing positivist and naturalistic paradigm. It hampered the exploration of cultural processes and forbade the analysis of the mental representations made visible through the landscape.

The methodological imperatives were certainly responsible for many of the simplifications which hindered the analysis of cultural aspects of spatial distributions during the first half of the twentieth century. The superorganic conception of culture was one of these interpretations (for a critical evaluation of the superorganic hypothesis, see Duncan 1980). Since geographers refrained from analysing cultural processes as soon as they had a mental component, they were reduced to presenting culture as a ready-made reality. In American anthropology, the superorganic view of culture had been used by Franz Boas – and was later popularized by A. L. Kroeber and Clyde Kluckhohn – as a reaction against the biological determinism of evolutionists (Hoefle 1999). Sauer adopted their view, even if it was not central to his conception of culture. His major contribution was the incorporation of a biological dimension into the conception of landscape and culture, and the refutation of the crude forms of environmental determinism.

By the middle of the twentieth century, many geographers grew impatient with the limitations imposed on them by the positivist or naturalistic methodologies developed in the late nineteenth or early twentieth centuries. When studying religious life, Pierre Deffontaines was conscious of the superficiality of the majority of geographical publications, since they did not consider the beliefs and attitudes of the people they were analysing. Some of his texts are perfectly clear in this respect:

> The most important event in the geographic history of the Earth was not such-and-such mountain folds, such-and-such sea-level change, such-and-such climatic transformation. It was the appearance with man of a kind of special sphere, more extraordinary than the pyrosphere, the hydrosphere, the atmosphere or even the biosphere, what could be called

the thought sphere, which R. F. Teilhard de Chardin called the noosphere, an immaterial envelope certainly, but which comes within the scope of landscape [. . .].

It is here a matter of the development of [man's] free thought, dominating nature, imposing his prominence on it, marking it through a special imprint . . .

(Deffontaines 1948: 7–8)

However, he did not try to build a more comprehensive framework for developing the cultural approach. First, a change in the prevailing paradigms had to occur.

Cultural geography receded during the 1950s and 1960s. It was quite understandable: geographers had focused on the material aspects of culture. Since progress made techniques increasingly similar, the relevance of the cultural approach for explaining the contemporary world was diminishing. The cultural approach appeared increasingly as a restrospective one.

CULTURAL GEOGRAPHY IN THE SECOND HALF OF THE TWENTIETH CENTURY

The materialist, naturalist and positivist limitations to a fully dimensional cultural approach gradually disappeared during the last half of the twentieth century. The impetus was largely external to cultural geography, coming from changes in the social sciences and other sub-fields of geography. As the sources of disciplinary authority shifted from a geographic ancestry to philosophers and social theorists, human geography expanded to include a wider array of methods and approaches. Hermeneutics, structuralism and post-structuralism brought more complex analyses of meaning into geographic research and transformed the conception of the geographic agent. In the process, cultural geographic themes of landscape and place were transformed as they shifted from naturalistic, geographic 'objects' to geographic phenomena inseparable from more complex geographic selves or subjects. The traditional concern for place and landscape became mediated through self and body (Sack 1997).

These transformations emerged from a period of relative dormancy in cultural geography around the middle of the twentieth century. The second generation of Sauerians followed diverging paths, but each represented an element of the Berkeley legacy, including landscape studies, culture history, historical cultural ecology and diffusion of material culture (Wagner and Mikesell 1962). More mentalistic topics, including language, communication and religion, were considered, but still within the constraints of positivism. For example, Wilber Zelinsky's *Cultural Geography of the United States* (1973: 73) emphasized the study of the distribution of both artefacts and ideas, but ideas were referred to by Zelinsky as 'mentifacts' that could be represented by locations on a map. At the time of the quantitative revolution, many geographers thought that cultural data could be processed in the same way as other geographical phenomena (Sopher 1972).

During the 1960s, however, the Sauerian legacy was increasingly defined by its detractors, most notably the spatial analytic vanguard of the quantitative revolution. From this critical perspective, Sauer's cultural geography was equivalent to its traditional antipode, the chorological view associated with Richard Hartshorne (1939). The spatial analysts blended these once antagonistic positions into a single, traditional geographic approach, described as proto-scientific, descriptive and idiographic.

In spite of their criticisms of cultural and regional geography, the spatial analysts shared their materialist and positivist character. They also shared a relatively uncomplicated concept of agency. In Sauerian cultural geography, agents were the conduits of culture. The spatial analytic conception of agency involved the application of a utilitarian calculus, which guided decisions concerning distance minimization, optimum locations, adoption of innovation and other foundational elements of a rationalized, modern social space. Communication remained an important concern, especially in diffusion modelling, but its form was that of units or bits of information moving through space and occasionally received by rational decision makers.

Ironically, the late twentieth-century revival of cultural geography has its origins in the challenges to this spatial analytic paradigm in human geography. The two most significant challenges came from Marxist geography and humanistic geography. Early Marxist thought in geography was predominantly structuralist and economistic, but it did lead to the introduction of topics associated with the social production of landscapes and the social production of meaning, themes that continue to resonate in the current post-Marxist period (Harvey 1989; Mitchell 1995; Domosh 1996).

For cultural geography, humanistic geography was the more significant of the two movements because of its emphasis on meaning, experience and interpretation (Tuan 1976). Geographical agency was enlarged to include the subjective dimension, as is evident in Yi-Fu-Tuan's (1977) consideration of sense of place and, later, in Augustin Berque's (1990) theme of *médiance*. Questions of meaning and experience were not new to geography and can be traced back to the 'geosophy' of John K. Wright (1947), the perceptual geography of historical geographers such as David Lowenthal (1961) and Hugh Prince (1971), and the explorations of geographical experience of Eric Dardel (1952). Also, the studies of everyday landscapes associated with J. B. Jackson (1983) and his journal, *Landscape*, offered a more experiential approach to this traditional geographical theme (Meinig 1979). However, the sustained momentum of humanistic geography came from the intellectual energy of hermeneutic movements outside geography in the human sciences, which drew on the continental philosophical traditions of phenomenology and existentialism (Entrikin 1976).

Geographers have also drawn a part of their inspiration from the exploration of language and its performance. This view is especially evident in post-structural analysis of culture as composed of codes and of texts as produced and used by the collectivity of speakers. Good examples of this connection were provided by Pred's (1990, 1999) exploration of the social codes of naming places and his probe of unconventional textual strategies or 'unbuttoned language'. A more technical analysis of geographic language and sociolinguistics may be found in Mondada and Söderström (1993).

Cultural geography: narratives and anti-narratives

In spite of its origins in French and German geography, cultural geography was a predominantly North American preoccupation through much of the mid-twentieth century. The intellectual currents prevalent at the time in French, German and British geography flowed towards a social geography in which cultural themes were addressed primarily in relation to matters of social structure, especially social class. Of course, notable exceptions existed, such as the landscape studies of the German geographer, Gerhard Hard (1970). Within North American geography, cultural geography remained relatively isolated in its continued association with the scientific biography of Carl Sauer and his academic progeny. The renewed concern with cultural geography at the end of the century, the so-called 'new cultural geography', returned the field to its more international origins (Cosgrove and Jackson 1987; Claval 1992a). However, the new cultural geographers continued to address the ghosts of the Sauerian legacy, in spite of their obvious discomfort in doing so. Such encounters have contributed to an apparent internecine conflict, or in James Duncan's (1994) terms, a 'civil war' in contemporary cultural geography.

As Duncan's inflammatory metaphor indicates, an intergenerational narrative that seamlessly weaves the work of Sauer and his students into the new cultural geography has remained an elusive goal. Its elusiveness is a consequence of both the intrinsic ambiguity and amorphousness of the culture concept and several dramatic epistemic shifts that have occurred in the field. The semantic complexity of culture has been well documented (Williams 1983). In part because of this confusion over meaning, geographers have tended to work with culture as an undefined concept (Wagner 1994). Some disciplines have staked out territorial claims to the concept, most notably anthropology, but its current use spans across the social sciences and the humanities. In its full semantic dimensionality, culture incorporates subjective meaning and social structural constraint, pre-existing codes and human creativity (Alexander 1990). Its borders with social structure on the one hand and moral values on the other are notoriously porous. However, attempts to reduce culture to economy, social structure and biology have served only to highlight its autonomous functions.

Epistemic shifts in cultural geography have been most evident in the growing complexity of the cultural agent. Within a relatively short period of time (less than four decades), cultural geographers have moved from the agentless realm of an implicit superorganic conception of culture, to the agent-centred concerns of humanistic geography and back to the relatively agentless world associated with the decentred subject of post-structuralism. A different, yet partially overlapping, characterization emphasizes the shift from functionalist and historicist interpretations of material culture to hermeneutic and radically reflexive accounts of self and meaning, place and landscape. Nature itself, which largely disappeared as a central concept in twentieth-century geography, has reappeared as a historicized, cultural construct (Olwig 1996; Gandy 1997).

These changes have been driven less by a specific geographic problematic than by metatheoretical arguments within the humanities and social sciences. It is in part for this reason that new forms of cultural geography have not replaced older traditions. Rather, each proceeds independently of the others, with occasional points of intersection that lead to the application of pejorative descriptors, such as 'old/new', 'theoretical/empirical' or 'explanatory/descriptive'. Interestingly, the core geographical concepts of landscape and place seem to move most easily across these categories and research traditions, as does a concern with communication.

Several intergenerational plots have been offered, but no single one has gained wide acceptance. Most narratives have been written from the perspective of one of the many factions that currently exist within cultural geography. In the most general terms they may be divided by their characterizations of Sauerian geography as either broad in scope, anti-positivist in method and inclusive in its membership, or as narrow, tending towards positivism and with membership determined by academic bloodline.

One of the most comprehensive recent efforts to offer reconstructionist narratives is found in Kenneth Foote *et al.*'s *Re-reading Cultural Geography* (1994). Its title plays on that of an earlier text by Phillip Wagner and Marvin Mikesell (1962), *Readings in Cultural Geography*, which set the basic categories of cultural geography during the era of the second Sauerian generation. *Re-reading Cultural Geography* traces the multiple trajectories of late twentieth-century American cultural geography and provides ample evidence of the dangers of making broad generalizations about the field.

Contributors to the volume offer numerous histories of twentieth-century geography and several plot-types emerge. They range across a wide spectrum of possibilities, including unification/integration, confederation and heterotopia, or the celebration of difference, and thus from narrative to anti-narrative. In this instance, the unification/integration argument is offered by Karl Butzer (1994), focusing on the topic of cultural ecology. For Butzer, the new cultural geography appears as a recent addition to an already impressively large scholarly edifice built by the Sauerians and their German predecessors. The hope for coherence derives in part from the cultural ecologist's capacious definition of culture, which includes all that is not nature. Thus the conception of culture as representation, a defining characteristic of the new cultural geography, is indeed part, but not all, of the realm. In the confederal thesis he wrote as a conclusion of Foote's collective book on *Re-reading Cultural Geography*, Marvin Mikesell (1994) emphasizes tolerance for thematic and epistemological diversity and belief in the existence of certain common concerns – for example, landscape analysis – that encourage cooperation rather than integration. The heterotopic vision of James Duncan (1994: 407), offers a postmodernist celebration of fragmentation and a diversity of epistemologies. He offers heterotopia as a vision of peace for the 'civil war' and argues that the intellectual projects currently grouped into the category of cultural geography are 'so disparate' that there is very little common territory 'over which to quarrel'.

Several recent debates illustrate the antagonisms that continue to exist and that suggest the oxymoronic quality of Duncan's peaceful heterotopia. For example, Marie Price and Martin Lewis (1993a) castigated the so-called 'new cultural geographers' for caricaturing and significantly narrowing the research interests of Sauer and his students. In advocating the relevance of Sauerian cultural geography for contemporary concerns, they challenge the interpretation of this work as a compilation of theoretically naive landscape descriptions and atheoretical culture histories. The scholarly exchange that later ensued over their challenge offered little in the way of substantive engagement, but did present a stark summary of the multiple and often conflicting narratives that coexist in contemporary cultural geography (Cosgrove 1993; Duncan 1993; Jackson 1984; Price and Lewis 1993b).

Unnoticed commonalities

Postmodern, post-structural and postcolonial studies in cultural geography have further complicated the plot. Great care is taken by proponents of these approaches to disassociate their work from all that has preceded it. For example, in a recent journal debate concerning an article on the cultural politics of nature in British Columbian forestry activities of the nineteenth and twentieth centuries, Andrew Sluyter (1997) criticized the author, Bruce Willems-Braun (1997a), for not recognizing his intellectual ties to the Sauerian tradition. The author responded by accusing his critic of attempting to discipline him by putting his work in a Sauerian definition of cultural geography. Willems-Braun stated emphatically that: 'My concerns lie with how "nature" and the natural landscapes are rendered culturally intelligible (as texts that can be read) . . . Sauer sought to locate "culture" in the physical form of landscape; I seek to explore the "cultural politics" involved in representing landscapes' (Willems-Braun 1997b: 706). For Willems-Braun, landscape has moved from the material to the representational and from the naively given to the politically contested.

   For the post-structuralist, individual and collective decisions involved in the construction of landscapes are embedded in discourses and thus landscape becomes 'naturalized' or 'materialized' discourse (Schein 1997). Culture is not a unified whole, but instead is composed of different practices of representation that agents act out as if performing a script. It is not clear, however, how agency works in the Foucaultian world of power relations. Is agency possible when decisions are understood as nodes within the cross-currents of discourse? Are individuals any more agents as script readers of discourses than they are as conduits of cultural processes? Can we even ask the question about a moral landscape or moral community with such a limited conception of agency? For example, how does one make a moral decision in relation to the environment or the potential for inclusion and exclusion within a community if the discourse that frames one's choices is itself immoral?

THE GEOGRAPHIES OF MEANING AND IDENTITY

The conflicts among cultural geographers undermine assertions about disciplinary continuity and mask innovation and change. The most evident and significant change has been the increased emphasis on meaning and interpretation. This shift towards the hermeneutic is a legacy of the quiet revolutionary, the humanist geographer. In certain traditional sub-fields, especially those that have remained strongly attached to materialist concerns, this hermeneutic turn has been relatively insignificant. For example, the cultural ecologists apparently find little to connect them to humanistic geography (Turner 1997). However, in most other sub-fields of cultural geography the effects have been profound.

Humanistic geography has been extremely important in preparing the disciplinary groundwork for the consideration of relatively new cultural topics that have shaped much of the contemporary geographic discourse. For example, a common theme in sub-disciplinary journals such as *Géographie et cultures* and *Ecumene* has been that of identity, and the source for such studies in geography has been the humanistic geographer, who has emphasized intentionality and the relation of subject, both individual and collective (Ley and Samuels 1978; Daniels 1985).

Common identities form bonds of solidarity. These bonds have a geographic connection in place and territory or as shared cultural geographies (Entrikin 1991, 1997). In forging imagined communities, groups create common identities among individuals who share a territory and a history. This seemingly basic concern becomes quite complex, however, when one seeks to provide a theoretical framework for understanding identity. Paul Ricœur (1992) offers a starting point in making a distinction between two types of identity, 'idem' and 'ipse'. The first refers to identity as the permanence and continuity of the self through time; it is the Cartesian cogito. The second emphasizes identity as constructed through the self's interpretation of life events; it is an interpreted life, one refigured through narrative. Such narratives form the foundational stories of collective life.

Moderns who live without the comprehensive meaning horizons once provided by myth and religion are left with greater individual responsibility to interpret and give sense to the various and often competing meaning horizons that make up contemporary cultures. Individual identity emerges from this process, not as a set of traits but as the self-awareness gained in terms of one's biography (Giddens 1991: 53). Thus personal identity becomes available to consciousness through a process of storytelling, of constructing narratives not only of self, but also of self in relation to the group or community. For the moral philosopher, Alasdair MacIntyre (1984: 221), the story of one's identity and the possession of an individual historical identity coincides with the possession of a social or communal identity. Modern identity thus becomes 'many tiered', representing a complex mix of universalistic and particularistic concerns (Taylor 1989: 8). A characteristic of such stories is their necessary relation to concrete places and events.

One would expect to find such themes in early twentieth-century regional geography, but disciplinary strictures concerning the 'natural science' of geography precluded such work. Indeed when American regional geography moved towards regionalism, or a collective identity associated with place and territory, it was seen as crossing the border into sociology or literature (Whittlesey 1954: 51). Not surprisingly, the leading American students of regionalism were sociologists, historians and planners, such as Howard Odum and Lewis Mumford. Similarly, the stories of how identity was forged in the neighbourhoods of growing cities were also left for others, most notably the urban sociologists associated with Robert Park.

The humanist geographer introduced these questions of identity to geography. By adding the intentional agent to the geographic lexicon, the humanist shifted the emphasis from the description of place, landscape or territory to their meaning for a subject, either individual or collective (Berdoulay and Entrikin 1998). The basic question of identity, 'who am I?', or collectively, 'who are we?', becomes geographic to the extent that such identity comes in part from that subject's relation to the world and the surrounding environment. As individual and collective identity become linked, one gains insight into shared attachments and conflicts over the meanings of landscapes, places and territories. Indeed it is argued that a strongly shared connection to local geographies is essential to the development of a collective identity (Chivallon 1995). The cultural becomes a potential motivational force, related but analytically independent from matters of biology, economy or society (Staszak 1999).

This basic relation brings into view a variety of research themes (all of which may be found in contemporary journals), for example, the question of landscapes of memory in which collective remembrances of home, war and nation serve as symbols of membership and group solidarity (Agnew 1997; Heffernan 1995; Withers 1996). Racial, ethnic, gender and sexual identity have also been associated with place, for example, in the conflation of place and ethnicity in ethnic neighbourhoods or the liminal urban spaces of sexuality or debates surrounding identity politics (Anderson and Gale 1992; Forest 1995; Bondi 1995; McDowell 1994). Interethnic conflict has centred on the symbolism of place. National territory has been defined through ethnicity and citizenship and transformed through international migration and the globalization of economies (Agnew and Brusa 1999). The relation of self to group and environment is given added dimensionality through its mediation in the body, itself a repository of cultural meaning (Nast and Pile 1998). Self and body have also been explored in terms of the culture of consumption and its connection to identity (Crang 1996; Bell and Valentine 1997). All these themes are given an added scalar dimension when set against the powerful forces of globalization that uproot traditional attachments and simultaneously homogenize and stimulate difference (Pitte 1995). The hybrid cultural forms that emerge from the mix of multi-scaled forms of life ranging from the local to the global have led to a reconsideration of the cultural geography of everyday life (Werlen 1997).

The growing significance of reflections on meaning and identity in cultural geography has occurred in conjunction with the evolution of feminism and gender studies. This connection is clearly evident in the new journal, *Gender, Place and Culture: a journal of feminist geography*. The early research in feminist geography offered a 'feminist empiricism' (Harding 1986), which sought to make women more visible within a social scientific geography. These interests quickly evolved, however, into explorations of the social and cultural construction of gender identities and critical examinations of the masculinist nature of geographical discourse, ranging across positivism, Marxism and humanism (Rose 1993; Bondi and Domosh 1992; McDowell 1992). The recent post-structuralist turn emphasizes the heterogeneity of women and their experiences and the necessity for a reflexive strategy in cultural geography that highlights the partial and situated quality of geographical knowledge (Haraway 1991; Rose 1997). Cultural themes are central to the consideration of the feminist geographer's positioned subject, whose identity is in part constructed through the discursive manipulation of symbols, meanings and representations, or through what might otherwise be described as the manifestations of cultural power.

THE POLITICS OF CULTURE

In the humanist perspective, emphasis has been given to cooperation and consensus, to the ways in which the individual recombines with the group and groups demonstrate collective spirit. Humanists turned to culture in order to address the social bonds that allow for group consensus and forge group solidarity. Solidarity emerges from the shared ways of life and experiences in place and territory that give individuals a sense of being part of a collective. It offers collective narratives that emphasize belonging and membership and invoke a strong communitarian sentiment.

Critics have seen such a perspective as being fundamentally conservative and at times overly sentimental and romantic in its concern with authentic and harmonious landscapes and places. The politics of culture has taken different directions in postmodernist and post-structuralist cultural geography. In the humanistic perspective, culture informs all areas of life, including the political. In post-structural formulations, culture becomes the medium of power. Rather than culture giving meaning to power, power becomes analytically prior to culture. Culture remains closely tied to communication, but communication is never just between subjects, but rather between subjects who are in a power relation.

In postmodernist and post-structuralist arguments, the primary concern shifts from solidarity to conflict. It is the openness and contentiousness of meaning associated with place and landscape that becomes the focus of study. The ability of any one group to impose meaning on a landscape represents a form of cultural imperialism and domination (Pred 1990). If culture is formed through stories that give meaning and order to experience, then power is manifested in the ability to narrate and prevent others from telling their stories (Said 1993). When interpreted in the realm of geography, landscapes as texts or discourse are continual sources of contestation among the many competing voices that compose a modern society.

Familiar humanistic themes are thus given quite different interpretations. For example, ethnic, gender and sexual identity are accentuated, but in relation to an oppressive other (Pile and Thrift 1995). Nationalism is explored, but primarily as a form of resistance against a state or other more powerful national group. Uneven and asymmetrical power relations make landscape and place sites of inter-group struggle rather than communal attachment.

PARTIAL VIEWS OF PLACE AND LANDSCAPE

During approximately one hundred years of history, the central concepts of the academic sub-field of cultural geography have remained remarkably stable, even as its approaches have changed dramatically. Its original formulation as a materialist, positivist, natural science of human artefacts has given way to its recent reincarnation as an increasingly idealist, anti-positivist, reflexive study of geographic meaning. The story of this transformation may be told in terms of a historical sequence of approaches, but the actual pattern has been one of horizontal proliferation and fragmentation rather than linear succession. Narratives of harmonious landscapes coexist with those that emphasize perpetual struggle and discord. What has remained constant through this change is a common vocabulary of landscape and place, and, to a lesser extent, territory and space.

The meanings of these concepts, however, have expanded greatly. They have changed from straightforward references to objects or locations to more complex representations of relations between subjects and worlds. Geographic understanding of culture has moved beyond distanced observation to include consideration of aesthetics, ethics and interpretation. Representation in its many forms and scales, from the image to the word (both spoken and written), and from the cosmic to the local, has become a central concern (Cosgrove 2001; Debarbieux 1995; Lewis and Wigen 1997; Mondada and Söderström 1993a). The expansion of cultural geography into these areas has blurred the boundaries between geography and other social scientific and humanistic disciplines, many of which have begun to explore increasingly the cartography of meaning and the cultural politics of landscape and place.

Similarly, the theme of language and communication continues to infuse cultural geographic studies, but in a form very different from the past (Claval 1995, 1999). Geographers no longer consider language simply as a fact to be expressed in terms of a distribution map. Rather language has become the source for the transmission and creation of meaning. The process of transmission – communication – has been a consistent theme through the study of diffusion, but its manifestations have changed significantly from a material emphasis on techniques of production, technical knowledge associated with environmental transformation and the creation of material culture, to the techniques of communication and the transmission of meaning. The globalization of culture relies on this latter technology, including geographic information systems. These new information systems transform geographies and the meaning of place (Curry 1998).

The 'cultural turn' has blurred the internal boundaries of geography. Social and economic geographers consider the production of cultural goods, such as film and music, and the production of cultural landscapes, such as historic preservation or urban entertainment zones, the particularistic customs of local production and exchange or the globalization of culture (Crang 1997; Lévy 1999a; Scott 1999). Geographers studying cities consider the ways in which images and narratives of place influence political action (Lussault 1993, 1997). Political geographers seek to understand the discursive nature of geopolitics, the landscapes of national memory and the geography of multiculturalism. The rebirth of cultural geography has also stimulated an ancillary concern with what might be referred to as a moral geography or a geography of ethics, in which concern for values and normative judgements comes into contact with cultural constraints (Proctor and Smith 1999).

These developments reflect a richer and more complex understanding of the geographical imagination. This term has been used in various ways by different authors to describe post-stucturalist, neo-Marxist and humanistic perspectives, but in its most general sense it describes accurately a geography that is about human ideals rather than simple descriptions of the world or catalogues of its contents. Such ideals separate humans from nature and differentiate communities (Tuan 1998). As such they exhibit a constant tension between the particularities of customs and habits and the universality associated with the sometimes utopian visions of human communities (Entrikin 1999). The cultural geographer's concepts of landscape and place contain this tension.

As these concepts become more complex, their representation in geographical literature becomes increasingly partial. For some, this partiality is a sign of progress, an indication of a less imperialistic cultural geography. For others, it is a sign of retreat. Making sense of this partiality offers a challenge for the cultural geographers of the twenty-first century. The natural scientific vision that gave shape and order to the field at the beginning of the century has gradually faded from view. It has not disappeared; rather it has become one among the many competing and often contradictory visions of contemporary cultural geography.

3 Economic geography: tradition and turbulence

Georges Benko and Allen J. Scott

The central concerns of economic geography revolve around the ways in which space – in its various manifestations as distance, separation, proximity, location, place etc. – dictates the shape and form of economic outcomes. In more concrete terms, we can say that the task of modern economic geography is to provide a reasoned description of the spatial organization of the economy and, in particular, to elucidate the ways in which geography influences the economic performance of capitalism. Obviously, these rather laconic formulations still leave open considerable room for debate about precisely how economic geographers practise – or should practise – their work, and as we shall see in this chapter, there have been many different advocacies in this regard over the developmental course of the sub-discipline.

The conceptual roots of economic geography as we now know it can be traced back, definitely if indistinctly, over at least the last three centuries. The first stirrings of economic inquiry in the seventeenth and eighteenth centuries already pointed to matters of geographic interest, though whatever spatial or locational content these early writings on the economy may have contained, it almost always functioned as background to more fundamental questions focused on the origins of national wealth and the causes of trade. In the second half of the eighteenth century and again in the early twentieth century, brief flowerings of a strong geographic sensibility can be detected in the work of certain economic writers, but even then economic geography, as such, remained very much a subsidiary concern. Up to the end of the nineteenth century, the wider discipline of geography itself was not much more accommodating in regard to anything that might be identified as a bona fide economic geography. Even as geography began to assume a modern disciplinary identity in the early twentieth century, it was not inclined to put undue emphasis on economic issues, except in so far as they could be subsumed within a burgeoning commitment to regional synthesis and the notion of geographic milieu.

Economic geography made its appearance as a fully recognizable branch of the discipline as a whole only in the period between the two world wars, and it was not until the 1950s that it started to evince really strong signs of self-assertiveness as a distinct field of inquiry (Scott 2000). It was, for all that, one of the first branches of human geography decisively to move away from a regional-synthetic to a more systematic-analytic approach and self-consciously to identify itself as a theory-building and hypothesis-testing enterprise. This break with the classical idiographic tradition in geography marked the beginning of a developmental trajectory over the rest of the twentieth century that has been driven forward by enormous intellectual energies, but that has been attended also by frequent and controversy-laden shifts of direction. As we shall argue here, this trajectory reflects a double dynamic. On the one hand, the historical course of economic geography can be understood partly in terms of an internal evolutionary logic that grows out of the elaboration, empirical testing and re-elaboration of particular theoretical concepts. On the other hand, the same historical course can also be seen as being notably responsive to external social and economic conditions and, above all, to the shifting practical problems and predicaments thrown up by capitalism in its ever accelerating development.

ECONOMIC GEOGRAPHY BEFORE ECONOMIC GEOGRAPHY

Primitive ideas about the effect of underlying spatial conditions on economic activity can be found in writings stretching back to the ancients and the Renaissance. It is only in the late seventeenth and early eighteenth centuries, however, as the science of political economy started to take initial shape, that anything approaching sustained examination of these relationships can be found.

William Petty's *Discourse on Political Arithmetick* (1690) was one of the first major pieces of economic analysis to develop any kind of systematic insight into issues of geographical interest. In this work, Petty lays out a number of ideas, which would recur repeatedly over the eighteenth century, about the phenomena of land and land rent and the consequent distribution of agricultural activities. Shortly thereafter, Pierre de Boisguilbert published his *Dissertation de la nature des richesses* (1707), which ascribed the basis of all wealth to agriculture and laid the foundations for the physiocratic doctrines taken up later in the century by François Quesnay and Richard Cantillon, among others. Cantillon was concerned especially to elucidate the relations between town and surrounding countryside in eighteenth-century France. A figure of notable importance at this time is Sir James Steuart, whose *Inquiry into the Principles of Political Economy* (1767) carried forward the ideas of Petty and Cantillon and fully anticipated the later theories of Johann Heinrich von Thünen regarding the spatial organization of agricultural land use around market centres (see below). Adam Smith, of course, crowned the accomplishments of the economists of the eighteenth century with his great synthetic work, *The Wealth of Nations* (1776), which definitively laid the foundations of the theory of competitive markets and free trade. The spatial element in Smith's writings is focused on the relations between soil fertility and land rent and questions of trade (including the impacts of the commerce of towns upon the surrounding countryside), but it is essentially derived from previous authors. Perhaps the most original geographical insight of *The Wealth of Nations* is contained in the brief passage where Smith proclaims that the division of labour is limited by the extent of the market, signifying that as transport technologies improve so it becomes possible for producers to sell their outputs on more spatially extended markets, thus enabling supply to expand and the division of labour to deepen and widen. This insight has been exploited frequently by modern economic geographers as a way of approaching the analysis of agglomeration economies (Scott 1988a).

By the early years of the nineteenth century, the geographical dimension begins to fade from the writings of political economists, perhaps because they were now so preoccupied with what we might call macroeconomic issues rather than with the internal subdivisions of nations and their economic characteristics. The great exception to this generalization is von Thünen in Germany, who, in his *Der Isoliert Staat* (1826), perfected the theory of rural land use as developed by Petty, Steuart and others, and demonstrated in great detail how the interplay between rent, transport costs and the prices of different crops induces a pattern of concentric rings of agricultural land use around major population centres. By contrast, von Thünen's distinguished contemporary, David Ricardo, (whose *Principles of Political Economy and Taxation* was first published in 1817), paid little or no attention to the geographical dimension. Even in his magisterial analyses of comparative advantage and differential rent – where geography potentially might have played a major role – the spatial dimension is reduced to a mere cipher. His theory of comparative advantage, for example, was more or less blind to the subtleties of geographical variation and simply reduced countries to aspatial containers of endowments. Further, as Ponsard (1958) has pointed out, Ricardo based his theory of differential rent largely on variations in soil fertility so that the spatial character of transport costs as generators of locational diversity was lost entirely. In the words of Dockès (1969), 'the abundant flow of ideas integrating the spatial and economic perspective disappears almost entirely in the nineteenth century like a river vanishing in a desert'. Even Marx, the great polymath of the mid-nineteenth century, was more or less indifferent to spatial issues, and as the century wears on, the principal concerns of the leading writers on economics (Jevons, Menger and Walras, above all) become yet more remote from geography. The goal of economic science at this point is directed primarily to formulating a coherent abstract theory of markets and economic equilibrium.

Hence only in a few isolated cases do we find much attention being paid to spatial matters at this time. One of these cases is represented by Alfred Marshall (1890), who, in a few fleeting (but visionary) passages, remarks on the significance of industrial districts and external economies as foundations for today what we would call regional competitive advantage. Another is the German engineer-economist Wilhelm Launhardt, whose article 'Die Bestimmung des zweckmässigsten Standorts einer gewerblichen Anlage' ('Determination of the optimal location of an industrial establishment'), published in 1882, points the way to location theory. Launhardt's book, *The Principles of Railway Location* (published in English translation in 1900–2), offers an early identification of the phenomenon of agglomeration via an analysis of the locational effects of improvements in the functioning of transport networks on locational outcomes.

Over much of the eighteenth and nineteenth centuries, then, as modern economic science gradually came into being, economic geography remained for the most part a rather disconnected and disparate body of ideas. Nevertheless, the ideas of writers like Petty, Cantillon, Steuart, Smith, von Thünen, Ricardo, Marx, Marshall and Launhardt are pregnant with possibilities for the elaboration of a truly thoroughgoing economic geography. All these ideas show up in one way or another in the great efflorescence of economic geography that occurred in the second half of the twentieth century. For whatever reason, however, economic geography remained stillborn over the 1700s and 1800s, and the different insights into the spatial foundations of economic activity that were elaborated by economists over this period of time failed signally to converge into a consistent and unbroken line of intellectual inquiry.

THE FORMATIVE PERIOD

Perhaps we might take the publication of George Chisholm's *Handbook of Commercial Geography* in 1889 as marking the beginning of a protracted formative period, in which – though it was not yet full emergent – something akin to what we think of as modern economic geography began to take shape (Barnes 2000). Certainly, with the dawning of the twentieth century, a widespread but still sporadic resurgence of interest in economic geography becomes increasingly evident, both in economics and in the rising discipline of geography proper.

By the turn of the century, as Jerome Fellmann (1986) has shown, a small number of economics departments in US universities were offering courses on economic geography. The Wharton School at the University of Pennsylvania (where Walter Isard was to establish a Department of Regional Science in the 1950s) was a pioneer in this regard, and J. Russell Smith (1913), a prominent member of the Wharton School, published one of the first major textbooks in the field. A further significant event was the launching of the journal *Economic Geography* in 1925, with its editorial offices at Clark University in Worcester, Massachusetts. The early volumes of the journal clearly reflect the then burning questions of resources and conservation. With the economic crisis of the late 1920s and early 1930s, however, the topics of industrial location and performance also rather predictably come to occupy an increasing number of the journal's pages.

In Europe, as in the USA at this time, the teaching of economic geography was frequently tied to specific social needs and, above all, the training of managers in commerce and product distribution. Numerous teachers of economic geography actually worked in schools of commerce during this period. The geography of the national economy figures prominently in this work. In the writings of the German geographer, Götz (1882), there is an attempt to comprehend the ways in which different national economies function and the role of the institutional environment. In 1904, Friedrich introduces the notion of *Raubwirtschaft* (the economy as destructive force) and also attempts to explore the methods and conceptual objectives of economic geography. The notions of economic landscape and economic space are introduced by Credner (1926) and Waibel (1933). In France, Hauser (1905, 1915) – both a historian and a geographer, in the traditional French manner – pursues a similar line of inquiry and is concerned especially with the location of economic enterprise in Germany and the USA. The role of the German *Konzerne* and the US trusts is highlighted in this work. The reflections of the great French human geographer, Vidal de la Blache, are also of some interest in this connection. In his *Principes de géographie humaine* (1921), Vidal suggests that any society, no matter what its level of development, is confronted with a basic dynamic: individuals are always tempted to form groups in order to take advantage of the division of labour. Equally, these groups are subject to geographic forces that lead differentially to agglomeration and dispersal. Vidal was concerned, too, with the role of transport in the spatial structuring of human society and in the geographical distribution of urban settlements. By the 1930s, a small number of French geographers were developing an interest in industrial geography, albeit in the context of a primary concern for regional synthesis (Blanchard 1934; Capot-Rey 1934). The study by Perrin (1937) of the industrial geography of Saint Étienne and its region anticipated, in a number of important respects, some of the same intellectual sensibilities that industrial geographers of the 1980s and 1990s were to put at the centre of their investigations.

In spite of these developments, the geographers of this period failed to move decisively in the direction of an analytical or theoretical economic geography. It was mainly among a group of German economists that real progress was accomplished in pushing forward the conceptual boundaries of economic geography in the first third of the twentieth century, though their contemporary impact was fairly negligible. Weber (1909), above all, formalized a viable theory of industrial location and, by the same token, laid some of the main foundations for the resurgence of economic geography after the Second World War. The point of departure of Weber's theory is his celebrated locational triangle. One vertex of the triangle is supposed to represent a market for a particular kind of output; the other two vertices are sources of raw materials used as inputs in the manufacturing process. The problem is to find the optimal location of a factory where the two inputs are assembled and from which the output is dispatched to the market. Weber showed that this location could be identified as the point where all transport costs are minimized and he devised a graphical technique for identifying the precise location of this point. As a general rule, the optimal location will lie within the triangle or on one of its edges, but Weber also argued that in instances where some idiosyncratic locational advantage (e.g. a source of power or a pool of cheap labour) could be obtained, a site outside the triangle might sometimes be preferable to the transport-cost minimizing point.

Weber's work was taken up by a number of his students and was echoed in a major publication by the US economist, Hoover (1937), but did not extend beyond a narrow circle of specialists. The reception of the work of two other major figures of the German school of location theory in the 1930s was not much better. These two figures, the geographer Walter Christaller and the economist August Lösch, both sought to derive a theory of the geographical distribution of market centres, each of which is taken as a point of exchange to which the surrounding agricultural population travels to purchase goods and services. The manner in which they each formulated this problem is remarkably similar in its initial basic postulates, though Lösch (1940) unquestionably carried the analysis much further than Christaller (1933). Both of them argued that the cost-minimizing behaviour of consumers would give rise to a regular spatial pattern of towns or 'central places' such that each town would be surrounded by a regular hexagonal market area. Moreover, in a world where differential demands exist for different types of goods and services, a regular hierarchy of central places will come into being, with many relatively small centres providing commonly demanded goods and services, and relatively few but much larger centres providing less commonly demanded goods and services. Weigmann (1931), in turn, developed a general equilibrium approach to the economy, conceived as a vast arrangement of spatial markets. He elaborated further the idea of the spatial economy as a domain of imperfect competition. Also, in 1935, Tord Palander published his *Beiträge zur Standortstheorie*, a book that pays close attention to the problem of transport costs. Palander emphasized the importance of market size and the complexity of location factors in a society founded on the division of labour; and towards the end of his book, he connects the problem of industrial location to issues of price-fixing and inter-firm competition.

Echoes of some of these concerns can be found in the work of a number of US economists in the period from the 1920s to the 1940s. Hotelling (1929), for example, developed a model of simple duopolistic competition in spatial context, and this model has been subject to many reformulations in succeeding decades. He demonstrated, in particular, that agglomeration is not necessarily a perverse outcome in a world where sellers of a homogeneous good are in direct competition with one another. On the contrary, he showed that two perfectly mobile sellers in a given geographic space will both tend eventually to locate side-by-side at the centre of the space as an outcome of their efforts to maximize the size of their individual markets. Two further important advances in this general area of inquiry were made by Reilly (1931) and Zipf (1949). Reilly's so-called law of retail gravitation was derived from the basic principle of Newtonian physics, to the effect that two material bodies will tend to attract one another in proportion to their mass and in inverse proportion to the square of the distance between them. The economic counterpart of this principle is that any given retail consumer will be drawn to one of two cities as a positive function of their size and a negative function of the distance of the consumer's location from them. It is then possible to map out the expected market boundary between the two cities. Zipf, for his part, proposed a rank-size law that in many ways ran parallel to certain of the propositions of Christaller and Lösch in the domain of central-place theory. The law involves an application of the Pareto function to the relation between the size of any city and its rank in the total set of cities in any given country, such that if the largest city's population is P, the population of any city of rank r is simply P/r. Finally, a number of US sociologists at this time were developing theoretical ideas about the city and urbanization that touched indirectly on issues of economic geography. The Chicago School of Sociology, in particular, dealt with issues of land use and intra-urban location, though it should be added that their approach drew more from ecological principles than it did from economics.

In general, geographers in the inter-war period were less concerned with the analytics of spatial economic organization and more intently focused on the description of given empirical situations and conveying a sense of the wider humanistic meaning of the geographic landscape. Something of this frame of mind was well expressed by Hauser when he wrote:

> Economic geography is in perpetual movement, a constant process of becoming . . . Location, lines of communication, the creation of new commercial powers, the increasing or decreasing importance of exports or imports, all these elements are ruled by endless dynamism and are always subject to transformation. This, we might say in passing, is both the great difficulty and the principle attraction of economic geography . . . It is impossible to constitute a science of economic geography, for how can we apply the name of science to a body of knowledge that is perpetually changing and moving?
>
> (Hauser 1947: 2–3, 18)

It was economists rather than geographers who most actively tested the conceptual boundaries of economic geography in this formative period. The work of a small number of economists, like Weber, Hoover, Lösch, Reilly and Zipf, and the geographer Christaller, represented the first stirrings of a genuinely theoretical economic geography and provided the foundation for what would come to be identified after the Second World War as regional science and spatial analysis. The concepts worked out in this formative period by economists are all the more important because they furnished many of the basic weapons in the ideological arsenal of economic geographers in the years following the Second World War, enabling them to challenge successfully the orthodoxies of classical geography and move decisively in the direction of nomothetic geographical science.

TOWARDS A SCIENTIFIC ECONOMIC GEOGRAPHY

The regional science movement

Some time in the late 1940s and early 1950s, a number of scholars in the USA began to revive enthusiastically the ideas of the German location theorists of the pre-war decades. This interest was reinforced greatly by the pressing economic problems of the immediate post-war years, all the more so because these problems frequently assumed a specifically territorial form. New insights into the bases of spatial income inequalities, urban blight and slum housing, economically lagging regions, the locational impacts of large-scale infrastructure projects, the operation of regional growth poles and so on were now urgently called for. The significance of problems such as these was further underscored by the dominant policy environment, which was turning increasingly to the guiding principles of Keynesianism and welfare-statism, and interventionist prescriptions of which called for much new active research into the regional and spatial constitution of the economy.

The year 1954 marks a critical watershed. This is the year in which Walter Isard established the Regional Science Association, primarily as a riposte to what he saw as the deficiencies of conventional economic analysis at that time – 'a wonderland of no spatial dimensions' (Isard 1956: 25) – and then as a source of practical ideas and information that could be used by policy makers as they faced up to the many new and difficult tasks of urban and regional planning in the 1950s. The ultimate theoretical goal of regional science, as Isard conceived it, was to rewrite neoclassical general equilibrium theory in such a way as to acknowledge that every supply, demand and price variable is associated with specific locational coordinates. In practice, however, this goal served largely as background atmospherics to the much more down-to-earth tasks of detailed locational analysis and the investigation of associated patterns of spatial interaction. Thus over the 1950s and 1960s, regional scientists carried out an enormously varied agenda of research on industrial complex analysis (Isard *et al.* 1959), regional input-output systems (Hirsch 1959), gravity-potential models (Warntz 1957), urban growth and land use (Harris 1956; Wingo 1961) and interregional migration (Sjaastad 1960), to mention only a few examples. Elaboration of the basic models of von Thünen, Weber, Christaller and Lösch was also very much part of this agenda. Thus Alonso (1965) produced an ambitious reworking of von Thünen, showing how his ideas could be deployed in the analysis of urban population densities and the distribution of residential land uses. Alonso's work subsequently helped to spark off a so-called 'new urban economics' in the USA. Echoes of this work can be found in France, where a series of policy-oriented studies of urban population patterns were carried out by engineers and planners over the mid- to late 1960s (Granelle 1969; Mayer 1965; Merlin 1966). In France, too, an early extension of the regional science movement beyond the USA was marked by the establishment in 1961 of the Association de Science Régionale de Langue Française, under the aegis of François Perroux and Jacques Boudeville.

At this time, these two economists were actively engaged in writing the basic theory of growth poles and growth centres and its application in regional planning (Boudeville and Antoine 1968; Perroux 1961). The conceptual framework for much of this work was identified by Perroux (1961), who wrote: 'Growth does not appear everywhere at once; it occurs at points or growth poles with variable intensities; it diffuses through different channels and with end results that vary over the economy as a whole'. In short, economic growth is functionally and geographically uneven and is strongly influenced by pre-existing patterns of urban and regional development. National growth is an expression of the economic performance of the regions that constitute the entire national space. In turn, regional economic performance is dependent on growth poles focused on lead plants with a high intensity of inter-industrial linkages.

Perroux's theory of growth poles enjoyed a considerable international reputation, almost from the moment of its inception. In parallel, work by Hirschman (1958), Myrdal (1959), Kuklinski and Petrella (1972) and others has added greatly to the original insights of Perroux and, above all, to his notion that development is a disequilibrium process. According to Perroux, Hirschman and Myrdal, growth poles are associated with two main dynamic processes, which (in the terminology of Hirschman) can be identified as polarization and trickle-down effects. The former of these effects tends to emphasize the play of agglomeration, centralization and inward migration; the second acknowledges that there is also a complementary trend to decentralized development in more peripheral areas. Depending on the choice of policy (e.g. maximum growth at the expense of regional equality or regional equality at the expense of maximum growth), the problem is to calibrate the relative influence of polarization and trickle-down effects over the entire capitalist space economy.

In a more neoclassical perspective, Borts and Stein (1964), among others, sought to affirm that regional inequalities in regard to factor payments (above all, wages) were simply temporary and self-correcting aberrations. In a world of perfect competition, they claimed, each region would assert its comparative advantage and any inequalities over space would soon be eliminated. The Borts-Stein model enjoyed a certain influence among economists when it was first formulated. The optimism of the model, however, appears somewhat hollow in light of the stubborn persistence of regional inequalities across the world, and especially in light of subsequent models based on notions of increasing returns effects, purporting to show that markets are in fact endemically prone to the creation of spatial economic inequalities.

Spatial analysis and quantitative geography

Just as regional science was making its historical appearance in the early 1950s, a small number of geographers were also beginning to experiment with some novel ideas about theoretical analysis and the spatial organization of the economy. The traditional idiographic core of geography was clearly still dominant at this time, but signs of rebellion were becoming increasingly apparent. One of the first systematic critiques of traditional idiographic approaches in geography was presented by Schaefer (1953) and carried forward by Ackerman (1958), both of whom advocated approaches that took the tasks of theory construction and abstract analysis seriously. This newly emerging vision of geography made it increasingly possible for economic geographers to build methodological and thematic bridges to the work of spatial economists and created an opening to an applied geography with special relevance to questions of regional planning.

More specifically, at this time, a group of geographers at the University of Washington (composed primarily of William L. Garrison and his graduate students) were beginning to recover some of the ideas of the old German school of locational analysis and were simultaneously in the process of discovering that it was actually possible to subject certain kinds of geographical questions to mathematical and statistical analysis. Accordingly, they now began to apply these quantitative tools to a variety of problems in location theory and central-place analysis. On this basis, they went on to attack some of the key problems of economic geography as it was then being formulated, including attempts to formalize many different kinds of models of locational choice, spatial flow, shopping patterns, hierarchical order and network structure. Garrison's students at the University of Washington – Brian Berry, William Bunge, Michael Dacey, Duane Marble, Richard Morrill, John Nystuen and others – were later to become central figures in professional geography generally in the USA in the 1960s. However, they were seen at this time by the discipline's more conservative majority as representing a rather unwelcome heterodoxy, and their work initially met with strong opposition. Given that they were, in any case, natural allies of regional scientists, they rapidly joined forces with the latter, and for a time their work could be encountered more regularly in the publications and conferences of the Regional Science Association than in the established outlets of the geographical profession. The existence of a flourishing regional science movement enabled the Washington school pioneers – and the geographers in other universities (notably Iowa and Northwestern) who were now joining them in increasing numbers – to achieve an early degree of academic legitimacy that might otherwise have eluded them (with incalculable end results for the subsequent course of the discipline of geography as a whole). As it happens, by the early 1960s, regional science and economic geography (in the guise of quantitative spatial analysis) were becoming more or less indistinguishable from each other.

Eventually, over the 1960s, quantitative spatial analysis ('the new geography', as it was then known) diffused widely through geography departments across the USA. The style of thinking and investigation of the new geography had strong impacts, not only in economic geography but also in other sub-disciplines of the field as well, notably urban geography and social geography. Economic geographers and their allies in the discipline were now moving rapidly into a hegemonic position in US geography departments and, for a time, their multifaceted efforts to devise formalized descriptions of the economic landscape essentially defined the discipline's research frontier. Almost all these efforts, moreover, were infused with notable enthusiasm for positivistic research methodologies and characterized by a search for coherent theories and mathematical models, together with a focus on formal hypothesis-testing procedures. Perhaps the classic work in this vein is to be found in the early papers of Berry and Garrison (1958a and b), who resolutely sought both to expand the theory of central places, as originally formulated by Christaller and Lösch, and to carry out robust tests of its empirical validity. The philosophical bases of positivistic geography were laid out by Harvey (1969) in a book that simultaneously summed up the entire movement and – inadvertently – sounded its death knell.

Triumph and decline of the new geography

During the 1960s, then, regional science and spatial analysis developed apace. A great outpouring of research effectively pushed the theoretical accomplishments of these fields very far outward, while also providing important guidelines for practical policy interventions into the space economy. The perceived practical significance of the work of regional scientists and spatial analysts at this time can be judged from the readiness of federal and local grant-making agencies in the USA (e.g. the National Science Foundation, the Office of Naval Research and the US Department of Commerce) to underwrite the costs of much of their research. A major reconstruction of human geography in general, and economic geography in particular, was now well under way. A matter of great urgency was the production of textbooks to expose students to this new approach. The movement was initiated by McCarty and Lindberg (1966), whose *Preface to Economic Geography* suggested that the new geography was to be essentially economic geography. This work was followed, in the early 1970s, by a series of other publications with very similar goals (Morrill 1970a; Abler, Adams and Gould 1971; Cox 1972; Lloyd and Dicken 1972).

By the 1960s, too, regional science and spatial analysis were starting to appeal to a certain number of geographers in Europe and elsewhere in the world. European geography in the 1960s was still strongly attached to the classical synthesizing modes of investigation in which it had excelled over the first half of the twentieth century. In the context of this tradition, economic geography had developed a modest presence, as represented, for example, by Smith (1949) in the UK, George (1956, 1961) and Claval (1962, 1968, 1976) in France and Manshard (1961) in Germany, but it was clearly reluctant to declare that it was engaged in any sort of radical break with traditional geography as a whole. By contrast, Swedish geographers had actually established an indigenous tradition of quantification and theoretical geography in the 1950s, and they were the first in Europe to welcome US-inspired forms of regional science and spatial analysis. Indeed even before the rise of the Washington school, Swedish geographers were already making original contributions to the field (Ajo 1953; Godlund 1956; Hägerstrand 195; Kant 1951). A little later, Törnqvist (1968, 1970) helped to introduce the idea of information circuits, with special emphasis on the notion of face-to-face communication for many kinds of high-level exchanges of business information. This idea has had a major influence on subsequent research into innovation, the location of service industries and the functioning of large-scale organizations.

British geographers, greatly influenced by the work of Haggett (1965), rapidly came into the fold of the new geography in the second half of the 1960s. As we have already noted, reception of the new geography in continental Europe proceeded more slowly and reluctantly, but from the late 1960s, it was more or less assimilated into geography programmes, at least in the major universities. In the Francophone world, a small group of geographers, notably Roger Brunet, Paul Claval, Yves Guermond, Bernard Marchand, Pierre Merlin, Denise Pumain and Thérèse Saint-Julien, among others, helped to diffuse the new vision of geography, and in 1972, the journal *L'Espace géographique* was established under the editorship of Brunet. Other geographers, notably Rochefort (1960) and Hautreux (Hautreux and Rochefort 1963), helped to initiate the new geography in France with their work on urban systems, and many of their ideas were expressed subsequently in French regional planning. In fact, the city and its problems came to occupy an increasingly larger place in the reflections of French geographers and economists such as Aydalot (1985), Bailly (1975), Beaujeu-Garnier (1980), Claval, (1981) and Derycke (1979). In turn, this stimulated a major interest among French geographers in applied geography or 'la géographie de l'action'.

Paradoxically, however, just as regional science and spatial analysis were attaining to something approaching widespread – though never universal – acceptance and approval among geographers, a powerful counter-reaction began to set in from a completely unexpected quarter. This oppositional movement was led at first by a small group of radical, progressive and left-leaning geographers – rebelling against what they took to be the methodological straitjacket and essentially conservative thrust of regional science and spatial analysis – and steadily gained momentum over the 1970s. It is surely no coincidence that this counter-reaction occurred at a time when the Vietnam War was reaching a peak of intensity, students began to question accepted forms of political and economic knowledge and social unrest was rife across US cities. It was further fuelled by the severe economic dislocations in both the USA and Europe that occurred as the 1970s moved forward and the crisis of Fordist mass production intensified.

CRITICAL VISIONS OF GEOGRAPHIC SPACE

The rallying cry of the new radical geographers of the early 1970s was issued by Harvey (1973), who, in a dramatic about-turn from his earlier position, now called for a complete reconsideration of the theoretical underpinnings of human geography generally. This call took the form of a fervent critique of the neoclassical competitive equilibrium theory that permeated regional science and spatial analysis, and an advocacy of Marxian economics as the essential foundation of geographical research. The great debate that then ensued in geography swirled around the role of space in enhancing or impeding social justice and environmental order and influencing the play of political power in modern society.

   The call was given further voice by the new journal *Antipode*, founded (again at Clark University) in 1969, and was taken up with much enthusiasm by geographers like James Blaut, Richard Peet (who also served as the editor of *Antipode*), Edward Soja, Richard Walker and Doreen Massey, to name only a few. Radical geographers conceived their primary academic mission as being nothing less than a full-scale redescription of the economic landscape in terms of Marxian economic categories (value, surplus, profit, accumulation, etc.), in combination with explicit invocation of the social and property foundations of capitalism and their expression in class struggle. As such, they paid particular attention to matters like conflicts over urban public goods, regional inequalities and core–periphery relations. As the crisis-ridden 1970s wore on, questions of job loss, unemployment and industrial restructuring also came to occupy much of their attention (Massey 1974; Massey and Meegan 1979).

   At the same time, US and British radical geographers were much influenced by a number of Marxist sociologists and economists, many of them working in French universities and research organizations. On the one hand, they borrowed numerous ideas from urban theorists like Castells (1972), Lefebvre (1974), Lipietz (1974) and Topalov (1973) about urban social movements, land rent theory and the capitalistic dynamics of the property sector. On the other hand, Marxian economists like Amin (1973), Frank (1968) and Emmanuel (1969) also had a major impact via their writings on uneven regional/international development and unequal exchange in capitalist society. Work by radical geographers on the regional/international front was further fortified by reference to the older heterdox tradition of development studies (Hirschman 1958; Myrdal 1959), which stressed cumulative causation as the mechanism underlying the formation of stubborn spatial inequalities in capitalism. It also took to heart the theory of the 'new international division of labour', as formulated in an influential book by Fröbel *et al.* (1980), which painted a stark picture of an emerging international system characterized by a core group of countries with a monopoly of skilled, high-wage, white-collar jobs and a surrounding periphery dominated by low-skill, low-wage, blue-collar jobs.

In spite of its roots in Marxian theory, radical geography presented much less than a unified front and many different tendencies were (and are) an intrinsic part of its make-up. For example, in the mid-1970s, a small group of geographers on the fringes of the radical movement began to advocate a neo-Ricardian approach to economic geography. Their specific claim was that the Ricardo-inspired model of Sraffa (1960) could be re-expressed in terms of a set of spatial and locational coordinates so that its account of production, pricing and distribution could be made to generate new insights about land rent and land use (Barnes 1984; Scott 1976). Others moved on to a variety of related problems concerning the impacts of capital investment, technological change and the spatial structure of the employment relation (Barnes and Sheppard 1984; Clark 1981; Clark *et al.* 1986). A further development of far-reaching importance at this time was the formulation of a feminist perspective in economic geography and an insistence on bringing fully into view the profoundly gendered nature of economic and geographic outcomes (McDowell and Massey 1984). Despite a certain waning of radical ways of dealing with economic geography after the 1980s, the effects of this feminist approach resonate within the discipline down to the present day.

THE RESURGENCE OF THE REGION: THE 1980s AND 1990s

The new economic and social conditions

Some time in the early 1980s, a yet further renewal of economic geography began to occur. After the crisis years of the 1970s and the transformation of many traditional manufacturing regions in the USA and Western Europe into 'Rust Belts', a series of new industrial spaces started to make their geographical appearance in areas that had hitherto been mainly on the margins of the older manufacturing centres. The resurgence of these new industrial spaces was initially most evident in the so-called Third Italy and the US Sunbelt, but it rapidly became apparent that the phenomenon was worldwide, with a number of erstwhile Third World countries (especially in East and South-East Asia) also participating in the trend (Scott 1988b). These new industrial spaces, moreover, were sites of a form of industrialization that differed in many important respects from earlier Fordist mass production. They could be seen, in short, as a sort of pioneer fringe of a post-Fordist economy, or what is more commonly referred to today as the 'new economy', with its characteristic foundations in flexible, decentralized networks of production units with high collective capacities for innovative change. Many of the most striking cases of these new industrial spaces were being colonized by sectors like high-technology industry, neo-artisanal manufacturing and services. The same sectors were now also beginning to function as leading edges of growth and development in some of the world's most dynamic economies.

This new conjuncture in the major capitalist societies thus entailed the emergence or re-emergence of the region as a distinctive and increasingly self-assertive economic unit and pointed to a real need on the part of economic geographers to reconsider the ways in which they had been carrying out their research. In turn, the conjuncture was related to a major sea change in the logic and dynamics of capitalist regulation, including a radical overhaul of the hitherto dominant policy system based on Keynesian welfare-statism. This turn of events occurred initially under the political leadership of Thatcher in the UK and Reagan in the USA, but eventually spread in one way or another to virtually all the advanced capitalist societies. One of the consequences of this overhaul was a renewed emphasis on localized economic development initiatives and a reassertion of the role of local political actors as agents of economic change. At the same time, major shifts were also occurring on the international front, as represented by the intensification of global trade and the proliferation of inter-country economic blocs like the EU, NAFTA, MERCOSUR and ASEAN. Globalization, too, was coming on to the agenda of academic discourse as a reflection of the great debordering of the major national economies that was now firmly under way.

The geographers' responses

One of the first concrete signs that the radical Marxian approach to economic geography might be losing its edge was the appearance some time in the early 1980s of a widening interest in 'localities' (Urry 1981). Localities research was primarily a British phenomenon, reflecting a concern during the Thatcher years for the changing (usually downward) fortunes of particular places and the political responses engendered by local economic crisis (see Cooke 1989 for a representative collection of papers). Initially, this research did not represent an explicit turn away from Marxian economic geography as much as a certain toning down of some of its more elaborate theoretical formulations. As it progressed, however, localities research became increasingly atheoretical in favour of a focus on the primacy of empirical context and data in geographical analysis (Smith 1987a). This thoroughgoing empiricism of the localities movement meant that its intellectual influence and lifespan were rather limited, but it marks an important moment of transition towards what we might call a new regionalism in economic geography.

At the outset, three independent but strongly parallel schools of thought can be identified as direct expressions of this new regionalism. One of them was represented by a group of Italian economists and sociologists who focused their research on the industrial renaissance that was occurring in Veneto, Tuscany, Emilia-Romagna and surrounding regions after the mid-1970s (Bagnasco 1977; Becattini 1987; Brusco

1982). A second group, known as GREMI (Groupe de Recherche sue les Milieux Innovateurs), formed around the economist Philippe Aydalot in Paris, devoting its attention to the topic of the region as a framework of industrial innovation (Aydalot 1986). A third group, composed largely of geographers, made its appearance in southern California, where it was concerned initially with attempts to decipher the roots of the economic vibrancy of the high-technology and motion-picture industries in the region (Scott 1986; Storper and Christopherson 1987). Central to the work of each of these groups were the concepts of agglomeration economies and the spatial concentration of industrial activity in specialized regional complexes. As a corollary, each of them was influenced greatly by Marshall's ideas about industrial districts and external economies, ideas that for the most part had lain dormant since the end of the nineteenth century.

Over the 1980s and 1990s, the pioneering work of these three groups of scholars was carried forward and modified in many different ways by economic geographers. Indeed, the enormous spate of literature over the last couple of decades on issues of agglomeration and the local economy has formed the basis of what some have referred to as a new orthodoxy in economic geography (Lovering 1999). This literature has pushed the theory of regional development to a high pitch of development and, simultaneously, has provided a mass of detailed research on specific aspects of the regional economy, such as traded and untraded interdependencies, the organization of local labour markets, the regional foundations of industrial innovation, the regulatory institutions that help to buttress modern industrial systems and so on. Much work is also now proceeding on the relationships between regional economic development and globalization, with due acknowledgement of the circumstance that while the global constitutes an essential context for the region, regions are coming to function simultaneously as basic geographic pillars of the global (Scott 1998).

The question of the regulation of regional economic systems has been influenced greatly by the work of the French Regulationist school, as represented, for example, by Boyer (1986) and Lipietz (1986). The main contribution of the Regulationists is their insight that the economic and the political are constitutive of one another through the interplay of a 'regime of accumulation' (a historically and geographically specific expression of a capitalist production system) and a 'mode of social regulation' (a political and/or quasi-political structure of governance). This insight was taken up eagerly by a number of economic geographers, who then deployed it in an effort to show how both old and new industrial spaces in the USA and Western Europe are associated with complex tissues of politico-institutional order, underpinning the effective functioning of local production systems, the operation of local labour markets, the formation of competitive advantage and so on (Benko and Lipietz 1995; Storper and Scott 1989).

CONCLUDING REMARKS

This is not the place to expatiate on current developments in the field or try to adjudicate the debates that preoccupy economic geographers today. That said, we may note, very briefly, a few major tendencies. To begin with, the new regionalism in the context of globalization processes continues to occupy pride of place in much current research. Furthermore, the ideas proposed by the new regionalism are being extended increasingly to questions of development in low- and middle-income countries. Additionally, in the 1990s and early 2000s, two new and competing claims about the spirit and purpose of economic geography have come into view forcefully. The first of these revolves around the work of Paul Krugman and represents an attempt to bring economic geography firmly back into the sphere of mainstream economics. In a series of publications, Krugman (1991, 1996) and his co-workers have sketched out a so-called new geographical economics, based on a model of monopolistic competition in a spatial context, and claimed that this can be taken as a revitalized statement of the dynamics of regional development. The second claim, which comes from within geography itself, is often identified in terms of a 'cultural turn' (Thrift 2000b; Thrift and Olds 1996). In this case, the main advocacy is that economic geography needs to be considerably more attentive to issues of culture than it has been in the past, and that much of the economic order of contemporary capitalism actually has its roots in human culture (rather than vice versa). In practice, adherents of the cultural turn tend to construct their approaches to the analysis of the economic landscape out of concepts like embodiment, performativity, identity and gender (McDowell 1997). Our tentative assessment is that whereas neither the new geographical economics nor the cultural turn is likely to become hegemonic in economic geography in the future, each brings to bear some useful sensibilities on the central questions of economic geography, even if, in their more extreme forms, they have been subject to a number of demurrers (Martin and Sunley 1996; Storper 2001).

As we have shown in this chapter, there is a long tradition of work in economic geography, beginning in the seventeenth and eighteenth centuries and continuing erratically down to the present day. In spite of this lengthy period of historical gestation, it is only in the decades following the Second World War that anything like a really coherent and assertive sub-discipline of economic geography can be identified. Even so, the developmental course of economic geography over the last few decades has been punctuated by many different shifts of direction, leading to constant upheaval, together with its attendant professional rivalries. Moreover, it would be an error to think of the shifting research edge in economic geography at any one time as a unified front. On the contrary, economic geography as a whole is always more like a palimpsest of both old and new ideas. Echoes of what went before constantly resonate throughout the field and theoretical advocacies from the past rarely die out entirely but have a disconcerting habit of reappearing in new interpretative frameworks.

To a significant degree, the great success of economic geography as an academic enterprise over the last half-century can be ascribed to its relevance as a tool for understanding critical aspects of modern capitalism, not to mention its direct and indirect practical usefulness for urban and regional planning and business applications. It poses urgent questions about fundamental aspects of the operation of modern economic systems and provides genuine insights that policy makers can exploit as they seek to promote more effective levels of capitalist performance. Even in an era of globalization, economic geography becomes more not less important, for the very good reason that globalization does not mean the deliquescence of everything into a space of flows, but in fact entails the strategic reorganization of the world's economic regions in ways that provide yet further opportunities for geographic differentiation and exploitation. Consequently, we may predict that economic geography has a vibrant future ahead. Equally, in view of the presumed continuation of capitalism's dynamic of creative destruction, we can be fairly confident in suggesting that economic geography is likely to be marked by as much turbulence in the future as it has been in the past.

4 Historical geography: locating time in the spaces of modernity

Mark Bassin and Vincent Berdoulay

The field of historical geography emerged in the border spaces between the disciplines of history and geography. The complementarity of history and geography has been widely appreciated since the Enlightenment, not least by Immanuel Kant, who was explicit in his insistence on their interdependence as well as their propaedeutic relevance for all knowledge. Since the eighteenth century, this perspective has been contested generally or reformulated in a variety of ways, and historical geography specifically has been annexed very differently by the two disciplines. The result is that 'historical geography' has alternated – and on occasion even competed – with a 'geographical history' of similar inspiration. All this serves to underscore the more fundamental problem in geography for the place and relevance that it should grant to the historical process.

The status of historical geography is a problem that has persisted for more than two centuries, sustained by its connection to the more fundamental epistemological problem of the significance and power accorded to time in geographical explanation. This connection, however, is only partial. Because temporality also relates to explanation in terms of processes (physical or otherwise), such as those utilized in the mathematical models developed by geographers, the question of time goes beyond that of the simple historicity of phenomena. In anchoring its approach in this historicity of phenomena, however, historical geography does not necessarily privilege temporality as a part of explanation or involve the adoption of grand theories or philosophies of historical evolution.

In fact, historical geography has been deployed in a number of ways. It has been treated as a discrete and autonomous sub-discipline in the geographical pantheon or has appeared as a transection cutting across all geographical inquiry regardless of specific theme. The research approach can be synchronic, as in the reconstruction of landscapes or regions at particular historical moments (Darby 1977), diachronic, if a process of evolution and development is stressed (Vidal 1917; Fleure 1947), or both, when a series of period-specific reconstructions are juxtaposed to illustrate the historical flow (Broek 1932). Whatever form it takes, the central question involves the position and importance of history as a part of the process of explanation in geography. To the extent that historical geography is concerned with the simple reconstruction of a landscape or region at a given moment in the past, the epistemological issue is less significant, for the problem relates principally to the use of archival sources. If, on the other hand, it is a question of using history in order to shed light on the evolution of phenomena, the problem becomes one of interpreting the causalities which unfold in the course of time (Sauer 1941; Sorre 1962; Hartshorne 1959; Driver 1988; Berdoulay 1995a).

HISTORICAL GEOGRAPHY TO 1900

Although historical geography was fully developed in the twentieth century, its origins in the preceding century are clear. Under the powerful influence of Carl Ritter and Alexander von Humboldt, geographical science in the first half of the nineteenth century maintained a vigorous interest in the historical process. At the same time, the growing success of history as a university discipline and a foundational element of the modernist ideology of progress contributed to an eclipsing of the other sciences of society, including geography. Thus the latter was generally restricted to describing the principal elements of the physical geographical arena on which the historical events were played out. Exceptions to this relegation of geography to a supporting role, such as Michelet's *Tableau de France* (1833), were quite rare. In the universities, historical geography tended to be limited to the identification of the political and administrative boundaries of the past, overlapping with the history of geographical knowledge which provided the material for its research. This situation changed only with the full institutionalization of geography in universities at the end of the nineteenth century.

Three early lines of inquiry may be identified, the influence of which may then be traced through the subsequent evolution of the subject. The first of these saw its task in what was effectively the reconstruction of past landscapes, that is to say a complex empirical description of the geography of a region at some given point in the past. 'Geography' in this sense could be understood broadly to involve the physical environment, flora and fauna, settlement patterns, agricultural and industrial organization, transport systems and so on, but very commonly was restricted to the natural milieu. Historical geography conceived in this spirit was often extremely closely allied to history proper. Indeed, the widely accepted view that historical accounts should take the physical lay of the land in question as their point of departure for an analysis of social, political, economic and even cultural developments meant that historians often began their works with preliminary chapters on historical geography. Such an approach encouraged the view of geography as a *Hilfswissenschaft*, or more specifically a 'handmaiden of history': a necessary but necessarily subordinate element of historical analysis. This was especially evident in so-called 'national history' – the opening sections of Thomas Macaulay's *The History of England from the Accession of James II* (1849) or S. M. Solov'ev's *Istoriia Rossii s drevneishikh vremen* (*History of Russia from the Earliest*

Times) (1851–76) offer notable examples – but it had been used since at least the eighteenth century as a companion to biblical studies as well (Wells 1708; Smith 1894). It is significant to note that this geography – invoked as the physical arena upon which the saga of human history was played out – was generally treated as static and unchanging.

A rather different sense of the term historical geography was expressed in the notion of the 'historical landscape', particularly associated with the emergence of *Landschaftskunde* or landscape science in Germany. A full consideration of this critically important aspect in the evolution of modern geography lies outside the bounds of the present chapter; suffice to say that, strongly influenced by Romanticism on the one hand and the advances in nineteenth-century natural science on the other, *Landschaftskunde* stressed the qualities of landscape as an evolutionary and organic entity. Any given regional landscape, therefore, was the product of the totality of elements – social as well as natural-physical – active on it, and was at the same time the product of an extended process of development and change (Wimmer 1885). From this standpoint, all present-day landscapes were historical landscapes simply by definition, a conclusion implicitly emphasized by Friedrich Ratzel, among others, in his discussions of the 'historische Landschaften' of contemporary Europe and North America (Ratzel 1906a and b), and one which was to find significant expression in the twentieth century as well. The focus of the study included descriptive 'reconstruction' to the extent that the moment of interest was fixed in the past, but the deeper concern was in understanding the ever active evolutionary and genetic forces at work in the formation and reshaping of discrete regional landscapes.

A final line of inquiry was concerned with what might be termed broadly environmental interaction as an aspect of human social development. The relationship of society to the natural milieu was always a central one for geography in the nineteenth century, and its teachings in this regard were exceptionally influential for historical science. Most notably, this influence took the form of determinist perspectives, which argued that the main lines of human historical development were directed, indeed effectively determined, by the physical and bio-geographical conditions of the areas in which this development took place. It did not matter fundamentally if these geographical influences were characterized theologico-teleologically, as by Carl Ritter (1862) in the mid-nineteenth century, or if they were given a more natural-scientific and Darwinian interpretation, as by Ratzel many decades later (1882–93; Bassin 1987a). In both cases, historians found a very powerful analytical tool, which provided a convincing and apparently objective causal explanation for the developmental scenarios and interpretations offered. 'National history' once again provided particularly fertile ground for this perspective, and the enormous and enduring popularity of the environmentalist histories by Buckle (1857–61) and others demonstrate its appeal to the popular imagination. Indeed, even Marxist historiography in the nineteenth century displayed a strong interest in environmentalism, which it re-dubbed 'geographical materialism' and set in the context of its own notion of economic determinism and the development of human society (Bassin 1992).

HISTORICAL GEOGRAPHY: 1900–45

The cross-section approach

It was only after 1900 that efforts began to be made to develop the historical-geographical traditions of the preceding century into a recognizable sub-field. Probably the most influential and widespread alternative – in the Anglo-American world at least – was the so-called cross-section approach, which sought to formalize the reconstruction of past landscapes both methodologically and scientifically (D. G. 1981). Adopting Immanuel Kant's *nacheinander-nebeneinander* distinction between history and geography, Hettner (1927), Hartshorne (1939) and numerous others argued laboriously that the task of historical geography was to slice 'historical sections through time' (Unstead 1907: 28), whereby the resulting tranche was intended to represent a full geographical picture of the region or country in question at the historical moment of incision. The methodological implications of this approach were twofold. On the one hand, it significantly enhanced geography's profile as a *Hilfswissenschaft*, by providing a clearly defined and undeniably useful niche for it to occupy in the edifice of historical sciences, the high scholarly quality of which was guaranteed by meticulous analysis of primary sources. At the same time, however, the Kantian dictum served to fix ever more securely the character of geographical inquiry as exclusively descriptive. This was a point about which practitioners at the time were entirely open, as is eminently clear from the following answer that E. W. Gilbert gave to the question, what is historical geography? 'The real function of historical geography is to reconstruct the regional geography of the past. Historical geography should confine itself to a descriptive geographical account of a region at some past period, and should not endeavour to make the explanation of historical events its main objective' (Gilbert 1932, cited in Green 1991: 12; see also East 1933). In this spirit, only the chronological narrative of history proper could lay bare the meaning and significance of the detailed chorological patterns and pictures provided by the geographer.

One of the most celebrated examples of the fruits of this approach was the work of the British geographer H. C. Darby. After a number of methodologically exploratory essays (e.g. 1932), the influential collection *An Historical Geography of England Before AD 1800* was published under his editorship in 1936. This volume assembled a series of 'period pictures' of England corresponding to a succession of sequential but discrete periods – e.g. 'Anglo-Saxon settlement', 'fourteenth-century England' or 'England in the seventeenth century' – with no real attempt to link these historical moments together. The full consummation of Darby's efforts, however, was achieved in his work on the Domesday Book of 1086 (Darby 1952, 1977), which involved the reconstruction of England's geography in the eleventh century on the basis of a major land inventory made by conquerors from France. The unique richness of the Domesday source, and the pinpoint accuracy with which the information could be dated, enabled Darby to produce a geographical account of enormous analytical significance, which both ensured his own scholarly legacy and significantly enhanced the status of historical geography.

The cross-sectional approach had its North American practitioners as well, represented most engagingly by Ralph H. Brown's minor literary masterpiece, *Mirror for Americans* (1943). Brown composed his work in the voice of a fictional narrator – Thomas P. Keystone – who describes the geography of the eastern seaboard of the USA using only those sources that would have been available at the time of ostensible authorship, in the early nineteenth century.

  Although many geographers were happy to embrace the radical epistemological cleavage between history and geography inherent in the cross-section approach as a satisfactory means of securing an independent scholarly identity for their sub-discipline (Darby 1962), others were troubled by the total banishment of an active chronological dimension from the analysis. One response was a sort of methodological compromise, in which a series of individual cross-sections were assembled in chronological order. We have seen that Darby's collection of 1936 took this form, and when the work was reissued in a new edition with a revised title in the 1970s, it was yet more pronounced. Now the 'period pictures' – e.g. 'Domesday England' or 'England *circa* 1600' – were linked by intervening chapters devoted explicitly to the problems of geographical change through time: 'Changes in the Early Middle Ages', 'The Age of the Improver, 1600–1800' and so on (Darby 1973). This option of assembling a sequence of cross-sections proved particularly appealing for American geographers (Friis 1940; Dodge 1932), and with his notion of 'sequent occupance', Derwent Whittlesey sought to formalize it into an intellectual-analytical perspective (Whittlesey 1929). Here the period pictures – now focusing on the geography of settlement – were not considered as discrete and self-contained entities, but rather as expressions along a single developmental line, each one reflecting traces both of what had been as well as what was to come. The sequent occupance approach exerted considerable influence in historical-geographical research in North America (James 1931; Platt 1928; Mikesell 1975). Among other things, it served to undermine the Kantian *nebeneinander-nacheinander* distinction, and in the final analysis proved to be a bridge to another important research focus in historical geography, namely the cultural geography of Carl Sauer and the Berkeley school.

Genetic-historical geography

We have already noted the emergence of *Landschaftskunde* in late nineteenth-century German geography. This perspective was considerably elaborated after the turn of the century and developed into what was to be one of Germany's greatest contributions to international geographical research. Traces of the spirit of organicism which had pervaded the earlier work were still very much apparent. Historical geographers identified the object of their attention as the 'genetic cultural landscape', and in their analyses they stressed its historical process of change and development from a hypothesized primeval state of the so-called *Urlandschaft*. Again, the geography of human settlement was uppermost in their concerns, but this was often studied through meticulous reconstruction of the evolution of the physical-geographical landscape, especially forest cover. In particular, Robert Gradmann (1901, 1931) and Otto Schlüter

(1952–8) produced classic multi-volume studies of the historical geography of Central Europe, but there were numerous other important contributions (Kretschmer 1904; Knüll 1903). The inspiration of this sort of evolutionary landscape science was translated into the North American context most influentially through the work of the Berkeley geographer Carl Sauer. Although Sauer's approach was more ethnographic than either Gradmann's or Schlüter's, and he was interested above all in the study of 'simple' indigenous groups of the American west and southwest rather than European or Anglo-American antecedents, methodologically his focus remained fixed on the cultural landscape understood as a genetic, evolving entity. This emerged clearly from a famous essay, 'The morphology of landscape', which explained cultural geography as the study not of period pieces but rather of the *historical process* through which a natural landscape is shaped by anthropogenic forces into a cultural landscape (Sauer 1925). Under Sauer's influence, the so-called Berkeley school took shape, which produced a series of studies in this spirit.

It was in Sauer's work, however, that the methodological distinctiveness of a historical geography which took the study of process as its main preoccupation began to dissolve. Whatever the explanatory limits of the 'cross-section approach' may have been, it provided historical geography with its own special sub-disciplinary, indeed trans-disciplinary, niche and function that was readily confirmed by both history and geography – a point that was well appreciated by punctilious methodologists such as Hettner and Hartshorne. The emphasis on the genetic or evolutionary essence of the subject, however, implicitly threatened to undermine this, for, simply put, an evolutionary perspective logically could not be limited to historical geographers. Very much to the contrary, it was at once a universalizing viewpoint, such that not only landscapes but all phenomena have to be examined in terms of a process or continuum of development. And this in turn meant that *all* geography was necessarily historical geography, at least to some degree. This point emerged, inadvertently but with full force, in Sauer's presidential address to the Association of American Geographers in 1941, as he endeavoured to present his own larger view of the nature of geographical science.

> If the object [of geography] is to define and understand human associations as areal growths, we must find out how they and their distributions (settlements) and their activities (land use) came to be where they are . . . Such study of culture area is historical geography. The quality of understanding sought is that of analysis of origins and processes . . . Dealing with man and being genetic in its analysis, the subject is of necessity concerned with sequences in time.

Sauer entitled his talk 'Foreword to historical geography', but what he was really advocating was an analytical viewpoint or epistemology intended to be valid for geographical investigation as a whole. Effectively all geography was historical geography, and although it was not necessarily Sauer's intention, the distinctiveness of the latter became blurred – a process which was much accelerated in the second half of the twentieth century, with results that were anything but negative. Earlier on, however, the French school of geography had emphatically adopted this point of view.

Historical geography *qua* human geography

Even without asserting itself as an autonomous sub-discipline with its own scientific rationale, historical geography played an essential role in the geographical process. This is illustrated very well by the French school of geography, which took shape in the teachings of P. Vidal de la Blache.

In France, as in other countries, historical geography was long confused with the history of geography, that is to say, with the history of the scientific study of the earth (Berdoulay 1995a). Vidal and his disciples, for their part, did not discount this association (Vidal 1880; Camena 1893). Yet their reading of contemporary German research heightened their sensitivity to the historicity of the geographical phenomena that they were studying and they sought to construct a human geography fully permeated by history. For them, in effect, the interaction between humankind and nature could only be understood when viewed analytically through the dimension of time. This was, however, a dimension of *historical* time, to the extent that, for Vidal and his followers, human social organization depended on the weight of custom and gradual evolution as well as historical contingency.

At root, Vidal's *géographie humaine* sought to make maximal use of that which history could bring to geography, an approach which ensured that the latter would become entirely historical. Above all, this approach rested on a general theory of human–nature relations. At issue here was a geographical possibilism, according to which determinisms of various shades are tempered by historical contingency and creative human initiative. By focusing attention on *genres de vie*, regions, countries, landscapes and so on, this theoretical approach emphasized the mediation inherent in human interaction with the natural world, making it at once interactionist and constructivist (Berdoulay 1995a, 1988). By adopting at the same time a conventionalist epistemology, as did Duhem and Poincaré, the Vidalian perspective retained its full freedom to interrogate and utilize the past. It was in this manner that geographers in France – in contrast to historians, who still emphasized political events – developed an analytical approach that focused on the daily life of the population and its material conditions throughout history (Febvre 1922). It is this point of view that the Annales school would adopt for history, a development which, in turn, would occasionally work to distort the historian's conception of geography.

However, as historical geography (effectively identical to *la géographie humaine*) displayed its relevance and expanded its study of the historicity of phenomena, it necessarily became diluted, to such an extent that its own status as a distinct field of knowledge was called into question. It is for this reason that the French school hardly developed a body of teaching devoted to historical geography, for why should the subject be taught at all if all human geography is historical? Indeed, in so far as the majority of geographers were concerned with contemporary phenomena, the liberty to search the past for insights into the present effectively led to an indifference regarding phenomena which appeared to lack any historical dimension. In contrast to a cross-sectional or genetic-historical approach, this historical geography became too often exclusively retrospective and excessively selective, a development which had the unintentional effect of obscuring the potential of subsequent changes in methodology and approach. This explains the frequent observation that historical geography has been neglected too often in France (Planhol 1972; Pitte 1994).

Nevertheless, the pertinence of this approach to historical geography is amply manifested at the very heart of human geography in France, as can be seen in a variety of significant examples. The best known of these are the regional monographs or works framed on this particular scale (Sion 1908; Gallois 1908). In the same spirit, the pioneering works of urban geographers may be noted. Abandoning the statistical-synchronic or functionalist approaches, they sought to trace the emergence and development of an urban ensemble back to the city's origins (Blanchard 1912; Levainville 1913). Less well known, but no less important, are those works which demonstrated how an approach to human geography which is at once historical and social could help explain political phenomena, thereby helping to ease political geography out of its insularity by exposing it to the determinations and contingencies of the historical process (Vidal 1917; Brunhes and Vallaux 1921).

Special mention should be made of rural landscape studies. This is certainly a domain where historical geography has made a major contribution and where interaction with historians such as Marc Bloch, G. Roupnel or, more recently, C. Higounet has been the most extensive. Although it used ever more sophisticated data and methods, this particular historical geography developed essentially through the never-ending critique of environmental (and, later, racial) determinism, a critique that was articulated in terms of a naively empirical and non-theoretical emphasis on economic and social factors. As part of this, the scope of the study was enlarged to include urban landscapes and commercial networks. This preoccupation with landscape and its organization represents the major thematic continuity of French historical geography, which continues to be pursued up to the present (Dion 1934; Meynier 1959; Pitte 1986; Trochet 1998a), and it is around this theme that international research contacts and exchanges are most developed (Flatrès 1979).

The study of viticulture, which has flourished since the 1940s, is indicative of this evolution. The synthesis of R. Dion (1959) emphasized the essential role played by historical but non-environmental factors – such as the Roman heritage or the medieval religious social structure – in the emergence and constitution of vineyards. Other scholars have demonstrated how much the construction of the most successful vineyards owes to the persistence of socio-economic strategies after the Middle Ages (Pijassou 1980; Enjalbert 1975). But one can see in this example a more general tendency – apparent outside France as well – for historical geography increasingly to become inseparable from cultural geography. Thus a variety of works draw on the growing fields of cultural studies and, once again, political analyses (Planhol 1968, 1993; Lézy 2000; Droulers 2001).

Despite the danger of undermining historical geography's pretensions to exclusive authority over the historical dimension in geographical studies, this approach has assured an important interaction with historians, most importantly at key moments of the latter's own intellectual evolution. The Annales school, associated with luminaries such as Lucien Febvre, F. Braudel, Leroy-Ladurie or G. Duby, has never concealed its debt to Vidalian geography (Pomian 1986), namely the inclination to posit a historical curiosity at the very heart of the totality of the subject of the human sciences. On the other hand, it is not at all certain that geographers have similarly profited in return from the success of the Annales school, as an examination of the renewal, or rather the diversification, of the scope of historical geography will demonstrate.

HISTORICAL GEOGRAPHY 1945–2000: NEW TRENDS AND DEBATES

The impact of the quantitative revolution

The evolutionary trajectory of historical geography in the second half of the twentieth century has been marked by continuities as well as breaks with the earlier traditions we have examined. French historical geographers pursued themes related to the landscape, and figures such as Darby and Sauer continued to exert a powerful influence; indeed, some of their most important work was to come from this period. Darby, in particular, carried his Domesday project forward, with seven volumes of his *Domesday Geography of England* appearing from the 1950s to the 1970s (Darby and Versey 1952–77), and the cross-sectional approach was taken up in the research of others as well (Glasscock 1975; Turner 1981). The same approach can be seen in China and other countries of East Asia, where historical geography turned its attention to the study of ancient regional geographical landscapes, documented through remarkable environmental, demographic and administrative records (Kinda 1997; Takeuchi 2000; Yang 2000).

It is the discontinuities with the pre-war period, however, that seem most significant, and the first point to be noted here is the unmistakable marginalization of historical geography in the discipline as a whole. From the 1950s, burgeoning uncertainties and insecurities regarding human geography's status among the social sciences inspired geographers to an ever greater preoccupation with methodologies and analytical approaches that were 'rigorous' and 'scientific'. This led to the proliferation of quantitative techniques, modelling, paradigms and 'theoretical geography' – in short, to a positivist arsenal, through the development of which it was hoped to secure the discipline's much desired qualification as a genuine science. These innovations occasioned considerable disruption within geography as a whole, and the implications for historical geography – in the short term, at least – were disastrous. From being a small but prosperous and highly respected research area, historical geography now came to represent virtually everything that was wrong in the discipline: backward-looking, traditionalist in approach and (speaking the vernacular of the day) notoriously 'idiographic', that is to say, reluctant to generalize insights and analyses of particular times and places into all-encompassing panoptic models, applicable everywhere, all the time and to everyone. A stigma of sorts developed around the 'empty concept' that historical geography was said to be (Dear 1988, cited in Dennis 1994: 155), a more-or-less outspoken scepticism, which not only coloured attitudes outside the sub-discipline (Zelinsky 1972), but also palpably affected scholarly practice within it.

Historical geographers were encouraged by their own spokespeople to question 'the adequacy of [their] traditional methods and techniques' (Baker 1972: 13), an injunction which, among other things, gave rise to an element of introspection and soul-searching (not to say self-excoriation) in historical-geographical discourse that remains down to the present day (Kay 1991). More positively, historical geographers responded to broader disciplinary priorities by seeking to incorporate new and popular methodologies to address their own historical interests, or alternatively exploring the historical dimension of research themes from other parts of the discipline. The relevance of quantification was emphasized (Norton 1984; Hamshere 1987) and its specific applicability in historical-geographical research was explored in a wide variety of specialized studies, ranging from agriculture (Turner 1981; Chapman and Harris 1982; Overton 1984) to the historical geography of urbanism (Whitehand and Patten 1977; Johnson and Pooley 1982; Dennis 1984). The strong disciplinary interest in spatial diffusion was shared by historical geographers as well, who utilized its theories and models in the analysis, again, of agricultural development (Denecke 1976; Overton 1985; Walton 1987) and also of the geography of epidemics and disease (Cliff, Haggett, Ord and Versey 1981; Cliff, Haggett and Graham 1983; Kearns 1985). Notable in this regard was the work of the Lund geographer Torsten Hägerstrand (Hägerstrand 1968, 1982) and the historical studies of 'time-space geography' which it inspired (Pred 1981, 1984; Miller 1982; Hoppe and Langton 1986).

The humanistic impulse

Although in the countries strongly affected by the quantitative revolution historical geography was never quite to regain its status as a distinct and autonomous sub-discipline, with its own special analytical approach and subject material, the marginalization it experienced in the immediate post-war decades did not endure. Indeed, with hindsight it seems clear that this marginalization positioned for a rather dramatic re-emergence, at the moment when the dynamism of the quantitative revolution began to falter and an increasingly irresistible mood of scepticism began to undermine disciplinary faith in its millenarian promises to deliver geography to the land of genuine science. Intimations of this turn could be seen already in the broad appeal of behavioural geography in the 1960s, with its focus on the psychology of the individual human subject, but behavioural geography carefully retained an essentially positivist methodology. It was only in the 1970s, with the emergence of a 'humanistic' geography, informed and inspired by the anti-positivistic precepts of twentieth-century phenomenology, that a clear epistemological alternative became available (Tuan 1976; Ley and Samuels 1978; Pickles 1986). Humanistic geography rejected – effectively if not always explicitly – the nomothetic assumptions of universal regularities and laws that condition all social behaviour and that can be mapped out in the form of abstract models. Instead, the need to appreciate the subjective, particularist and interpretative element in all geographical phenomena was emphasized, and a preoccupation with unique individuality replaced the quest for universal regularity. In the course of this shift, historical geography found itself on the new cutting edge (Billinge 1977; Gregory 1978b; Harris 1978).

Some of the determining characteristics of a 'humanistic' historical geography were sketched out in the work of one of its most influential precursors, J. K. Wright. Wright coined the term 'geosophy,' which broadly referred to the study of subjective geographical knowledge, but specifically involved at least two distinct concerns. On the one hand, geosophy examined the historical evolution of geographical knowledge, attempting to ascertain quite precisely what different historical periods and civilizations knew or thought they knew about the natural world in which they operated. Wright's own *magnum opus* from the 1920s was precisely such a study, and other examples of geosophy *avant la lettre* can be identified as well (Wright 1925; Brown 1943). Yet as Wright made clear in a celebrated essay, geosophy was above all quests for 'the place of imagination in geography' (Wright 1947). Geographical knowledge in this sense represented not so much a partial – and partially accurate – awareness of the objective reality of an external and objectively existing universe as a collection of impressions, ideas and beliefs which together comprised a subjective life-world for the individuals and cultures in question. The key dimension, which humanistic geography took over from behavioural geography, was the process of perception, through which all environmental experience was internalized, organized and interpreted. To be sure, this did not necessarily spell the end of historical geography's traditional preoccupation with the materiality of the landscape, but it did signal a truly major shift of concern onto the *mentalité* of the individuals and societies in question. Under Wright's inspiration, ideas *per se* became a prime ingredient of historical-geographical research, and the disciplinary walls separating historical geography from the history of geography, and indeed from intellectual history itself, began to crumble accordingly.

This process was clearly apparent, albeit in rather different ways, in the work of those who developed his insights, notably Glacken (1956, 1967), Lowenthal (1961) and Tuan (1974, 1977). The concern for perceptions and a sensitivity to subjective experience opened a variety of new research avenues to historical geography. There was continued strong interest in the agricultural landscape, but now the analysis was focused on the agents operating in these landscapes as much as the palpable effects of their activities of cultivation and transformation. The role of perception in the process of frontier agricultural settlement was examined, focusing on the mindset and evaluation of the settlers themselves (McManis 1964; Heathcote 1965; Powell 1971, 1977; Blouet and Lawson 1975; Jackson 1978) or, alternatively, on the perceptual or mythic environment that was created for them (Bowden 1969, 1975; Powell 1977; Baltensperger 1992). The perception of urban spaces and landscapes was also explored (Krim 1969; Domosh 1987, 1990), as was the salience of the gender distinction in the experience of landscape (Norwood and Monk 1987; Kay 1991; McEwan 1996).

Perhaps even more important than the 'perceptual environment' for historical geography was a powerful new interest in what might be called landscapes of values and meaning. In many respects, this was a direct development of the particular brand of landscape study fostered by Carl Sauer, an approach which traced the transformations of a natural landscape through the activities of human societies and analysed the resulting 'cultural' landscapes as palpable social artefacts. However, while Sauer's attention had focused for the most part on the effects of the material economic pursuits of the culture in question, humanistic historical geography was interested in examining what the configuration of the built environment could tell about a society's attitudes, beliefs and even moral values. The seminal work of J. B. Jackson (himself directly influenced by Sauer) in the USA and W. G. Hoskins in Britain was particularly influential in encouraging and shaping this particular analytical approach (Jackson 1972, 1984; Hoskins 1955; Meinig 1979b). Scrutinizing various aspects of what Jackson termed the 'vernacular landscape', historical geographers explored the influence of religious persuasion (Jackson 1978; Ben-Artzi 1992; Raivo 1997), ethnicity (Conzen 1990) and political dogma (Zelinsky 1990; Wyckoff 1990; Nitz 1992) on the shaping of countryside and city. On a rather more abstract level, it was suggested that the cultural landscape can bear the clear imprint of a shared ethos and the communal ideals that serve to animate the members of the social unit (Hayden 1976; Meinig 1979a; Vance 1990). Increasingly, historical geographers used the term 'ideology' as a sort of collective designation for the subjective attitudes they saw reflected in the landscape, and increasingly they emphasized its importance as a central element in their investigations (Olwig 1984; Biger 1992; Wynn 1992; Denecke 1992).

Iconography and geographies of representation

Humanistic geography, despite its novel preoccupation with the subjective factors of cultural values and attitudes, remained focused on the real-world expression and influence of these qualities, that is to say, on the materiality of cultural landscapes which could be touched, explored and mapped. The growing popularity in the 1980s and 1990s of the term 'ideology', however, signalled a fundamental shift in historical-geographical practice, the effects of which are still very much with us today. Increasingly, it was the qualities of the ideology itself – or *mentalité*, as it was often called – that became the focus of attention (Baker 1992), and in the place of palpable material landscapes, historical geographers focused on the processes of landscape construction and signification taking place within the respective ideological framework. In the telling expression of one practitioner, landscape was best understood not as the ground beneath our feet but rather as 'a way of seeing' (Cosgrove 1984: 1), while another spoke of it as a 'vast repository out of which symbols of order and social relationships, that is ideology, can be fashioned' (Duncan 1985: 182–3). It was precisely the symbolic aspects of the landscape which were of interest. It was likened to a 'text' saturated with cultural and social meaning (Duncan 1990; Barnes and Duncan 1992), and for its analysis an elaborate iconography began to be identified (Cosgrove and Daniels 1988). Although the link back to the tradition of humanistic geography was still clearly asserted (Daniels 1985), the innovations were at least as important as the continuities.

Instead of *perception*, geographers were now concerned rather with the project of *representation*, and this substitution of a simple word betokened an analytical and epistemological shift of substantial dimensions. Although both terms referred to the study of geographical ideas and attitudes, representation now assumed an intentionality absent from naive perception, which suggested that the images under consideration were deliberate, if not necessarily entirely conscious creations intended to serve a particular purpose. Under the strong influence of postmodernism and postcolonial studies, most notably Said's (1978) work on the deconstruction of orientalism, representation was understood most fundamentally as the manufacture and manipulation of geographical images for the ultimate purpose of sustaining the social and political hegemony of western civilization. For the most part, the 'imaginative geographies' (Gregory 1995b) which resulted were directed outwardly, towards the non-European colonial periphery, and a body of historical-geographical research has argued that stylized geographical representations of this periphery were fundamental to its actual appropriation and control by the West. Representation of this sort involved the naming of places (Carter 1988), photography (S. Ryan 1996; J. R. Ryan 1997) and mapping – the latter developed most influentially in the historical cartography of Harley and his disciples (Harley 1988, 1992; Edney 1997). At the same time, however, the representation of landscape had an important role to play in the structuring of domestic social control as well. This was apparent *inter alia*, in the rich traditions of European landscape art, and geographers joined historians of art (Barrell 1980; Bermingham 1986) in exploring how social relations in the countryside were naturalized and effectively legitimated through depictions of rural landscapes in the eighteenth and nineteenth centuries (Prince 1988; Daniels 1986, 1988).

The establishing and charting of power relationships were not, however, the only purposes that geographical representation could serve. In connection with the growth of interest in national identity through the 1990s, the ways in which identities have been articulated historically through evocations of landscape has attracted considerable attention from geographers. Of course, this concern was apparent already in 'traditional' humanistic historical geography, which examined how nationalist ideologies influenced and were manifested in the built environment (Zelinsky 1984, 1986; Konrad 1986). While this particular interest has not disappeared (Morris 1997), the emphasis shifted onto the *idea* or *ethos* of the nation and the various ways in which geography functioned as an important constituent element. The identification of the nation with natural realms and characteristic landscapes – or landscape ideals – has been explored by historians such as Nora and Schama, who acknowledge the extensive contributions of geographers, and by geographers themselves (Nora 1984–92; Schama 1995; Lowenthal and Prince 1965; Lowenthal 1975; Nash 1993; Lowenthal 1994; Heffernan 1995; Withers 1996; Matless 1998). The 'construction' of national territories is recognized as a protracted historical-geographical process, which involves the demarcation of a space which is distinctly national and the signification and valorization of different regions and places within it. This process is a critical element of the larger process of national self-definition, and, like the larger process, it is heavily contested within the nation itself, as illustrated in studies from countries as wide-ranging as Germany (Herb 1997; Schultz 1997, 1998), Finland (Paasi 1996), Iran (Kashani-Sabet 1998), Poland (Kristof 1994) and Russia (Bassin 1991a and b, 1993, 1999). Finally, geographers have considered the historical 'construction' of national landscapes through the medium of landscape art (Osborne 1988, 1992; Daniels 1993, 1998; Bassin 2000). All this interest in representation contributed another dimension of geographical reflection – that concerned with the formation and development of the culture of modernity.

Modernity revisited

By virtue of its interest in the origins or antecedents of phenomena and their evolutionary process, historical geography contributed both implicitly and explicitly to the contemporary interrogation of modernity as a socio-spatial phenomenon. The profound transformations in society and its territorial organization indicated by the notion of modernity have long been taken for granted. The unequal distribution of modernity's benefits was most commonly attributed to the mental or cultural backwardness of the regions in question, an assumption which historical geographers deduced out of a 'grand narrative' of technological and economic progress. However accurate this assumption may or may not have been, they were able to document thoroughly the spatial dimension of social modernization.

Doubts which now surround the legitimacy of actions undertaken in the name of modernity have compelled researchers to develop a more nuanced perspective. Distancing themselves from stereotypes of backwardness, they concentrated on the forms of power which limit the initiative of certain peoples as well as the social or cultural logic which determines their choices. Power relations can be scrutinized from a very critical perspective, inspired to varying degrees by Marxism (Gregory 1984). The historical geography of the myths, attitudes and values which are fundamental for modern territorial ideologies contributed to the interrogation of various projects and practices of spatial planning (Morissonneau 1978; Claval 1990; Piveteau 1995).

Other scholars, developing a perspective offered by ethnography, have been interested in the multiple interactions between traditional and modern forms of knowledge relating to territory and the environment (Buttimer 1992; Claval and Singaravélou 1995; Berdoulay 1995b; Takeuchi 2000). The play between local and global scales appeared to be conditioned by this multiplicity of spatial knowledge. Historical geography has figured centrally in these sorts of interrogations, and has continued to do so as they have been rearticulated more recently in the context of postmodernism. Postmodernism offered a critique of modern society, above all by denouncing the power exercised – in the name of the grand narrative of triumphal western science – against 'minority' categories in the population, such as women, homosexuals, people of colour, Third-World peoples, etc. It demonstrated how the modern categories of gender, ethnicity and so on are socially constructed and figure as part of a spatial competition to acquire material or symbolic advantages (Anderson 1993). In order to escape the conceptual categories of modernist social science, this research makes careful, indeed oblique use of common language (Pred 1990). More generally, the recourse to history that this involves is paradoxical, in so far as postmodernism seeks to demonstrate that spatial preoccupations are more fundamental to the contemporary world than those of time – in other words, that geographical knowledge is more important than historical (Soja 1989). In sum, it is as if historical geography serves to justify the precedence of geography over history.

Certainly, the attention to representation and discourse made it possible to revisit the geography of the past, western or otherwise. By concentrating on the production, modification and reinterpretation of the landscape, it is possible to show the extent to which it is tied to social organization. Understood as a text inserted into diverse discursive fields, landscape proves to be a means alternatively for reproducing power or contesting it, as illustrated admirably in Duncan's study (1990) of the development of Kandi in Sri Lanka in the early nineteenth century, or Ogborn's study of eighteenth-century London (Ogborn 1998). Above all, the development of western technology has hastened the destabilization in the modern world of the very foundation of the organization of territories and representations (Capel 1994). In effect, the historical geography of certain innovations – money, photography, the use of steel and glass in construction – shows that, in everyday life, the presence of one element is inconceivable outside its relation to one or several absences. It is precisely this relation, at once contingent and material, which characterizes the experience of the daily life of modernity (Strohmayer 1996, 1997a).

Postmodernism has stressed historical geography's potential value for situating individual initiative and reflexivity. The works of Giddens (1979, 1991) argued that the affirmation of the subject and the consequences of his or her agency in the course of the development of modernity have spatial dimensions which played an essential role. Parallel to this, the perspective of 'time geography' sought to underline the necessity of understanding human action as a continuous flow of behaviour in space and time (Pred 1986). But the operationalization of this sort of research became increasingly difficult, indicating that the cultural approach is perhaps the better one for dealing with the question of reflexivity (Gregory 1981; Harris 1991; Berdoulay 1999). In any event, postmodernism enabled historical geography to pay the necessary attention to the phenomena of reflexivity and social organization and control, as well as to the effects of the specific language that is employed (Hannah and Strohmayer 1991).

Colonization and planning

The critique of western modernity discovered a particularly useful terrain for analysis in the experience of colonialism. To be sure, this analysis condemns the colonial systems put in place by western societies for the purposes of dominating non-European populations and/or their respective resources (Bruneau and Dory 1994; Godlewska and Smith 1994). However, historical geography has been able to document the structures of regimentation and control of colonial populations, which were frequently more numerous than those of the colonizers themselves (Demangeon 1923). Along with this essentially political and economic orientation, a rather broader perspective has taken shape progressively.

By situating colonialism and the imperial experiences of various countries in the context of a developing modernity, historical geography has integrated cultural perspectives on the transformation of territories and landscapes. It opens the way for the study of the interactions between colonizer and colonized. Since the 1980s the postcolonial intellectual movement – securely anchored in the literary critique of Edward Said (1978, 1993) and inspired by postmodernism – has developed this particular perspective. By focusing attention on the need to decolonize the knowledge of the countries which experienced domination, it implicitly invites the imperial West to reconsider its view of its own existence. Even the preoccupation of this movement with literary discourse does not make it impossible to extend the interrogation to include the production and transformation of regions and landscapes in the colonizing realms themselves. The important point, however, is that by understanding this phenomenon fully in its global dimension, historical geography demonstrates that it is not entirely subservient to social theories that may be relevant in particular cases (Driver 1988, 1998).

It is now clear that the colonial activity of western nations represents a complex phenomenon which cannot be fully explicated in terms of a simple power relationship, and the lessons of which have not been fully examined. The colonization of sparsely or non-populated regions, for example, poses the problem of the initial structuring of spaces formerly untouched by social organization, as illustrated by the study of the colonization of North America (Claval 1990; Berdoulay and Sénécal 1993). In fact, this phenomenon turns out to be even more general. Historical geography demonstrates to what extent the planning of space corresponded to a project with ambitions that could be quite radical. Wheatley (1971) has analysed the morphology of the first generation of cities – especially in the great arenas of nascent urbanization in Mesopotamia, the Indus Valley, Egypt, north China, Central and Andean America and Yoruba – as a spatial arrangement, which had the ultimate effect of fundamentally transforming society by creating out of a fragmented but relatively egalitarian organization one which was cleanly stratified. Subsequent experience through the ages has repeatedly confirmed the efficacy of these urban arrangements, in the context either of colonization or free autonomous development.

From these studies it appears that the organization of colonial spaces not only leads to the transformation of these realms but also to the transformation of the colonizing population itself. Thus the understanding of colonization underwent a transformation, in the sense that it now came to represent a crucible of planning theory, which – as anthropologists and sociologists such as Rabinow (1989) and Marié (1989) indicated – flourished along with the affirmation of modernity. For many Europeans, and in particular the French, the colonies appeared to constitute laboratories for experimentation with planning projects that were difficult to realize in a metropolis where political and social inertia stymied the possibility of innovation. Colonial space, perceived to be relatively unshaped and administratively malleable, could be modified for the purposes of economic and social development. In this manner, the colonies were able to play the role of an incubator for modern urban and regional planning (Berdoulay *et al.* 1996; Berdoulay and Soubeyran 2000). In this case one can see historical geography superimposing itself on the history of urbanism and urban and regional planning. More broadly, the convergence between historical geography and the history of that knowledge which establishes and legitimates practice becomes ever clearer, for the latter is not limited to the development of planning.

Convergence with the history of geography

The history of geographical thought is one of several means of assuring the reflexivity to which the geographer aspires. This reflexivity, indeed, can be seen as possessing a dual nature: there is a reflexivity of the populations studied, who organize their own knowledge of their place in the world, and there is a reflexivity of the historian-geographer, who studies this knowledge. Thus if the history of geography is once again merging with historical geography, as was the case in the nineteenth century, then this is happening today in a very different spirit. At the moment, the most important point is the appreciation of the discursive dimension of this knowledge (Berdoulay 1988; Livingston 1992). Along with the languages they mobilize, these discourses possess an inertia that goes beyond the place and moment of their elaboration, as well as a powerful impulse for organizing the reality of the populations which utilize them. They contribute to the construction of representations of the world, which themselves generate practices.

Research into the history of cartography and cartographic conceptions has developed rapidly, the more so as it facilitates the analytical integration of those ideological discourses which underlay it (Dion 1977; Harley 1989; Wood 1993). Maps themselves, however, mobilize a language of signs which is entirely their own (Dainville 1964). It is in these semiotic processes that certain modes of appropriation and historical construction of regions are expressed (Casti 1998). The construction of representations of the world owes a great deal to the literature of travel and exploration. In addition to the factual information they present in order to legitimize the discourse, these depictions contain numerous elements which are pertinent to contemporary geographical reflection on the construction of the 'other' and, in turn, on the ensuing transformation of the identity of the author and his or her reference group. The reciprocal relations connecting author, reader and subject population are complex and ambiguous: travel literature can modify the image of the other as much as the image of the people or country that produced it. In close interaction with a more purely scientific literature, this travel literature invokes geographical ideas, which echo the historical geography of communication and transportation (Alegria *et al.* 1998; Berdoulay and Gomez Mendoza 1998).

From this same perspective, the study of the construction of geographical ways of seeing cannot be limited to the internal logic of the discourse. One is therefore interested in bodily practices and the techniques which establish them. The history of geography thus studies a mix of cognitive, explorative and experimental procedures which specify the displacement, movement and acquisition of information. It is these aspects which give this information credibility and scientific value (Bousquet-Bressolier 1995; Berdoulay and Gomez Mendoza 1998). This perspective crosses the line into historical geography, for it is in relation to it that it is possible to explain practices, their contexts and some of their consequences.

The same convergence between the two sub-disciplines can be seen in regard to the images mobilized by scientific discourse. These images span various fields of intellectual, artistic and practical knowledge. They are manifested in literary or artistic works, but also, in a more banal fashion, in newspapers, posters and ordinary discourse. They rest on rhetorical processes – notably metaphor – and function as models of intelligibility (Dematteis 1985; Buttimer 1993). Those which concern modernity and its challengers are expressed in geographical discourse: they are situated at the centre of a double polarity, between a rationalist and mechanical vision of the world and a more romantic and organic vision (Da Costa Gomes 1996). But these interpretative keys also help to understand actions taken in order to transform environments and landscapes, and carry out the 'internal colonization' which leads to the transformation of national society (Gomez Mendoza 1992). If one approaches these images in their concrete dimension, as they are expressed in pictorial, architectural or landscape representations, then historical geography remains close to the reflections which animate the history of geographical ideas. In this manner, historical geography could help to lead us to a modification of our approach to the valorization of landscape heritage (Berdoulay and Bielza 2000).

In sum, the boundaries between historical geography and the history of geographical thought are blurred in a wide variety of research. Historians of geography concentrate generally on what the ideas owe to the socio-geographical context, and in particular the social construction of knowledge (Berdoulay 1993; Buttimer *et al.* 1998). Contemporary research is becoming more and more attentive to geography and the reflexivity of geographers, as well as to the agents (however modest) of the transformation of the earth through the knowledge and ideologies which they produce. For why should geography not apply its own approach to itself? Within historical geography, this sort of research leads to a geography of geographical knowledge, which has yet to be developed. Historical geography, for its part, does not hesitate to study the contribution of geographers towards understanding the genesis of regions and landscapes, an approach which in turn nourishes reflection on geographic thought.

CONCLUSION

No consensus has emerged from geographical science in the twentieth century regarding either the importance or the approach of historical geography. Indeed its very existence as a sub-discipline has not always been self-evident, as it alternated between an ancillary role in geography and history and a fragmented contribution to various branches of geography on the one hand, and a more or less distinct individuality on the other. Both of these alternatives were equally marked by incessant methodological debates. Paradoxically, it was at those moments when it lacked a clear identity as a sub-discipline that historical geography acquired a remarkable import: to the extent that it could share the approaches of geography as a whole, it contributed considerable empirical knowledge, demonstrating the extent to which the present is a product of the past. Yet this immediately gave rise to a second paradox, for the strengthening of the influence of the historical perspective led to the weakening of historical geography's position, the more so as the latter was largely concerned with socio-economic problems that were ever more criticized as excessively structuralist. A number of works that explicitly subscribe to historical geography have shown how a historical dimension can contribute to the study of problems that are not explicitly historical. At root, the attempt to limit study to an exclusively historical geography heightened the awareness of the richness of the geographical laboratory which is constituted by the past.

After the relative disaffection for historical geography in favour of the quantitative revolution, which privileged the production of spatial models that were either synchronic or included a temporal dimension only as a measure of the speed of the processes, there is a new interest in the complexity of historical-geographical phenomena. Despite this, there are very few examples of geographers who accord history a particular epistemological status which would locate historical geography in a separate and autonomous sub-disciplinary domain (Guelke 1997). Rather it represents for some a field where the perspectives of the humanities, the 'historical mind' (Harris 1971), or more generally the freedom to question notions or theories elaborated in the first instance in regard to the contemporary world, can be developed most easily. This refers particularly to contemporary interest in understanding the affirmation of the subject or self that accompanies the ascent of modernity and its current crisis. Finally, in the same way as they do not acknowledge those classical subdivisions of geography which deal with the contemporary world, many geographers see no special content whatsoever in historical geography, apart from that of reflecting on the past.

In this, such geographers are effectively encouraged by the disappearance of sub-disciplinary, indeed interdisciplinary, boundaries. Historical geography's recent evolution has demonstrated the potential of this development, and suggestive results can be seen in the study of landscape, representation, ethnogeographies and the theory of modern geography and planning. The differences between cultural and historical geography, or between historical geography and the history of geographical thought, have come to appear insignificant. Must we thus conclude that historical geography *per se* no longer has a place in the broader discipline? Even if it is not considered a clearly defined sub-discipline, does it have nothing of its own to offer?

The cognitive nature of geography reminds us that it mobilizes methods and perspectives, and to deny ourselves this diversity would be to impoverish our capacity for understanding. In this spirit, historical geography should continue as a field for investigation. Its epistemological autonomy is debatable, to be sure, but it possesses the merit of directing attention to the historicity which permeates human experience, its praxis and its applications. Is not the very fact that modern geography has increasingly abandoned the explicit and deliberate use of narrative, preferring to leave it to the historians, symptomatic of a certain intellectual deficit (Berdoulay 2000)? Is not the recent interest in narrative a summons for the revalorization of an essentially historical perspective?

5 Political geography: spaces between war and peace

Peter J. Taylor and Herman van der Wuste

THE CASE FOR POLITICAL GEOGRAPHY

When geography was established as a discipline at university at the end of the nineteenth century, political geography was quickly recognized as a specific domain. German modernization of the university through the nineteenth century had created an academia of specialized knowledge in which geography's intellectual credentials were initially seen as problematic (Taylor 1985b). Pressure to become specialized even led to proposals to focus solely on physical aspects of the discipline, but the geography that eventually emerged from the German universities was holistic, including a human geography based on studying societal change in its physical setting. Friedrich Ratzel, the major proponent of this approach, first demarcated the territory of human geography in his *Anthropogeographie*, and towards the end of his career, after the publication of various other works, came his *Politische Geographie* in 1897. This long text (more than 800 pages in the extended second edition of 1903, published just before his death) effectively brings political geography to life as a sub-discipline of human geography (Ratzel 1903).

During his years as a student in the life sciences, Ratzel was deeply affected by the enthusiastic reception of Darwin's teachings in the German academic world. As he occupied a newly established chair in geography, he developed a perspective that was informed by the lessons he drew from Darwin, a sense that geography had to be a human geography embedded in human history, and his experience in the Franco-German war of 1870–1 and as a travelling journalist in the more exotic parts of Europe and the Americas. By the time he wrote *Politische Geographie*, he was still strongly marked by the evolutionary perspective, but he was certainly not an all-out environmental determinist. At this juncture, Germany's unification in the second Reich was still fresh and Germany's international position had again become a major issue, not least in Germany itself. The forces that pushed for great power status were growing stronger. Ratzel was among the supporters of this movement (Büttmann 1977).

Politische Geographie portrays the state as the hard core of the sub-discipline. A state is any political organization connecting a part of humanity and a part of the earth surface. States may range from a tiny settlement of Africans and the land its inhabitants use, held together by some authority, to the complex current combinations of population and land in the western world. States tend to grow in surface area as their populations reach higher levels of civilization. Such states crowd out others at lower levels. The more developed the state, the better organized its part of the earth's surface. This surface and the nature of its borders are key state assets. State development is conditioned by context: its physical (maritime versus landlocked, flat versus mountainous) and political features (power relations with relevant others like large powers and neighbours).

Ratzel's *Politische Geographie* essentially explores on two levels: the globe and the state. It has an extremely wide definition of what a state is. The description of states encompasses the world and delves into history. However, its portrait of the political world in the end clearly reflects the contemporary power distribution. The index of the book lists references to some 63 contemporary political units – states or colonies (in actual practice nothing else was left at the time). Just six are mentioned ten times or more: Germany and Britain (21 times each), Austria (14), France (13), USA (13) and Japan (10). Given this power distribution, all states are in rivalry. The rivalry is about territory. Territory is bordered space, newly appropriated again and again. The struggle envelops the world as a whole. At the global scale one rule applies: the more civilized state grows at the expense of the less civilized.

Ratzel's effort to present political geography as a relevant sub-discipline of human geography does not mean that relations with the other sub-disciplines are ignored, nor that the shared interests with neighbouring disciplines are overlooked. Indicative here is the subtitle of the second edition: the geography of states, traffic and war. He connected his interests in political geography with other parts of geography. The book essentially deals with landscape typology, population geography and also cultural (levels of civilization) and economic (resource base and transport) geography. In addition, it relates political geography to adjoining disciplines. Ratzel stated in his introduction that for political geography the insights of sociology and *Staatswissenschaften* (legal and economic aspects, the study of war) cannot be avoided. His work was reviewed within those disciplines (e.g. a pre-publication of part of *Politische Geographie* in Durkheim 1898).

Over time political geographers have put states in the context of wider social, economic and political arrangements more consciously. They have struggled with the conceptual problems involved in the definition of state, problematized the state as the penultimate unit of political community, become interested in politics below state level and refined the analysis of the problems that Ratzel put on political geography's research agenda. In this chapter we are concerned with political geography's substantive development in these terms during the twentieth century.

At several junctures political geography has teamed up with various other parts of geography. Over time the relation with physical geography has generally subsided, although political geographers with military concerns have never given up on those interests. By and large the same goes for population geography. Links with cultural and economic geography have generally been maintained (e.g. in the study of nationalism and international trade). Relations with urban geography are growing as a result of the increasing importance of cities as specific arenas for political action and as the essential nodes in the global urban political-economic planning and control network (Knox and Taylor 1995; Taylor and Flint 2000). In some respects, political geography has been linked to the discipline of political science (including international relations) born in the same period. This refers to topics like elections, administrative systems and foreign policy orientations, and also to the way in which the territorial nature of politics can be perceived and shifts in methodological practice, like the relative preference for the analysis of purely quantitative data. More recently, political geography has been connected with the newly reinstated political economy that was coming apart as Ratzel crafted his sub-discipline. Over time political geography's stock within the discipline, within academia as a whole and as a subject of interest generally, has fluctuated. The following sections deal with political geography's changing fortunes during the twentieth century.

NINETEENTH-CENTURY ROOTS AND TWENTIETH-CENTURY BRANCHES

The intellectual roots of political geography stem from the late nineteenth century. Its initial programme was shaped by contemporaneous patterns of thought and specific social circumstances. Some of the central concepts that made up the intellectual climate of the period returned in some shape or fashion later on, and it is useful to mention those concepts and briefly summarize their further use during the twentieth century. We will concentrate on 'progress', 'functionalism', 'environmentalism' and 'regionalism' in turn. As regards the social circumstances that gave rise to a focus on political geography within the young discipline of geography or human geography, it is obvious that state-building, broad-based nationalism and colonial rivalry, all of them constitutive for the emergence of human geography more generally, induced at the same time a more specific political interest.

   Social progress was an important notion throughout the nineteenth century, stemming from various sources within the Enlightenment and suggesting trajectories that societies would follow, which would improve their overall quality of life. There were more deterministic and more voluntaristic versions, and precisely which societal qualities would improve was perceived differently. They could be material circumstances or spiritual values, or an extension of peaceful relations among humans on the global scale. When Ratzel wrote, an important part of the debate on social progress was conducted against the background of evolutionism (Darwinian or otherwise) and Ratzel was an ardent follower of those debates. In that context one can consider progress to be the sequence of outcomes of rivalries about shaped and reshaped niches or of ever more successful adaptations to external conditions. His contemporary, the French geographer,

Reclus, was confident that in the long run humans from all corners of the earth would relate to each other more easily, and he looked forward to a globalized society made up of voluntary small-scale associations (Claval 1998: 80–3).

In the twentieth century notions of social progress – however misguided and perverted – have inspired the great challengers to a political order based on market democracies: the communist experiment (1917–91) and the populist right regimes of the Fascists and the Nazis (1922–45). Social progress has been the basic drive behind all the efforts to construct viable welfare states in market democracies, and in many cases was a major inspiration behind the decolonization process in the colonial world after 1945. Progress for all was also a rallying cry during the triumphalist stage of American capitalism following the Second World War, when the only interesting map seemed to be that of the position of units (countries or parts of countries) in different stages of economic growth or on the road of modernization or political development.

Functionalism became an important perspective on human affairs in the late nineteenth century. The French sociologist, Durkheim (1893), was a major inspiration for this school of thought. According to him, social groups or whole societies are somehow kept together ('integrated'). In order to achieve this, the constituent parts must contribute to their overall operation, and such contributions are deemed indispensable. The metaphor in the background is that of a living organism; the more general intellectual inspiration, once again, the debate on evolution. Durkheim's sociology laid its foundations at the same time that French academic geography emerged as a competitor. Ratzel's work was hotly debated in this context. Ratzel himself also used this perspective when he portrayed the state as an organism with a boundary and a capital city that performed indispensable functions. This pattern of thought was later manifested in the development of systems analysis.

Functionalism was extremely important in a whole series of disciplines during most of the twentieth century. The same applies to political geography. In 1950, Hartshorne, a key figure in the development of the discipline of geography, drafted an influential research agenda for political geography's study of the state, an agenda that was put forward entirely in functionalist terms (Hartshorne 1950). At the same time, in the field of sociology, Merton set out the ways in which functionalism could be used properly (Merton 1957: 19–84) and Parsons brought forward his version of structural functionalism that was the major perspective in American sociology during the 1950s. The main question functionalism seems to answer is how complicated social units can be stable, equilibrated, can continue to operate etc.

During the period 1950–75, an interesting combination of the notions of progress and functionalism was put forward in the domain of political geography (and related fields of study) by the idea of political development. Just like development more broadly conceived, it was assumed that societies followed a certain trajectory in which new requirements arose. These would be covered by new structures that would provide the contributions to integration necessary during the following stretch of the road, and so on. The main question is not concerned with stability but with change. In 1975 a prestigious large-scale research project, executed by political scientists, political sociologists and historians, came to a halt when the different stages could not be identified for a series of countries and a more global perspective was instituted (Tilly 1975). In geography during the 1960s, some studies with a similar ambition were executed, particularly looking at intra-country differences in levels of development. A good example of this latter trend is presented by Soja (1968) in his work on Kenya.

After 1975, the notions of progress and functionalism – certainly at the state level – were largely abandoned. In world system studies, one of the major research programmes of the social sciences of the last quarter-century in which political geographers took an active part, both concepts can be identified, but at the global scale only. Another major shift in recent decades is the radical questioning of both ideas. In many (though not all) studies conducted under the label of postmodernity, large question marks are raised regarding these ordering devices that were so dominant for so long.

Environmentalism expresses the idea that social life is conditioned by the physical milieu in which it takes shape. Ratzel's geography – including his political geography – is obviously constructed around this relationship. Ratzel's reception of Darwin went through Haeckel, the important German Darwinist who himself developed the idea of ecology. All living creatures, humans among them, are looking for a niche within a natural environment that, in turn, is transformed by the activities of the whole set of creatures that are interacting in very different ways. In Ratzel's state-centred political geography, the physical milieu plays two different roles simultaneously. On the one hand, it acts as the resource base that is vital to the state's chances of survival. On the other, the wider physical milieu, part of which a state dominates at a certain point in time as its territory, provides states with better or worse chances to develop: secure ports, major arteries etc. In Ratzel's view, these configurations, and consequently the positions of all states, change as state territories change through competition. What at one stage is an external asset or liability becomes part of the resource base, or vice versa.

During the twentieth century, this set of ideas has been important in a number of ways. In the first half of the century, the physical resource base played a large role in the assessments of state power and thus in the ways in which the international system was perceived from various corners. In the last part of the century, the physical environment again became a major concern in politics and elsewhere. The assessment is now less in terms of an exploitable resource base than as a vital condition of survival from a perspective of sustainability. As this condition can by no means be limited to the individual state's territory, the physical environment has become a transnational concern – to a point.

In the first half of the century and again, with renewed vigour, at its end, the position of a state *vis-à-vis* other states within the physical environment at large has been an important problem. Geopolitics, as it was coined in Germany after the First World War, following Kjellen's lead (Holdar 1992: 307–23; Sprengel 2000: 147–68), has been a perspective of all states, large and small. Several schools of thought have been formed, some of which were closely allied with the foreign policy elite and thus represented an effort at applied geography, based on a technocratic impulse (Korinman 1990). Others were more distant and reflexive towards the holders of power. Around the turn of the century, Mackinder (1904) introduced his global vision based on the positional differences of Britain and Russia and the debate has never really subsided. In time, arguments were no longer derived only from purely physical conditions (central to Mackinder's approach was the impact of the development of transport technologies), but economic and cultural spatial variations were added. Whittlesey (1939) emphasized the formation of states on the basis of specific core areas.

Regionalism is the last of the nineteenth-century heritages that had an impact on political geography's development in later years. During the entire nineteenth century, the growing uniformity of social practices within well-established states, and the crafting of new states imposing new homogeneities across older local traditions, was a major practical and intellectual challenge. In addition, the more intensive contacts between Europe and the remainder of the world forced Europeans into the consideration of generalized interpretive maps expressing differences and similarities. Orientalism knew different versions for the Near, Middle and Far East (the start of the general current debate on this issue is Said 1978). Now there was a new urgency for a regionalization of the world on different scales, for different purposes.

French geography harboured the most distinctive and refined elaboration of the regionalist motivation. As French regional geography became firmly established and codified in the early twentieth century (Claval 1998: 84–152), it concentrated on the internal variation within France and consequently acted as a counterweight to a general trend in the social sciences to think of societies as unquestionably coincident with states. But Vidal de la Blache, the founder of the French regional school, originally had been much more susceptible to the idea of regions at different scales, the fates of which should be interpreted as interconnected. Vidal started with Ratzel, whose works he read and commented on meticulously. While Ratzel moved from the life sciences into geography, Vidal was originally a historian and therefore less inclined to emphasize the physical constraints than the historical experience of those who populated and thus formed a region. Vidal's effort to build a respectable geographical discipline occurred in the political context of the defeat of France in 1871 and the loss of the Alsace region. His regional motive was embedded in a political battle concerning a better administrative practice in France. His historical inclination imbued his geography with a 'cultural turn' that conditioned a lot of work in this vein during the twentieth century. During the last years of his life, his probing towards a regional geography based on the new requirements of modernization and industrialization, instead of the longstanding *genres de vie*, opened the door to alternative regionalizations that have been pursued vigorously since.

On a larger scale, the idea of Europe, the Atlantic Community, the world of Islam, the Pan-regions of the interwar years, the First, Second and Third World since the 1950s until 1991, the core, semi-periphery and periphery and countless other ways to divide the globe meaningfully have been made in journalism, politics and geography. In political geography such classifications have been presented as the outcome of interaction patterns in international relations and political-economic global forces (role in the world-system), or longstanding givens (clash of civilizations) that condition the degrees of freedom of political players who find themselves in one of those positions (Nierop 1994; Brook 1995).

Progress, functionalism, environmentalism and regionalism embodied intellectual perspectives firmly established at the outset of the twentieth century, widely used outside political geography. As political geography branched out in the course of the century, these traditions were taken up, reinvigorated and repeatedly combined in new ways. At the beginning of the twenty-first century, the notions of progress and functionalism may look tarnished for the moment, but this is by no means a guarantee of their definitive demise. Environmentalism has found a new lease of life as a result of the new urgency of the age-old problem of the limitations imposed on humankind by nature. Regionalism has re-emerged in a new vein as a result of the cultural turn in the social sciences and as a product of the new global political economy. These new versions of environmentalism and regionalism provide much food for thought, not least for political geographers. Recent general overviews of the political geography of the twentieth century and of political geography's twentieth-century history are provided by Taylor (1993) and Dikshit (1997).

FROM THE GREAT WAR TO THE WORLD WAR

The Great War, later called the First World War, was a catastrophe for Europe first and foremost. It ended a long period when war among the European powers on their own territory had only been an intermittent, short-lived, nearly always secondary concern. In that period, the prospect of a commonwealth of nations and states, peacefully cooperating and connected by bonds of shared high culture, mutual commercial interest and a legitimate set of international norms administered by supra-national legal institutions, had been growing for increasing numbers of people. This commonwealth was still very much centred around Europe, and benign colonial government was supposed to last indefinitely. Such a bright future had already been clouded by worrying signs of mass-based nationalism, colonial rivalries and arms-racing, but it was still there. The outbreak of the First World War was a great shock in itself, but also because of the suddenly demonstrated willingness of large sections of the public to be part of the deadly game.

The consequences of the First World War were enormous: the European state system was shattered, the government and legitimacy of many states were in shambles, economies were largely destroyed and previously unheard of human loss was suffered, particularly among the armed forces on both sides. At the same time, the war provoked unprecedented mobilization and participation in state affairs and consequently levelled several thresholds on the way to mass democracy. The interwar years were lost years, in many respects, filled with efforts to get European civilization back on track, but they also marked a fierce competition between different visions of how states should now be run and how international society should function. The tenets of Marxism-Leninism, Fascism and Nazism challenged the evolving modes of conduct that regulated the capitalist democracies. The capitalist economy went through a severe crisis. In the colonies there were signs of rebellion. The USA became increasingly perceived as a (positive or negative) role model, a civilizational force to be reckoned with, a power that could no longer be ignored. The Second World War finally undid the European-centred state system and set the stage for a truly worldwide system of states organized in three worlds of development, with the USA as the hegemonic power. The whole period encompassing the two major twentieth-century conflicts has been called a European civil war. As this war progressed it really became a global conflict – a world at war.

The First World War involved the citizenry at large to an unprecedented degree. Foreign affairs, traditionally the preserve of a highly circumscribed elite, to some extent and intermittently, became a matter of public debate, scrutiny and concern. This had happened before (e.g. in Britain and France, with respect to colonial issues) and foreign affairs afterwards remained of only modest importance in mass politics, but there is reason to look at 1918 as an important divide in this respect. The French political geographer, Yves Lacoste, considers the domestic public debate on Germany's place in the European state system after the war as the first manifestation of 'geopolitics', in his view shaping the public discourse on a state's place on the map – that is, its territory, social life and cultural identity, and the external threats and opportunities that surround it (Lacoste 1993: 1–35). Among the foreign policy elite, including the military, the discourse that emphasized geographical features like site qualities and situation in the setting of policy became important, though by no means universally shared. In that way, geography at large, and political geography in particular, contributed to an applied approach in foreign policy, in the same way as geography's contribution to other policy sectors like town planning around the same time (Claval 1994: 27–8).

The central concerns of political geography during the war years and the interwar period can be summarized easily. The general question was what kind of geographical features produced what kind of political order: the segmentation of states and other territories, the power distribution, the risks and opportunities in terms of violence and economic loss or peace and economic benefit. The applied question was how one's own state performed in such equations and if and how the outcomes could be affected by policy. The relevant geographical features could be of several kinds. First of all, and most importantly, they could be derived from the physical world or from the quasi-immutable realms of civilization. At the same time, the idea was promoted that the geographical features of states could perhaps be arranged in such a way that positive effects were maximized. This referred first and foremost to state borders in relation to population distribution. But there were also questions concerned with the location of capital cities as a state's headquarters, and the administrative map distributing sub-territories and competences to tiers of government in order to maximize governmental efficacy and efficiency and improve the sense of political community (Fawcett 1919; Holmes 1944).

In the remainder of this section we will address these various subjects and the different approaches taken in their study. The geographical features that gave rise to these macro-views about political order and its consequences for individual actors are based on three different types of features: the distribution of land and sea and its consequences for mobility; the distribution of climate and its consequences for resource bases; and the distribution of distinctive civilizations and its consequences for social development. All of them are mentioned in Fairgrieve (1915), with particular emphasis on the ensuing distribution of available energy. Then there is a question that was perhaps not much studied at the time, but that was clearly of great relevance for contemporaries: the identity of one's own state as read from its geographical features. The aggregate of such identities was obviously relevant to the nature of the political order at large (Steinmetz 1920, 1927; van der Wusten 1991: 30–41). The construction and reconstruction of state borders (and also the controlled migration of people) in order to produce a 'better', more viable state system was a major bone of contention during the period in which political geographers were deeply implicated (Bowman 1922). The location and functions of capital cities and the units in an administrative system are the final points of interest in interwar political geography that were occasionally explored by political geographers.

Mackinder (1904; Parker 1982) already briefly mentioned in the preceding section, was the first proponent of a macro-view of political order in which the fate of states is predicated on their location, with respect to the broad distribution of land and sea on earth and the available transport technology. The published version of his famous lecture has a map entitled 'The natural seats of power'. His argument runs as follows. On the Eurasian continent there is a pivot area (later called the heartland) – central Siberia north of the central Asian mountains – that cannot be reached by naval power and therefore is easily defended against incursions from that side. As the development of transport technology facilitates land transport more than sea-based transport, incursions of pivot area powers into zones dominated by naval powers will become relatively easier than incursions from naval powers in the direction of the pivot area. Consequently, the road to world dominance opens up for the power that dominates the pivot area. The Russians are the current tenants of that area, but this is not necessarily the case for ever. The lecture was given at the Royal Geographical Society in 1904, just a few weeks before Japan and Russia entered into a war in which Russia was defeated.

In 1919, when Mackinder was involved briefly in the Russian civil war as a British official in South Russia, he elaborated his views (Mackinder 1919) – which have been quoted often – by expressing the fear of German dominance of Eastern Europe, followed by German-Russian dominance of the heartland, which would then lead to German-Russian world dominance. What a disaster for the newly proclaimed democratic ideal! In a paper published in *Foreign Affairs* in 1943, Mackinder once again adapted his basic views to the turn of events, in which he speculated again, on the basis of land and sea distributions, about the fate of countries after the war given the unexpected alliance of major land and sea powers against Nazi Germany and Japan.

Mackinder's views were certainly not unknown before the First World War, but they only found international renown after 1914. In Germany, a large public debate followed the peace treaties. The issue at stake also aroused geographers. In Munich, Haushofer, a retired military man who had been in Japan before the war, began his efforts to establish a field of geopolitics as a body of applied or applicable knowledge aiming at the restoration of Germany's international position. The main vehicle for this purpose was the *Zeitschrift fuer Geopolitik*, published between 1924 and 1944 by Haushofer. The *Zeitschrift* published a lot of work by political geographers and the later claim of German geographers that political geography was somehow totally different from geopolitics cannot be sustained (Kost 1999: 290). Haushofer recognized Mackinder as a very important influence. Always an important topic in the *Zeitschrift* was the macro-view of the political order. It included proposals and speculations about Germany's potential friends and foes in Europe, inspired by Mackinder's opportunity map of land and sea positions, and also an interest in the development of the colonial world. Haushofer's views were immediately criticized (e.g. in the Netherlands by Ter Veen 1931), with French geographers taking the lead. Parker (1988) has reviewed their positions. More recently he has detailed the similarities and differences in Vidal de la Blache's reaction to Ratzel, Goblet's and Ancel's reaction to Haushofer and the German threat, and Lacoste's post-1968 effort to start a new critical geopolitics, reiterating the case for a distinctive French set of reactions to the intellectual and political challenges of these diverse periods (Parker 2000). During the Second World War geographers in the USA denounced Haushofer's geopolitics as a major support of Hitler's expansionary drive. More recent research – without denying the links between Haushofer and the Nazis, particularly during the early years – has considerably nuanced such views (Bassin 1987b). In the USA itself Spykman (1944) published a book towards the end of the Second World War that reads as a recommendation for the later containment policy. It is based directly on Mackinder's ideas about the relevance of sea and land masses for the conduct of foreign policy, depending on one's geographical position, although he adds some new twists to that debate, introducing the category of 'rimland' as power-enhancing.

A second geographical feature that was repeatedly used to interpret the political order and a country's place in it was the distribution of climate and the covariant resource base. In emphasizing the connection, it was suggested that agricultural opportunities still counted for much in long-term development. In addition, the distribution of minerals and other non-renewable resources were taken into account and found to be spread unevenly across the world. A good early example of such views, in which the availability of energy was made into the most crucial condition of social development, is Fairgrieve (1915). A host of such studies, interpreting the resource bases of individual countries and their distribution as the major indication of power and, consequently, their chances in war, appeared in the interwar period (Leith 1931; Dickenson 1943).

This provided an important background for the macro-view of political order that suggested a threefold or fourfold division of the world into pan-regions, each based on one major power, plus a zone of dependencies for each recruited from the different climatic zones (O'Loughlin and van der Wusten 1990; Taylor 1993: 47–8). Every resulting bloc could thus be quasi-autonomous and would not have to be afraid of outside interference. Systemically there would no longer be a reason for rivalry between major powers. This view was considered as an attractive option and also as an evolving reality. The major powers identified were the USA, Continental Europe – in some views dominated by Germany (Britain being on the decline and not to be reckoned with) – Japan and, perhaps, also Russia, with a dominating role on the Indian subcontinent. Such thoughts were discussed in circles of the interwar enthusiasts of European integration (like Coudenhove Kalergi) and elaborated by Haushofer and those around him (Heffernan 1998: 125–38). Haushofer (1931) stressed, in addition to the material and power-political basis for such a bloc-like political order, the necessity of an ideological basis, or pan-ideas, that could be derived from civilizational characteristics. It is obvious that such ideas tied in with one traditional US option, known as the Monroe doctrine, and the longstanding Japanese preference for a zone of influence in Pacific Asia, which later (before 1945) was on the way to realization in the co-prosperity zone, and still materialized later, to a point, in Japanese post-war external policy (Rumley *et al.* 1996; Grant 1998).

One other organizing principle for macro-political order was the quasi-stable geographical distribution of civilizational realms. The emphasis was not so much on the possibility of clashes of civilizations as on the internal possibilities of order maintenance based on cultural homogeneity and the possibilities of fruitful mutual cooperation based on such differences. This approach was already part of the macro-order we just encountered as the consequence of a geography of pan-ideas. It was also a view that inspired French politicians and geographers, who clearly saw the demise of Europe's central position in the world order after the First World War and began thinking about new forms of cooperation across traditional frontiers (Parker 1988). When France organized the last world exhibition before the Second World War, in Paris in 1937, two of the most dominant and imposing pavilions of the show were the German and Soviet ones, facing each other and clearly demonstrating the totalitarian impulse that drove their respective regimes (Strohmayer 1996). It was a symbolic preview of the disaster that followed and a demonstration of the odds against a political order merely based on benign civilizational distinctions in the political climate of the times. A similar train of thought was developed in Russian geography in the years before the revolution and carried on in some emigrant milieus after 1917 (Hauner 1992). Russia's civilization was here perceived as a unique blend of European and Asian elements. It was deemed necessary for Russia to keep the resulting spirit alive, to be conscious of its unique identity and from that position to contribute to the common civilizational concert. The current debate on Russia's position in the post-communist world carries a number of arguments used in these earlier discussions.

In the interwar years, much of the groundwork was laid for a subject that now, once again, challenges political geographers considerably: the connection between a country's geographical features and the identity that its inhabitants derive from their shared territory. The interest itself goes back to the nineteenth century and is not related to state territories alone, but to all territories that have been the subject of efforts to ground a common identity for social groups. The builders of national myths were always keen to exploit the geographical and historical context in which they operated. In the interwar years professional geographers became active in this field when they mused on situational features like maritime or mountainous surroundings, position *vis-à-vis* large powers, defensible borders, landscape types and so on as conditions for the development of state, nation and regional populations. The foundation of a number of new states in Central and Eastern Europe, from Finland to Yugoslavia, invited indigenous geographers to concentrate their minds on this question (a well-known example is Jovan Cvijic in Serbia). A number of geopolitical points of view were thus developed. In hindsight these were very much part of the process of nation-building that was progressing in these countries. The current interest in the subject is on the whole much more critical, aiming at revealing the myths of nationalism and the ideological needs and biases in such constructions. A lot of this work also has to do with sub-state units or cross-state border units always aiming at the recognition of their separate identity and their unique qualities.

The series of peace settlements that followed the First World War (often slightly erroneously referred to as the Versailles Agreement) was negotiated by statesmen who had taken the advice of geographers. In the American delegation Bowman played a significant part, while de Martonne supported the French, and there were others elsewhere, such as Ogilvie on the British side, Cvijic supporting the Serbs and Marinelli for Italy. The experience of the war and the Paris conference gave rise to acrimonious debates later on in the International Geographical Union, where Germans and others were hardly on speaking terms for an extended period of time. This was the beginning of the end of German hegemony within the geographical discipline, which was completely reversed after Hitler came to power, and geography, like other academic disciplines, suffered the loss of many who fled and others who were deeply compromised. The Versailles Agreement brought to life a number of new states and rearranged many borders. In its aftermath, the first organized population exchanges between states, more recently called ethnic cleansing, occurred, sometimes under international supervision. The new borders were the result of negotiations that ended in referenda in quite a few cases, based on detailed maps concerning the distribution of ethnic groups, language groups and the like (Bowman 1922). Obviously such maps were contested pieces of information. Later on geographers were also active in the analysis of these referenda and their consequences. In 1938 the American geographer, Hartshorne, who at that moment resided in Europe, writing his famous *The Nature of Geography*, also published a paper on the fate of the referenda and the borders since Versailles (Hartshorne 1937).

In the interwar years there was very little interest in electoral geography. Siegfried, who was in fact an outsider in the world of French geographers and was only recognized as a kindred spirit much later, had published his analysis of voting patterns under the Third French Republic in 1913, largely anticipating a major outcome of work in political sociology concerning the stability of voting preferences, as reported by Lipset and Rokkan (1967). Taylor and Johnston (1979: 21) mention two more geographical papers, published in 1916 and 1918, as the precursors of the post-war interest in electoral geography. In the Netherlands there was one electoral geography paper in the interwar period, published by a German refugee in 1936. If there was any interest in these matters at all, it was with the referenda organized for the sake of state formation after the First World War.

Finally, state symbols and the state apparatus were points of interest for geographers. One question, which again had to do with the emergence of new states or their profound reorientation as a result of the First World War, was the choice and location of capital cities. The new Bolshevik and Kemalist regimes moved their capital cities to the inland positions of Moscow and Ankara. Helsinki and Prague found themselves far from the middle of their countries, while the position of Belgrade, Vienna, Budapest and others changed, *vis-à-vis* their national borders. There was a slight interest in such matters from political geographers (Cornish 1923; Whittlesey 1939; Spate 1942).

The administrative system slowly became a focus of interest during the interwar period. It had already been a research subject in the late nineteenth century, for example, in France, where arguments of historical continuity and state efficiency gave rise to a lively debate on the optimal administrative units (Claval 1998: 54–5). Gradually such considerations focused on the question of the ever growing cities and their functionally dependent surrounding regions. The debate about metropolitan government with respect to London had continued throughout the second half of the nineteenth century (Barlow 1991), but from the early twentieth century this became a much more general issue. As the new subject of physical planning and town planning became professionalized in its modernist guise during the 1920s, an international debate on the administrative institutions in ever enlarging urban areas took place. Geographers were certainly not the only participants, but they played a part (Hall 1988: 86–173). After the Second World War, when the large expansion of the welfare state necessitated a much more sophisticated localized bureaucracy in order to implement all the different sectoral policies, this constantly recurring problem became a major point of interest for political geographers. Political geography became the geography of public administration in this instance, where notions of state-bureaucratic efficiency, local identities and the advantages (political, fiscal and the like) of inclusion and exclusion determined the outcomes of ongoing disputes (for a long-term analysis of two contrasting cases, see Terhorst and van de Ven 1997).

MAJOR TRENDS IN THE SECOND HALF OF THE TWENTIETH CENTURY

As in human geography generally, the Anglo-Saxon world led developments of political geography after the Second World War. It is from within this linguistic and cultural context that the most influential ideas were launched and trends initiated, even if their origins can be traced elsewhere. A famous example is the use of von Thünen, Weber, Lösch and Christaller in economic geography since the late 1950s. A comparable example in political geography is the use of the French historian Braudel's work (dating from the 1940s onwards and being closely related to French regional geography) on the emerging map of the centre-formation and the expansion of capitalism (Braudel first set this out in 1949 and in its final version in 1979) by the US scholar, Wallerstein (1974, 1980, 1988), in his world-systems perspective since the 1970s. This in turn provided the basis for Taylor's reordering of the subject matter of political geography since the 1980s (Taylor 1985b, reprinted and extended in 1989, 1993, 2000). This growing importance of the USA, Britain and the rest of the English-speaking world is partly due to the terrible setbacks to German science during the Nazi years and the general hegemonic position of the USA after the Second World War (Taylor 1996).

Our reading of the development of political geography after the Second World War is primarily geared to the Anglo-Saxon world. In more recent years there has been a significant increase in the participation of political geographers from other parts of the world in these debates and this will be reflected in our overview. Towards the end of the section we will mention briefly some of the developments elsewhere, notably in France, Germany and Russia.

For the most part, the second half of the twentieth century has not been an easy time for political geography. Despite its strong historical credentials, the sub-discipline has struggled to prove its worth in terms of changing notions of contemporary relevance. In this struggle, political geographers have faced and overcome three specific challenges that fundamentally threatened the existence of the sub-discipline as a viable intellectual project. First, political geography emerged from the Second World War with its reputation tarnished by association with Nazi *Geopolitik*: the 1950s and early 1960s represent an apolitical rehabilitation. Second, the quantitative revolution in geography left political geography behind in the 'social-scientization' of human geography: the late 1960s and 1970s represent attempts to modernize political geography into scientific norms. Third, empiricism resulted in incoherence in content, a mish-mash of topics loosely connected as 'political': the 1980s and 1990s represent an opening up in political geography of a new pluralism in theory and practice. But in facing up to each challenge, political geographers created new critical problems for the viability of the sub-discipline. We will consider the new approaches emanating from the challenges in turn.

The functionalist solution to the *Geopolitik* débâcle

As we have seen, during the Second World War, political geographers locked horns with Anglo-American geographers condemning German *Geopolitik* as a 'pseudo-science', lacking the intellectual objectivity of political geography *per se*. This debate was settled by the outcome of the war, but it was by no means clear that the attempt to distance the sub-discipline from its Nazi progeny was wholly successful. Certainly political geography remained an unacceptable area of study in the Soviet bloc throughout the cold war. Even in the USA, Richard Hartshorne (1954) had to remind his readers, in his review of the sub-discipline for the fiftieth anniversary commemoration of the Association of American Geographers, that political geography was 'an essential part of geography', an assertion unnecessary for other sub-disciplines covered in other chapters. Although Hartshorne went on to concede that political geography was 'one of the less-developed parts' of geography, in fact, the early 1950s was a particularly creative period, when political geographers – including Hartshorne himself – made important attempts to relaunch their sub-discipline.

The embarrassment of *Geopolitik* was dealt with by the omission of geopolitics of whatever national provenance. By and large, the geographers of this period withdrew from concern for global and large-scale regional geostrategy and focused upon the scale of the state. Of course, eschewing geopolitics had to go beyond this scale selection: political geography had to be overtly free from political bias. The creation of an apolitical political geography was achieved by using a functional approach to the sub-discipline. Hartshorne (1950) laid out such a project by identifying 'the primary function of any state' to be its organization of the state-area. He proposed a politico-geographical analysis of states that involved identifying the centrifugal and centripetal forces to show how diverse areas are bound together as 'an effective whole'. At approximately the same time, Gottmann (1951, 1952a and b) was developing similar ideas on the interaction of 'circulation' (the 'movement factor') and 'iconography' to produce the spatial patterning of states. More dynamic than Hartshorne's model, this was developed by Jones (1954) into a 'unified field theory' as a chain of links: political idea–decision–movement–field–political area. These contributions of the early 1950s were to dominate political geography for over two decades and were reproduced in student readers in the 1960s (Jackson 1964; Kasperson and Minghi 1969) as well as being influential in textbooks into the 1970s (Bergman 1975; Muir 1975).

Although a relaunch, there is in fact much continuity with earlier political geography. In many ways the functionalism is a neutered version of the organic theory of the state, regionalism is overt in the emphasis on political area and environmentalism is represented in concern for physical features as political forces. These all come together, along with progress, in the form of 'the development of the European state system' in Pounds and Ball's (1964) model, in which environmentally favoured 'core areas' become modern states. Although this work is historically sensitive, subsequent propagation through Pounds' (1963) and de Blij's (1967) textbooks, where the model is extrapolated to the rest of the world, is very functionalist, with obvious teleological overtones.

Debates within this school of political geography have been rather predictable. The best critiques have been presented by Burghardt (1969, 1973), who argues that functionalism in both the Hartshorne and Gottmann varieties are premised on the pre-existence of sovereign territories without historicizing this outcome of European state-making. Where the latter is done by Pounds there is the problem of confusing specification of core area, notably mixing historical cores with contemporary economic cores in the same model. In the event, this functionalist approach was not undermined through internal sub-disciplinary debate, but it was found wanting as a response to wider disciplinary changes.

We will use Jackson's (1964) 'readings on the nature of political geography' as a transition publication, reflecting this school of work but looking to go beyond it. There are nine publications from the trio of relaunchers introduced above, but Jackson in no way follows their prescriptions closely. Geostrategic thinking makes a minor comeback but, most important of all, this is part of a reinsertion of politics and power into political geography. Jackson chooses to begin, not with the functionalist models, but rather with two papers on the nature of politics and the nature of political power respectively. This is a serious attempt to link political geography into contemporary political science: although the subject of the book is the nature of political geography, geographers contribute only 13 out of 34 chapters. This reflects both the paucity of substantive research stimulated by the functionalist models and the changes happening in geography in the 1960s, in short, opening up to wider disciplinary influences.

Systems with scales as a solution to 'moribund backwater'

In terms of the upheavals happening in geography in the 1960s, political geography was unlucky in its 'sister' social science discipline. Whereas both economics, with its location theories of primary, secondary and tertiary activities, and sociology, with its urban ecology models, could furnish theoretical frameworks for new spatial analyses, there were no equivalent location models to be borrowed from political science. Hence political geography is conspicuous by its absence in key texts of the 'new geography' which emerged in the 1960s: the sub-discipline does not warrant a chapter in the influential *Models in Geography* (Chorley and Haggett 1967) and is ignored in Haggett's (1965) *Locational Analysis in Human Geography*. Perhaps not surprisingly, Berry (1969) pronounced political geography to be 'a moribund backwater'.

Political geography was not entirely bypassed by the spatial school and its quantitative revolution, however. While state boundaries, capital cities and heartlands did not lend themselves readily to analyses using the latest methodologies, there were areas of the sub-discipline that could be so investigated. Pre-eminent among these was the geography of elections, with its data neatly recorded in electoral areas. Traditionally studied through map comparisons, it was but a short step to convert to statistical models, in particular, correlation and regression analyses (Roberts and Rumage 1965). Such empiricist studies at the national scale did not overcome the lack of spatial theory, but this was achieved at the local level. Building on political sociology studies of structural effects, especially the neighbourhood effect, Cox (1969) and Reynolds (1969) led the way to a new emphasis on the locational context of voting decisions, thus drawing this area of political geography into the emerging school of behavioural geography. However, unlike geography's other sub-disciplines, where location models revolutionized practice, in political geography these location models remained a minority preoccupation. Nevertheless they did have an important effect on the sub-discipline in terms of scale of analysis.

The local, and especially the urban, had been neglected severely in political geographies that were concerned with the state whether the focus was internal or external. Partly as a response to the politicization of human geography in general (Harvey 1973), the early 1970s saw the beginnings of an urban political geography (Cox 1973) emphasizing community conflicts (Cox, Reynolds and Rokkan 1974). Cox, in particular, developed this approach into a general political geography. Drawing on location theory's assumption that location choices are market choices (Cox 1978), Cox (1979) considered how resulting advantages and disadvantages were affected by public policy, by governments intervening under pressure from public conflict to do something about a 'location problem'. This was the most ambitious attempt to restructure political geography since Hartshorne (1950) and, unlike the latter, there was a total discontinuity with the sub-discipline's heritage. This is where the conceptual revolution of the 1960s finally caught up with the sub-discipline to create a completely 'new political geography'.

Not all reactions to the more rigorous approaches stemming from the 1960s were so disruptive. In particular, the functionalism of the 1950s could be translated into the new concerns for systems in geographical analysis. These resulted in yet another update of organic theory, but with a less teleological twist from the recently expanding field of electrical engineering that was basic to computer science. This new discourse is explicitly illustrated by Cohen and Rosenthal (1971) – in their development of Whittlesey's (1939) law-landscape ideas – who provide a systematic framework for studying traditional political geography problems. Other uses of systems thinking were quite disappointing, using Easton's (1963) concept of political system (input-output structures) to little effect (Bergman 1975; Muir 1975). The exception was Johnston's (1979) attempt to integrate electoral geography into a broader political geography via the use of 'spatial systems'. Although a contribution in the spirit of the 'new political geography', it is intriguing that this study's ahistoricism harks back strongly to Hartshorne's (1950) functionalism.

One dominant feature to come out of these 1970s political geographies has been the use of political scale to organize subject matter. With the introduction of the local/urban and the rehabilitation of the international/global operating alongside the traditional concern for the state-scale, there emerged a ubiquitous three-scale organization, beginning with the traditional texts of Bergman (1975) and Muir (1975), continuing with the new texts of Cox (1979) and Johnston (1979), and including also a new text informed by the current neo-Marxist geography by Short (1982). Although clearly a very neat division of subject matter – no doubt the basis of its popularity – separation of political processes by geographical scale was always very problematic, to say the least (Taylor 1982). In many cases it masked relatively shallow thinking about the nature of political geography. In reality political geography had emerged as a wide range of topics in search of a framework – presaged in Jackson (1964), with its 34 chapters divided into 14 different sections – and 'systems with scales' did not provide an answer.

In the debates on these responses to the quantitative revolution, there was some recognition of better individual pieces of research and some interesting fragments of theory, but an overall lack of coherence was identified as a serious malaise by both Cox (1979) and Claval (1984). This is hardly surprising given that the sub-discipline has been largely reactive rather than proactive in this period of intellectual change – in Claval's words, 'the field has developed in a rather chaotic manner' (Claval 1984: 8). The result was an uncoordinated political geography. Cox (1979: vii) refers to 'an assortment of ill-related topics' and not the 'tightly organized body of knowledge' to be expected of a sub-discipline. However, the time for the latter was passing. Just as calls for coherence appeared, the intellectual tenor was moving beyond such standardized authoritarianism.

We will use Burnett and Taylor's edited volume as the transitional publication between reactions to quantitative spatial analysis and the later pluralism. Here the chapters (22 of them) are all by geographers, so there is no resort to non-geographers to fill in the gaps. The content is variable, ranging from traditional topics like frontiers and geopolitics to elections and ethnic separatism, but the key point is the presentation of alternative approaches within the same text. Public choice models occur alongside neo-Marxist approaches to the state and standard social science modelling. This eclectic mix can be seen negatively as incoherence or positively as a vibrant pluralism. As we look at the 1980s we see that it is the latter interpretation that begins to predominate.

The pluralist solution to the coherence critique

The 1980s are important in the history of political geography because, for the first time, an international institutionalization emerged. This took two forms. First, an international journal dedicated to the sub-discipline, *Political Geography Quarterly*, was launched in 1982 and prospered to the degree that it soon outgrew its original title to become just *Political Geography*. Second, a series of international conferences were held under the auspices of the International Geographical Union (IGU) through the creation of the World Political Map Commission, which first took shape as a study group. (The study group and the commission itself were entitled 'world political map' rather than 'political geography' to get round the Soviet bloc's aversion to the latter term.) The first conference was in 1982, in Haifa, and the second, a year later, in Oxford, produced the necessary application to the IGU for recognition and support. These two institutional innovations, both as outlets for the latest research and as settings for research network formation, are generally recognized as key influences in the late twentieth-century resurgence in political geography.

The new journal opened with an editorial essay which reflected the variety of contemporary political geography – 21 themes were initially identified in its proposed research agenda for the 1980s (Editorial Board 1982a), to which others were soon added (Editorial Board 1982b). Eschewing the idea of promulgating a 'new orthodoxy', the essay identified pluralism as the 'most healthy aspect of the recent growth in political geography' (Editorial Board 1982a: 2). This stance has been reflected in the contents of the journal over nearly two decades (Waterman 1998) and has been affirmed in a recent editorial (Slater 2000). Waterman's survey points to the wide variety of interests reflected in the pages of the journal. He suggests that there is conceivably 'still a lack of focus in the new political geography', but he does not see much harm in this: 'Though this may arguably frustrate some of the more doctrinaire members of the discipline concerned with dogma, it is still, in general, to be welcomed' (Waterman 1998: 387). This is also illustrated by the range of topics for special issues of the journal (table 1). The series started with the classical issue of redistricting and ends with the same topic, with GIS added. In between there is just about every kind of topic that has been of concern to political geographers over the years.

Since the early 1980s, the IGU World Political Map Commission has organized one or two international conferences every year. Special sessions and extra meetings took place in connection with the IGU congresses in Paris (1984), Sydney (1988), Washington (1992), The Hague (1996) and Seoul (2000). Two more conferences have been held in Israel and there have been various meetings in Central Europe (Prague, the Slovenian-Italian border), Eastern Europe (Moscow), India (twice in New Delhi, once in Punjab), Asia-Pacific (Tokyo) and Latin America (Rio de Janeiro). Various gatherings have been organized jointly with national groups of political geographers in France and the USA and with individuals in Canada and Switzerland. Many conferences have resulted in specially edited collections. A few examples are Rumley and Minghi 1991; O'Loughlin and van der Wusten 1993; Claval and Sanguin 1997; Becker and Miranda 1997.

Pluralism does not mean all approaches are equally important in the development of the sub-discipline. In this field Wallerstein's (1979) world-systems analysis as adapted by Taylor (1982) has been particularly influential, specifically through a world-systems political geography textbook (Taylor 1985b), which is now in its fourth edition (Taylor and Flint 2000). For pluralism not to be incoherent there is a need for examples of strong theory to anchor the variety. World-systems analysis played this role in political geography, which had been castigated as 'theory deficient' (Reynolds 1981). The only other text to ground the sub-discipline in a clearly articulated theory was by Cox (1979), but this suffered through its disengagement from political geography's heritage. In contrast, world-systems political geography incorporated both traditional – capital cities, boundaries, geopolitics – and recent themes – neo-Marxist state theory, elections, urban conflicts – by reinterpreting them in world-systems terms. The result was a political geography that was systematic while also being historical and global as well as local, the latter through treating geographical scales as integral to political processes and not as separate arenas. This way of rearranging political geography was not without opposition. At the outset Dear (1986: 295–97) made a strong effort to counter this trend and steer political geography back to its traditional concerns with the state. Still other texts have attempted to ground political geography in other areas, notably political economy (Short 1982) and socio-cultural theories (Painter 1995).

A journal, conferences and general texts only tell part of the story, of course. Political geography now has a very large literature on specific themes and topics. Reynolds and Knight (1989) provide the latest comprehensive review of substantive studies in political geography, but this is now becoming dated. Today we can identify four areas that stand out in political geographical contributions to contemporary geography: contemporary state studies, research on nationalism, continuation of electoral analyses and full rehabilitation of geopolitics.

Reviving the traditional concern to understand the state has involved much pouring of new wine into old bottles. For instance, combining national and local levels, Paasi (1996) has applied recent socio-cultural approaches to territory and boundary in a study of Finnish engagement with its political border with Russia. Another traditional political geography theme, federalism, in relation to contemporary political upheavals is represented in a collection of essays edited by Smith (1995). This volume looks at recent ethnic challenges to states, notably in the former communist states, and considers the relevance of federal theory as an ideology and practice to manage political change. In contrast, Staeheli, Kodras and Flint (1997) bring together essays that focus on one country, the USA, and its move towards a neo-liberal devolution. In all three studies, local communities and groups are viewed as interacting with state-level processes to create new geographical outcomes.

Although a central topic of the sub-discipline, research on nation and nationalism has not been a major substantive contribution by political geographers. This is beginning to change. A collection of essays, *Geography and National Identity* (Hooson 1994), and the publication of Colin Williams' (1994) essays in one volume has heralded a new beginning for geographical research in this area. This in turn has very broad ramifications, as recent work links up with both the cultural (e.g. Johnson 1992) and the geopolitical (e.g. Dijkink 1997) dimensions of geographic inquiry. It is in this area that political geography has spawned one of geography's most interesting exercises in intellectual self-reflexivity. Falah and Newman (1995) take their opposing national positions into a collaborative venture that explores the limits of research for understanding in a powerful nationalist context (Israel/Palestine).

Quantitative electoral geography has survived the many methodological upheavals of the last two decades. Well represented in the basic text on US political geography (Shelley *et al.* 1996), the main centre for this research has been in the UK, under the leadership of Ron Johnston. His work and that of his colleagues has focused on two areas. First, the changing geography of British general elections has been traced (Johnston *et al.* 1988), showing the continuing importance of place and region despite party de-alignment among the electorate. Second, the spatial organization of elections has been explored further through combinatorial analyses (Rossiter *et al.* 1999). More generally, the great global wave of democratization has not escaped the scrutiny of political geographers (O'Loughlin *et al.* 1998).

The post-cold war context, however, has had most impact on research in geopolitics: there has been a final rehabilitation of geopolitics back into mainstream political geography. This has been represented by three groups of researchers. First, following on from debates surrounding world-systems political geography, a broad political economy approach has been developed, centred on the concept of world hegemony (Agnew and Corbridge 1995; Taylor 1996; Agnew 1998). Second, a quantitative social science school has searched for international patterns of political behaviour, such as diplomatic organization (Nijman 1993; Nierop 1994). Third, a critical geopolitics has been created which uses post-structural approaches to power and space to create a genuinely new and radical school of thought (Dalby 1990; O'Tuathail 1996; Dalby, Routledge and O'Tuathail 1998). The latter is fulfilling political geography's largely latent potential for interdisciplinarity through strong links with dissident international relations scholars.

This variety in both topic and methodology is not to everybody's liking, of course. Dear (1986) set the tone early on: 'My core contention is that the central object of analysis in political geography is the state'. But he also stated: 'I am not prepared to privilege any particular theory or method in discourse'. As Waterman (1998) sees it reflected in the pages of *Political Geography Quarterly* over the years, political geographers are still concerned with matters of state, to a considerable extent, but it is certainly not the exclusively privileged topic of interest, and they use a wide array of methodologies. At the same time, the architects of the sub-discipline, for example, those looking for a grand design in their regular general reviews for *Progress in Human Geography*, generally prefer a wider set of themes within the constraints of a privileged methodology.

Unlike the other two sections, it is not appropriate to conclude with a 'transition publication' because we cannot know at this time where pluralistic political geography is leading. Nevertheless one recent student text (Agnew 1997) represents an ideal publication for taking stock of where we are after a century of endeavour in the field of political geography. This volume is avowedly pluralistic in approach. Agnew identifies three 'theoretical viewpoints' (the spatial-analytic, the political-economic and the postmodern) and five 'main areas' (approaches, states, geopolitics, movements and identities and nationalism) to effectively create a 3 × 5 political geography grid within which he locates his 15 readings. This is pluralism triumphant in contemporary Anglo-

Saxon-led political geography, a far cry from the biology-embedded, state-centred view that loomed large during a major part of the sub-discipline's history.

Political geography's development in France partly recaptures the history of the subject as it unfolded in the Anglo-Saxon world, but it was also firmly embedded in the French geographical tradition. In the early post-war period Gottmann (1952) wrote his state-centred overview of political geography in a functionalist vein. His perspective is in many respects similar to Hartshorne's programme and Jones' additions at the time. But Gottmann soon moved to the USA and then to Oxford and it was only much later that his voice was again heard in French geography (particularly through the efforts of Prevelakis 1996).

Since the 1970s there has been a sustained interest in political geography from different corners. Lacoste has always had a strong concern with the possible use of geographical notions, and particularly cartographic material, in setting the terms for foreign and military policy and in affecting the public discourse on major political events. In his journal *Hérodote* he has tried to educate the public by geographical analyses of current affairs since 1976. In his view, geopolitics is this public geographical debate on the nature of the state, foreign affairs and international conflict and the public perceptions that it seeks to influence. This has a lot in common with the critical geopolitics that we encountered earlier. It should be added that geopolitical debate in France has recently become particularly lively. Whereas French geography in the inter-war years often strongly opposed Haushofer's views in these matters, academic debate framed around the classic geopolitical questions (certainly not stemming solely from within geography, but also from international relations) is now widespread in France.

Claval has combined his interests in urban, regional and cultural geography with his study of political geography and has produced a series of books, papers and book chapters on various parts of the subject over the years. He has been invaluable as a bridge between the non-French speaking world and French geography, open to both sides. He has written on military strategy (Claval 1994), but also on the significance of large urban centres and the global urban network in setting the terms for political units (Claval and Sanguin 1997). In this way he continues the traditional French opposition to a political geography too exclusively concerned with the state and its power politics. Claval is still an active writer, but his organizational efforts that brought French and other political geographers together in a series of conferences are now continued by Sanguin.

Currently, French geography is slowly opening up to the Anglo-Saxon world. A good example is the work of Lévy, who writes from a perspective somewhat similar to that of Lacoste, but is much more at ease with the post-modern literature now coming out of Anglo-Saxon geography (itself influenced by French linguists and philosophers). French political geography has remained French: it is steeped in the regionalist tradition (not merely at the sub-state level but at all geographical scales). Lévy's last book is another effort to come to terms with the notion of Europe from a distinctive regionalist perspective (Lévy 1997).

German political geography has long remained in the shadows, for obvious reasons. The history of the connections between the Nazis and geopolitics did not invite a return to this subject matter. To the extent that there was an interest, it was long channelled into problems of administrative geography (the struggles about competences between administrative tiers and the like (see Boesler's work, for example). Only in the last ten years has there been a sustained interest to re-enter the debate about political geography. More than in other countries, the historiography of geopolitics has been a research topic for political geographers. In particular, Sandner and a number of his co-workers have been active in this field, and valuable overviews have appeared in *Political Geography* (vol. 6, 107 ff.; vol. 8, 311 ff.). In the 1990s there was also a renewed effort to resuscitate classic geopolitical concerns by experts connected with defence policy and the military academies, as well as in the press. As in France, the debate has been lively, but there appears to be less academic interest. In recent years German political geographers have become more intimately enmeshed in the networks of the Anglo-Saxon world, and interests have developed in line with such relationships. A recent indication is Reuber's (2000) programmatic statement that is clearly geared to current concerns in the English-speaking world, as can be seen from the references.

In Russia political geography was a forbidden fruit until the mid-1980s. The geographical establishment in the USSR was adamant in its disapproval of any activity in its realm that might connect geography with politics. As the tide turned, political geography became extremely useful and also a pressing concern. It became helpful as politicians in a newly established system of mass democracy looked for a captive audience. Electoral analyses soon provided clues as to the map of stable preferences. A whole series of such analyses has been published in Russian, but also in English and French, particularly by Kolossov (O'Loughlin, Kolossov and Vendina). In addition, political geography became a pressing concern as the geopolitical map changed and new interpretations of re-establishing Russia's place in the world were needed. Among politicians and the informed public a continuing debate ensued in which geographers could play a role. As was mentioned earlier, there has been a debate in Russia concerning the country's position and mission, connected to its geographical position, from around the beginning of the twentieth century. Although it was not called geopolitical, it was clear that after the revolution the USSR's international position was constantly discussed with an eye to its geographical features. As the USSR disintegrated, notions from the first debate (Russia as bridgehead between Europe and Asia – its European vocation, its Asian heritage) again came to the fore. The geopolitical interpretation of Russia's safety and the correctness of its boundaries in all directions gave rise to vehement political debate. A much discussed programmatic statement on a nationalist basis is by Dugin (1999), and a recent reinterpretation of the whole debate is in a work edited by Kolossov (2000).

In general, one may conclude that in the second half of the twentieth century political geography outside the Anglo-Saxon world developed in relation to the concerns of its own environment. This is most obvious for the various perspectives on geopolitics, but it is also relevant with respect to other items on the research agenda of political geography. At the same time, these different political geographies are opening up and are linked to the English-speaking world. This mixing of experiences and perspectives adds to the pluralism that we have already encountered.

6 Social geography: looking for society in its spaces

Chris Philo and Ola Söderström

INTRODUCTION: CAPTURING 'THE SOCIAL' IN GEOGRAPHICAL INQUIRY

We geographers are [people] of many creeds and tongues. We have plenty to say, but we seldom say it in unison or in harmony.

—G. H. T. Kimble

G. H. T. Kimble was referring here to what geographers say about 'the regional concept', but his observation also applies with particular force to the cacophony of claims that geographers have made over the twentieth century on the subject of social geography. Indeed, all manner of things have been said about social geography (*géographie sociale*; *Sozialgeographie*), not just in different languages, but from a great variety of positions, regarding both the nature of geography and (though rarely stated explicitly) the character of society. It is impossible to provide an account that does justice to this diversity, and any such account, including our own below, inevitably will imply too much coherence and 'harmony' in how social geography has been practised in given periods and between different places. Given our own linguistic abilities, we focus principally on social geography as written in English and French, and, in striving to combine our reflections on work in these two languages, we probably end up suggesting more symmetry between elements and trajectories within the two than is warranted. At the same time, we risk neglecting 'alternative histories' associated with social geography, as developed in parts of the world that do not speak English or French, and we are acutely aware of the rather different accounts that might emanate from other regions of Europe or from regions outside the West. Moreover, we offer very much an interpretative narrative, conveying an argument about changes, gains and losses in social geography across the century, preferring to debate the contributions of particular individuals, papers, books and projects than to produce lengthy lists of citations.

One way in which to describe the task of this chapter would be as 'mapping' onto geography concepts from social theory, sociology and other disciplines (social history, social anthropology and political science), showing how they have impacted upon the conduct of human geography. To some extent, and certainly with reference to social theory, such mapping has already been undertaken by the likes of Derek Gregory (1978, 1994), while Peter Jackson and Susan Smith (1984) have charted the borrowings from social theory and elsewhere which have arrived in social geography. Valuable as such exercises are, they risk portraying geography as dominated by social theory and other disciplines, and being a net importer of conceptual goods. The result somewhat obscures the work of geographers trying to make sense of 'the social' by their own means, including their own *bricolage* of elements culled, admittedly not always that self-consciously, from a diversity of sources in social theory, other disciplines and popular discourses. Our account seeks to keep the lens focused on the geographers themselves, endeavouring to show how they have tried to capture the social in their own scholarship, first by defining ('constructing') it in different ways and, second, by inventing or using different concepts, in the course of which they have more or less deliberately created different geographies of the social (or different social geographies). Instead of taking something called the social for granted, we chart metamorphoses in the *idea* of the social within geography, and more especially within the sub-discipline named 'social geography', and our aim is to clarify what the social in geography has been, what it has not been and what in the future it could become.

We suggest that geographers prior to the 1970s tended to have a 'black box' sense of the social, in that it was only invoked in the guise of material social facts perceived to be outward expressions of society's inner workings, and in so far as such material social phenomena were believed to exhibit definite environmental bases, regional characters or spatial distributions. We identify different ways in which these material social geographies have been conceived, particularly around notions such as landscape, organization and structure. We also note some exceptions to these trends, particularly stemming from the Vidalian tradition and in one Anglo-American version of regional social geography. We then suggest that geographers from the late 1960s through to the 1980s began to enlarge greatly their substantive and conceptual senses of what the social entails, and in so doing started to problematize the whole terrain of groups, classes, relations, systems, structures, experiences, struggles and the like which *is* the social and which connects to countless worldly spaces in such a complex fashion. The focus then shifted to taking seriously the immaterial social dynamics of society's internal workings, in that many geographers increasingly realized that they needed to look inside the black box of the social if they were to understand properly its geographical associations. In so doing, we hint at the emergence in the 1980s of a more sophisticated approach to understanding the mutual articulations of the social and the spatial (see also chapter 1), one which rebounded all over human geography but still held particular implications for social geography. Finally, we comment briefly on the excitements of the 1990s, a period during which human geography's intellectual landscape became so twisted and torn that it is hard to comment on its new shape with any confidence, but we still speculate about certain dangers attaching to a 'culturally turned' social geography wherein the social itself risks complete dissolution.

Our impression is that different traditions of social geography research and attendant shifts in geographers' understandings of the social, have surfaced at different times in different places across the globe. While the main text concentrates on work in English and French hailing from Europe and North America, there are arguably 'alternative' social-geographical traditions to be traced in other languages in other parts of the world. Were we to concentrate more on these alternative social geographies, it is likely that our simple interpretative narrative in the main text would need to be qualified, contradicted and reframed in various ways. The history of social geography in German-speaking academia, for instance, certainly shows deviations from particular phases in the narrative pursued below (Bobek 1948; Hartke 1956; Werlen 1995). The history of social geography in regions outside the West is probably less well documented, and there is arguably a rich historiographic field for historians of the discipline to consult, but the suspicion must be that – given the European origins of academic geography (Livingstone 1992; Stoddart 1986) and the hegemony, however regrettable, of western intellectual constructions within academia the world over – the cast of social geography as it has developed outside the West has been in some measure an imitation of major trends, ideas and practices within English-, French- and German-speaking social geography. Some scholars have now began to explore what they term the 'colonization' of geographical inquiry, in places such as India and South Africa, by the prevailing orthodoxies of European and North American geography (Crush 1994; Raza 1972; Wesso 1994), while wondering about indigenous geographical orientations which, on occasion, have offered an alternative to these alien impositions. In South Africa, from around 1980, the call in some circles was for a 'dewhitened, de-colonised and critical human geography', positioned as a 'geography of the common people' or a 'people's historical geography', and research in this vein became strongly attuned to the grounded experiences of struggle and basic survival endured by those marginalized under apartheid (Crush 1994: 339–46). This approach, resting 'on a textual relationship with a particular social group (the "common people")' (Crush 1994: 344) and talking about many different fragments of this group, such as the street hawkers of the apartheid city, clearly comprised a version of social geography differing in many (if not all) respects from that pursued contemporaneously in Europe and North America.

A few 'Third World' geographers, who have become well known in the West, have long debated the goal of freeing geographical scholarship in their own regions from western discourses, and in so doing have opened a window to alternative visions of social geography. Milton Santos, the Brazilian geographer, seeking to establish a viable social-spatial theory of underdevelopment, once wrote as follows:

> 'Underdeveloped space' has a specific character; the priority of importance varies, even if the same forces are involved; because their combinations and results are different. This is something which Western geographers have great difficulty in understanding. Why should we not then rally expertise from the underdeveloped countries themselves: to develop theories which would make sense to them both as geographers and as citizens? At the moment, 'official' geography operates as though the West had a monopoly of ideas.
>
> (Santos 1974: 4)

Santos' own conceptualizations, endeavouring to track the links between modes of production, social formations and space, duly signalled exciting new possibilities for human geography in general and social geography in particular, as did his more grounded thinking (Santos 1979) about the 'dual economy' comprised of two different circuits (an 'upper', formal one and a 'lower', informal one) of production, exchange and associated social life. Yet in fostering what Richard Peet (1998: 127) terms 'a kind of dialectical-existential structuralism' borrowing from both Karl Marx and J. P. Sartre, Santos arguably repeated a reliance on western ideas rather than forging a genuinely South American or Brazilian take on human or social geography. The thorny deeper issues here, of course, are those integral to debates within postcolonial theory about the extent to which it is ever possible for people of colour beyond (and also in) the West to escape completely from white western intellectual constructions (whether academic, popular, literary or poetic), to find their own distinctive and somehow untainted 'voices'. To extend Gayatri Chakravorty Spivak's (1988) famous question, we must ask, 'Can the subaltern geographer speak?' Are there, and can there be, genuinely other social geographies 'out there' to be written down, to challenge the various mainstream social geographies and trajectories within these, as discussed in this chapter?

MATERIAL SOCIAL GEOGRAPHIES: FROM THE 1800S TO THE 1970S AND BEYOND

Much passing for social geography from the late 1800s through to the 1970s and beyond can be cast as 'material social geographies', preoccupied with the environmental determinants, regional differentiations and spatial distributions of a narrow range of material phenomena perceived as social: tangible, immediately observable, countable, measurable, mappable phenomena, which are outward expressions of human society. We should signal immediately that, notwithstanding complicated connections between environmental determinism and the historical materialism of Marx (Bassin 1996), our critical stance on the material focus of social geographies up to the 1960s is not meant to apply to a Marxian social geography with a materialist basis (see below), except perhaps when considering certain aspects of work by one French Marxian geographer. Explicit early references to 'social geography' can be found dating back to the late 1800s, notably in continental Europe and in the projects of the Le Play school, and considering these references means giving some thought to the 'invention of the social'.

Inventing the social

A deceptively obvious first remark is that the constitution of social geography as a sub-discipline required the prior fabrication of its two ingredients: geography as a human science and the social as a category of thought and action. Only the second point needs to be tackled here. The term 'society' took on its present generic sense during the nineteenth century, prior to which it had referred, for those frequenting royal courts, to notions of high society or, for the economists at the beginning of the nineteenth century, to a freely and contractually created association (Rabinow 1989: 19). This latter meaning seemingly emerged through the scientific study of a new world, a *terra incognita* (Topalov 1991). Using direct field observation, for example, Louis-René Villermé's famous 1840 study of workers' conditions in the textile industry sought to import the methods of natural science into the analysis of society (Perrot 1972: 31). The social thus began to be constituted through a series of knowledge strategies: medical surveys, studies of workers' economy and housing, social taxonomies and statistical analyses (Sion 1908). This movement entailed the discursive construction of 'macrosocial totalities' (Desrosières 1993: 90), allowing for new thinking about specific social groups and their conditions, looking beyond the realm of the individual and personal morality. 'Moral statistics', the measure of the norms, habits and behaviours of particular sectors of the population, helped to produce a disengaged perception of social problems and a language for their rational management.

In France, the school of the French engineer and sociologist Frédéric Le Play was among the most important of the actors in this process. Closely linked to the movement of social Catholicism, Le Play and his followers developed a systematic programme of studies examining the housing and economy of working-class families (Ewald 1986); the core of the social reform project favoured by Le Play and his followers was the 'patronage' system. Hinging on the social responsibility of the 'patron', stressing workers' private property and the recomposition of the family cell, this paternalist system was supposed to ensure the well-being of the workers and, eventually, harmonious relations between social classes (Kalaora and Savoye 1989). Le Play also held high political positions in the Second Empire and, as founder of the Société d'économie sociale in 1856, he started the journal *La Réforme sociale* in 1881, one year before his death. According to Gary Dunbar (1977), it was in this journal that the term 'social geography' occurred for the first time, being used in 1884 by Paul de Rousiers when reviewing Elisée Reclus' *Nouvelle Géographie universelle*, published between 1875 and 1894. Social geography as a term, therefore, was not invented by geographers themselves, but by a school of empirical sociology in the context of a project of social reform, although it did appear in response to the scholarship undertaken by a geographer, Reclus, whose place in the history of social geography is itself worthy of brief comment. Although certainly not a revolutionary in terms of methodology, Reclus paid considerable attention to urban phenomenon and the role of social organization in the use of natural resources, thus anticipating studies in social geography which were to emerge several decades later (Errani 1984: 34). Yet for various reasons, notably to do with his nomadic life (Chardak 1997), the intellectual paths opened by Reclus were not really pursued. As such, Reclus' embryonic social geography was, as we will see, one of the many false starts suffered by the sub-discipline in France (Lévy 1996; Raffestin 1983).

Negating the social: environmental social geographies

It was in a paper read to the York meeting of the British Association in 1906, subsequently published in 1907, that something approaching a clear statement about 'social geography' first appeared in the Anglo-American literature. The author of this paper, G. W. Hoke from Ohio, self-consciously pivoted between the achievements of nineteenth-century explorer-geographers and theories of environmental determinism, but he still provided this modern-sounding account of the field under review:

> The following discussion will be based upon the proposition that social geography deals with the distribution in space of social phenomena, and that its working programme may be stated as the description of the sequence and relative significance of those factors, the resultant of whose influences is the localization in space of the series of social phenomena chosen for investigation.
>
> (Hoke 1907: 64)

The starting-point here was 'the localization in space' of the variety of social phenomena under study and their clustering in specific worldly locations; the next step was to establish the factors which combine to influence and control the clustering of said phenomena. The relative strengths of influence exerted by different factors were to be ascertained in the process, along with the temporal ordering of which factors come into play at what stage in exerting their own locational influence. It would not be too difficult, then, to regard these suggestions as a blueprint for the practice of the spatial social geographies to be considered below.

Yet in other respects, Hoke's paper was a 'hoax' (Philo 1991b) when it came to specifying a distinctive social geography, given that he advanced no clear view about what was to be taken as comprising the social phenomena to be studied by such a (sub-)discipline. Consider this observation:

> When an individual buys a farm or locates a factory, their chief problems are those of distribution, and are, to that extent, geographical ones. Locating the site of a city, laying out the course of a railroad, the settling of territorial disputes and a host of other important human activities make large demands upon the subject of social geography in its various aspects.
>
> (Hoke 1907: 65)

As well as intimating that he anticipated Fitzgerald *et al.* in using social geography as an omnibus term akin to human geography, Hoke's attention was drawn to phenomena such as farms, factories and railroads, which are taken more commonly as the province of economic geography, or to phenomena such as territorial disputes, which tend to fall into the bounds of political geography. Moreover his focus was very much on material things – buildings, boundaries, cities and other material 'marks' on the landscape – and the impression is that he took such things to be social merely by virtue of being human creations. In consequence, his conception of the social was underdeveloped, and we have to assume that Hoke simply took it for granted and supposed that nothing needed to be said about its interior constitution prior to mapping its exterior manifestations.

The scale at which Hoke operated was the regional, as was evident from his references to the worlds of 'Appalachian Highlanders' and Balkan 'steppe riders', and the environmentalist cast of his social geography was evident in the factors which he claimed influenced such regions. Hence he talked about 'the physical circumstances of the land' within given regions (the mountains, the forests, the plains), and spoke of land as 'the active and dominant constraining element' in the lives of groups such as American 'Indians' (Hoke 1907: 65). Yet he was no simplistic environmental determinist, for he acknowledged that 'the influence of the environment is profoundly modified by the social status of the population', while also referencing the role played by such elements as a given population's (culture-)history, (folk-)psychology and technological capabilities (Hoke 1907: 66–7). As such he remained close to the orthodoxy associated with that pioneer of French geography, Vidal de la Blache, who had acknowledged five years earlier that 'there are cases in which the repercussion of social causes command over geography' (Vidal de la Blache 1902: 21). Even so, Hoke still unveiled the contours of an environmental social geography, echoes of which sounded in numerous other contributions to the earliest stirrings of this sub-discipline prior to the 1930s.

Within Anglo-American literature, Percy Maud Roxby sketched out a loosely environmentalist agenda for human geography as a whole, in the course of which he identified four principal ways in which human beings adjust to the physical or natural properties of given regions: the racial, the economic, the political and the social. Intriguingly, he commented:

> Economic geography serves one of its highest functions if it is closely linked with other aspects of human adjustment to physical environment which have so far received less attention. Of these one of the most interesting and profoundly important is that which for want of a better term we usually call social geography.
>
> (Roxby 1930: 285)

The potential for an environmental social geography was duly signposted, subsequently to be picked up in Britain by Gilbert and Steel (1945). A few years earlier, a not dissimilar statement had appeared in a presidential address to the Association of American Geographers, delivered in 1922 and published in 1923. This was Harlan H. Barrows' call for geography to be reframed as 'human ecology', which, despite the use of the term 'human ecology', so closely associated with the Chicago school sociologists, virtually ignored their work in laying down a starkly environmentalist manifesto for the discipline. Indeed Barrows (1923: 3–4) declared that geography should 'make clear the relationships existing between natural environments and the distribution and activities of man [*sic*]', and should seek 'to show the interactions between man and a particular environmental complex' (meaning landforms, climate, vegetation and so on). Barrows listed three lines of human-environmental interaction – the economic, the political and the social – but he ascribed most importance to the first and least importance to the last. When reviewing 'the divisions of systematic geography', he commented:

> Theoretically at least there is a definite field for social geography, which would study the connections that may exist between the social life of peoples and their natural environments. *But the facts of 'living' are intangible* and for the most part find any connections which they may have with the natural environment through the facts involved in 'getting a living'. . . . [T]his body of relationships appears to form a potential field for geography rather than an assured field.
>
> (Barrows 1923: 7–8, emphasis added)

Within Barrows' environmentalist frame, social geography was transparently a second-class sub-discipline, given that the social was taken to entail 'facts of living', which leave few imprints on the tangible landscape, and only meaningfully linked with natural-environmental conditions through the economic activities of production, commerce and transport. It was precisely such a negation of the social that Roxby questioned, of course, but there is the intimation in Barrows' position that an environmentalist take on the discipline as a whole, certainly at this time (Matless and Philo 1991), was in itself an obstacle to any vision of the social that could form the basis for a social geography worthy of note.

It is often supposed that the social was also neglected by the Vidalian school in France, which can be explained by its specific conception of the relation between individuals and their environment. More recently it has been argued that what has been called 'classical' French geography adheres, at its root, to a Lamarckian environmentalism (Lévy 1999b). In the environmentalism of Jean-Baptiste de Lamarck, adaptation to the environment was taken as the mechanism of history rather than (Darwinian) selection, and the use within the Vidalian tradition of the term 'milieu' as an alternative to 'society' was entirely consistent with this view. The Vidalian school, dominant for so long in French-speaking areas, can thus be qualified as a kind of 'natural science of ways of living', a science in which attention to social matters was inevitably somewhat secondary. At the turn of the century, French human geography was only a recently formed discipline, and considering something specifically delimited as social geography would have appeared then a somewhat exotic exercise. Even when the term was used by authors such as Emile Levasseur or Camille Vallaux there was, as in the small British debate mentioned earlier, a tendency to assume a quasi-equivalence between social and human geography (Racine and Raffestin 1983: 305). So where and what was the social in this classical French geography? The answer, it might be argued, lay at the centre of the disputes over academic territory between Emile Durkheim and Paul Vidal de la Blache. The end of the dispute – or so the story goes – produced a compromise division of labour between geography (dealing with the earth and places) and sociology (dealing with people and society). In Vidal's words, 'la géographie est la science des lieux et non des hommes' (Vidal de la Blache 1913: 297), and in those of the historian Lucien Febvre (1922), 'la géographie a pour objet la Terre et non la Société'. Often parochially described by geographers as an instance of the imperialism of sociology, this *affaire célèbre* is perhaps somewhat more complicated.

Vidal became a lecturer at the École Normale Supérieure in 1877, then professor at the Sorbonne in 1889. In 1891 he created the journal *Annales de géographie* and entered the Académie des Sciences Morales et Politiques in 1906. An indirect confrontation between him and Durkheim began with the latter's critiques of Friedrich Ratzel's *Anthropogeographie* in Germany and Vidal's above-mentioned statement concerning the relations between geography and society (Vidal de la Blache 1902). Yet the history of the relations between Durkheim, the founder of academic sociology, and the Vidalian school, is more than just the history of a confrontation. Various offers of collaboration were made by the Durkheimians, in line with their leader's conception of sociology as divided into two parts: social morphology (including disciplines such as demography and geography), on the one hand, and proper sociology (divided into different objects of study: religion, law, family), on the other (Durkheim 1909). These proposals for collaboration were rejected by Vidal on the grounds that a scientific division of labour, with the drawing of clear boundaries between sociology and geography, was necessary. A few years later, the confrontation between the two schools became more heated. In 1906, Marcel Mauss and Henri Beuchat published a paper in Durkheim's *Année sociologique*, which in substance elaborated on Durkheim's discussion of Ratzel, as well as criticizing geography for considering the relations between nature and humans as a direct one, thereby neglecting the mediating role of society. In a review of a group of regional monographs produced by the Vidalians, François Simiand (1910) went on to conclude that human geography lacked conceptual precision and epistemological foundations and would do better limiting itself to natural phenomena.

   Territorial claims and boundary policing in the academy were not the only things on the agendas of Vidalians and Durkheimians during the period, however, and Antoine Vacher and Albert Demangeon crossed the border from geography to sociology as collaborators, contributing from 1905 to the *Année sociologique* and to research on topics such as family budgets (Mucchielli 1998: 406–7). Several themes of interest to the geographers also moved closer to ones studied by the sociologists: artificial, urban environments became legitimate topics of interest; the idea of economic regions was added to that of the natural region or *pays*; and the everyday workings of the region were explored, not only its 'soul'. One of the heirs of Vidal's teaching, Jean Brunhes, a professor in Switzerland and France, was an important figure in this contrasting image of environmental social geography arising in French-speaking areas. Brunhes began his career in the city of Fribourg in Switzerland in 1896, where the University of Fribourg had been an important incubator of the principles of social Catholicism (Brunhes himself was a propagator of the Vatican's 1891 *Rerum Novarum*). This association with principles of social reform, along with the links between the Le Play school and Fribourg, certainly explain part of Brunhes' own inclination towards taking seriously the inner workings of social life rather than concentrating solely on naturalized *genres de vie*. For Brunhes, society was not a transparent entity sitting between person and milieu, as it was in other forms of classical French geography, but a constituent part of human geography: 'any geographic fact contains and implicates a social problem' (Brunhes 1913: 3). Social geography was thus addressed explicitly by Brunhes: it was one of the four components of human geography, and its main task was to trace the influence of social organization and customs on the adaptation of people to the environment. This was an influence seen in terms of connections, not causality:

> Between the facts of the physical order, there are sometimes relations of causality; between the facts of human geography, there are not more than relations of connection. Forcing, so to speak, the bond linking phenomena amounts to doing false science, and a critical mind will here be very useful in order to identify the many cases where connectedness is very different from causality.
>
> (Brunhes 1956: 296)

Such a statement distanced Brunhes from a naturalistic definition of geography, as too did his emphasis on the immaterial dimensions of the social, 'the psychological factor in the connections between natural phenomena and human activity' (Brunhes, 1956: 298), which he considered to be at the origin of geographical facts. For all this, as Annette Buttimer (1971) observed, there was still a clear gap between Brunhes' proclaimed theoretical principles and his practice of geography, the latter continuing to be limited by the (tacitly agreed upon) division of labour between sociology and geography. The contribution of Brunhes nonetheless demonstrates that classical French geography was far from being monolithic in its neglect or, worse, negation of the social.

It is interesting that, after a period of rejection in the 1970s and 1980s, classical French geography has recently been re-evaluated. Saving Vidal from Vidalism seems to be the implicit project, in that the epistemological astuteness of Vidal's own writing has been 'rediscovered' by some historians of French geography (Robic 1991). However, if we recognize the enduring impact of the classical paradigm – and not just that of Vidal – on human geography in twentieth-century French-speaking geography, the impression is that its peculiar environmentalism was indeed an obstacle to the development of a fully fledged social geography. After 1914, French social geography duly entered a deep and mostly untroubled sleep, which lasted 30 years until Pierre George's Marxian social geography, or 60 years until the crisis of the classical paradigm, depending on how we consider post-war French social geography (Frémont et al. 1984; Lévy 1999b).

Packing the social into regions: regional social geographies

As already indicated, the guise of social geography during the earlier years of the twentieth century was commonly regional, examining the character of phenomena regarded as social within nameable and delimitable portions of the world. The Vidalian tradition keyed into this vision of regional social geography as well as possessing the environmentalist focus. Yet a subtly different regional angle, one where the issue of environmental influences receded, began to appear during the middle years of the century. This was most obviously the case in the difficult claims of Richard Hartshorne (1939, 1959), an American geographer who spent some years in Germany, in the course of formulating his stance on geography as the study of 'areal differentiation'. For Hartshorne, the great geographical project was all about identifying how areas of the earth differ from one another, the assumption being that it is feasible to identify obvious variations between regions which effectively demarcate the spatial divisions of the earth's material skin. He did not suppose that regions in this vein necessarily equate with existing political and administrative divisions, although they might on occasion; rather he insisted that the task was to inspect variations within (and co-variations between) different 'surfaces' of reality – the physical, the economic, the political – in the hunt for regional unities and boundaries which only the scholar would be able to discern (Jones 1995). He believed that 'the interest of geography in each of the many features which contribute to [areal] differentiation is in proportion to its relation to the total' (Hartshorne 1939: 399), and he fully expected certain categories of phenomena to be more decisive as regional discriminators than others. A strain of environmentalism remained in his work, since 'the marked differences in the natural environment of different parts of the world, and the partial dependence of most cultural features on the natural environment' (Hartshorne 1939: 399), meant that physical phenomena – and hence physical geography – were believed to be most commonly the crucial markers of regional distinctiveness.

Economic and, to a lesser extent, political phenomena – and as a result both economic and political geography – were also thought to be important as sources of areal differentiation, but a definite shift in his reasoning occurred when he came to consider social phenomena and the possible contribution of social geography (or as he called it 'sociological geography'):

> When one considers the theoretically possible field of sociological geography from the point of view which we have been following, it may appear doubtful that the development of studies of that character can make important contributions to geography. In areas of primitive [*sic*] development one might study the geography of clothes or implements, or conceivably of manners and customs, and religions. For the important [*sic*] parts of the world, however, such studies would apparently have little geographical significance. Men wear hats in Chicago that allow their ears to freeze because the winters are not cold in London.
>
> (Hartshorne 1939: 404–5)

The last statement here referred to how people in Chicago might buy hats made in London, or hats that imitate London fashions, but find that such hats are not designed for cold Chicago winters, the broader argument being that these hats – and by extension other 'sociological' phenomena – are basically placeless, having scant necessary connection with any particular part of the world, and thereby next to useless as indicators of 'real' differences between worldly regions. The impression is that, despite the tantalizing reference to such immaterial things as manners, customs and religions, Hartshorne was casting around for things more material (with a measure of corporeality), which he could define as 'social' and then examine for their contribution to areal differentiation. Unsurprisingly, once having anchored the social around phenomena such as hats, his 'sociological geography' appeared a trivial exercise which could add little to geography's grander endeavour. As with Hoke, Barrows and others, therefore, he was unwilling to countenance phenomena which were immaterial, unavailable to a visual economy (Jones 1995), and here, too, strong links ran between a set understanding of geography and limited conceptions of both the social and social geography.

One attempt *was* made to develop a more substantial regional social geography in the mode of Hartshorne's areal differentiation, by J. Wreford Watson (1951), a Scottish geographer who worked for some time in Canada. Wreford Watson set off from the clearly Hartshornian assumption that '[t]he really significant things . . . are not the phenomena in themselves, nor their interactions with each other, but *the way in which they provide distinctive character to the regions which they fill*' (Wreford Watson 1951: 482). Where he departed from Hartshorne was in reckoning that all manner of phenomena, material and immaterial, can give rise to the distinctiveness of regions:

[I]t is impossible to stop at the concrete. The human factor is something more than the works-of-[people]. It includes ideologies as well as technologies. And in not a few instances it is the *immaterial* force that is the really significant thing in the geography of a region, which gives that region its distinctive character, and separates it from others.

(Wreford Watson 1951: 468, emphasis added)

In overcoming the virtual fear of the immaterial which afflicted other geographers of the time – certainly Anglo-American geographers – Wreford Watson called for geographers 'competent to deal with the immaterial social factors in the geographic scene' (Wreford Watson 1951: 469), and in so doing immediately opened up for scrutiny a whole panorama of social phenomena which were less than immediately tangible, about which others had been so silent. Proceeding from a preliminary definition of social geography as 'the identification of different regions of the earth's surface according to associations of social phenomena related to the total environment' (Wreford Watson 1951: 482), he announced:

Social geography, by its title, will obviously confine itself to the social patterns; that is, to those made by people coming together in groups; to the patterns of population, settlement, social institutions and organizations. . . . Not all of these are immediately self-evident. They are not all expressed as material objects in the . . . landscape. But those which are; houses, barns, factories, villages, cities, communications, are first noted. Then perhaps the statistical data on population, race, language, and religion can be gathered, and fitted into the picture. Lastly, the study of social groups and their activities is made, and incorporated with the rest.

(Wreford Watson 1951; 481)

This passage reflected a conviction that geographers should talk to sociologists, there being 'adequate reason for equating social geography with the sociological aspects of geography', and displayed a readiness to take seriously such staples of sociological analysis as 'social groups (home, work, play, worship groups), and social institutions and their function' (Wreford Watson 1951: 484).

Importantly, Wreford Watson applied these notions when reconstructing what he termed 'the social geography of a city', in this case Hamilton, Ontario. He sought to identify the 'social regions' of Hamilton, conducting a regional geography at the intra-urban scale and asserting that the city was constituted by 'patterns of changing areal structures and of changing group interactions' (Wreford Watson 1951: 488–9). He began to tease out how these structures and interactions created a city divided into a series of localities ('social regions'), associated with different types of social group present in the social hierarchy of Hamilton society; it might even be said that he offered an embryonic social-geographical treatment of class, albeit depicting class in descriptive categories like 'stable working class', rather than ones with more of an analytic edge (after Marx). It is impossible to see classes in a straightforward manner, even if one can infer their effects in the visible landscape, but Wreford Watson was in no doubt that class – and other bases for social groups, notably ethnicity – did lie behind many regional differences within Hamilton. His study spoke of 'social contrasts' and he considered the paradox that inner-city Hamilton contained many clubs, lodges, churches and cultural facilities patronized by well-to-do people from the suburbs, but not by poorer, often immigrant families who could be found living right next door. This led him to write of these facilities as being 'socially remote from those who are geographically near, but socially near to those who have become geographically remote', and he drew a diagram to illustrate this paradoxical spatial intermixing of wealth and 'respectability' with poverty and 'deprivation'. Such a line of inquiry, with its concern for the more subjective dimensions in the minds of Hamilton's poor inner-city dwellers, which created 'social Himalayas' separating them from spatially proximate facilities – '[s]ocial distance thereby qualifies geographical distance' (Wreford Watson 1951: 497) – has many parallels with more recent research in social geography tackling both the 'objective' bases of disadvantage in the city and the 'subjective' experiences of people coping with it.

Similar preoccupations – regional economic and social differentiation, the relations between geography and sociology – were central to French-speaking geography of the mid-twentieth century. The interest in cities and the consideration of economic regions in the last years of Vidal's life (he died in 1918) broke with a strict environmentalist orthodoxy and opened, if timidly, the possibility for a more obviously social geography. This possibility came to be more fully exploited after 1945, in the context of post-war reconstruction, the electoral successes of the left and the growing influence of Marxism among French intellectuals. New words started to be used at this time to define the social: 'organization' and 'structure' entered the language of geographers such as Pierre George and Abel Chatelain with fresh connotations, showing that society possessed a conceptual 'thickness' which it had not had under classical Vidalian geography. The social tended to become an articulated whole and an active producer of geographies, and no longer a mere 'thing' entailing a transparent entity between milieu and person. George was the central figure, particularly because he introduced Marxian categories of analysis into geography, something that came much later in English-speaking geography. Already in his *Géographie économique et sociale de la France*, published in 1938, he had used terms such as 'industrial proletariat' and 'capitalist exploitation' (Frémont *et al.* 1984), and inequality – the social differentiation of *genres de vie* – was clearly a central question for him. Moreover this was a question which he took as basically an economic one – 'nowhere is it possible to separate the social from economy' (George 1946: 6) – and therefore it might be argued that he placed Marxian economism above Vidalian environmentalism. In what is probably the first French book dealing explicitly and exclusively with social geography, George (1946) offered a classification of the world into social regions on the basis of different modes of production. He identified regions where 'traditional rural societies' dominate (the most common case), regions comprising the 'complex societies' of Europe (both urban and rural) and regions supporting the 'societies of the future' (USA, Russia, Japan). Each of these regions was characterized in terms of social structure (George 1946: 45) and social process (notably industrialization and urbanization). In this formulation, social geography became a description of the mosaic of social structure, and data on industrial production, population density, tons of fertilizer in the agriculture of a region and the like became a standard part of disciplinary discourse. The surface of the earth was seen thereby not only as a natural product, but also as a social one. These additions to the classical paradigm in terms of measurement and quantification made French geography a more 'useful' discipline, at least potentially, and this move prepared the way for the connections between geography and planning in France in the 1960s.

Herein resided George's signal contribution to an analysis of the social in geography, but despite his new terminology, talking of structure and organization, and some of his general statements – 'society is a form of human organization for the exploitation of resources' (George 1946: 4) – it remains difficult at a distance of years to appreciate precisely what it was for him that was hidden in the black box of society. Certainly, Marx's economism influenced George more than his humanism, and social representations in the form of 'ideology' (an important Marxian category), for example, never came into the picture. This is probably why another geographer of the same period, Chatelain (1946), in a comment on George's book, called for a more complex social geography composed of two parts: a geography of class and a geography of social life. Citing the absence of any serious social geography of the city of Paris, and asking 'when will we have a social geography of the French bourgeoisie?', Chatelain also urged geographers to develop empirical work ('grand syntheses can wait') (Chatelain 1946: 270). Yet apart from his own inquiries and occasional works by others, such as Étienne Juillard's thesis on the evolution and crisis of rural life in Alsace (Juillard 1953), Chatelain's call remained all but unanswered. One reason for this silence was that in the immediate post-war years the boundaries between sociology and geography, as drawn by Vidal, Febvre and Durkheim, were still both hermetic and hegemonic, as revealed by explicit discussions about the relations between sociology and geography in the 1950s and 1960s. Max Sorre in 1957 and George himself in 1966 both devoted books to this discussion, but they stayed within a broadly defined environmentalist and regionalist definition of geography, wherein geographers were expected to develop synthetic studies of regional entities while sociologists were supposed to develop in-depth analyses of the 'nature and origin of social phenomena' (Sorre 1957: 8). To this distinction, George (1966: 8) added a methodological one: namely that geography, concerned with what is visible and graspable (contra both Brunhes and Wreford Watson), should use quantitative and empirical methods, whereas sociology, not being so constrained, could be more speculative and thereby use qualitative methods. In other words, neither Sorre nor George fundamentally questioned Febvre's old partition.

It is perhaps telling that it took a woman geographer, Renée Rochefort, to break with this orthodoxy. Conducting research for her doctoral thesis in Sicily during the late 1950s, she came to see the distinction between social and natural phenomena as untenable. As she explained in an oft-quoted passage:

> I understood that irrigation, unquestionable technological progress, admirable element of the efficiency of geographic landscapes, was, for this very reason, a means of blackmail, of threat, of exploitation of Man by Man [sic]. It was impossible, not to try to understand why, i.e. to penetrate into a complex path of laws and networks of social forces.
>
> (Rochefort 1963: 21)

Choosing 'work' as the theme of her research in Sicily was itself indicative of the innovations introduced by Rochefort into the discipline, since work was an abstract and unusual category in the context of French geography at this time. Inevitably involving consideration of both the natural and social worlds, it effectively united the traditional 'notion of *genre de vie*' and what she called the 'more modern notions . . . of class, social category and life standards' (Rochefort 1961: 3). Work was, in other words, a 'transitional notion' for Rochefort. It helped to shift attention to central social problems: 'we know more about the exportation of Sicilian hazelnuts to Sweden than about unemployment' on the island, she observed (Rochefort 1961: 5). The notion of work served more generally to move geography out of the Vidalian paradigm, and one explicit aim of her geography was to 'keep geography alive and avoid its transformation into this register of contemplative reflections, in this cartographic file that the non-specialist sometimes wants, too quickly perhaps, to forget about' (Rochefort 1961: 2). For this purpose, and unlike what Sorre and George wrote in the same years, it was indispensable to get into the intimate genesis of things. Although Rochefort did not directly attack classical French geography, the introduction to her work on Sicily might be read by a Vidalian believer as a catalogue of blasphemies: humanity, and not space, was to be at the centre of geography; geography should be not only descriptive but also predictive; and she accepted the value in there being zones of interference between disciplines and in the heterogeneity of real world spaces. That said, she did recuperate some of the most interesting aspects of the French school, notably because, in contrast to George, she insisted on the importance of *mentalités* and the necessity to collaborate with ethnologists and anthropologists. She referred to literature (Pirandello, Tommaso di Lampedusa), stressed the importance of fieldwork and wanted to express in her text the mood of the 'roadmender in Vulcano in wintertime, bored to death on his desert island' (Rochefort 1961: 6). Yet given all these innovations, Rochefort was still another false start for French social geography: hers was a lonely voice. Her engagement with problems of daily life, injustice, poverty and people's grounded feelings about these difficulties was probably the main reason why other geographers felt unable to integrate her proposed innovations into their own research. More of an engaged and subtle empiricist than a theoretician, she did not create a school of thought with a series of followers, and her gender may have had some part to play in this, given the prevailing masculinism of the discipline in France, as elsewhere.

Ethnographic fieldwork of the type encouraged by Rochefort continued to be very marginal, and still is today in French-speaking countries. Even so, it was practised to some extent during the 1940s to 1960s by the so-called 'tropical school', since for the main figure of this school, Pierre Gourou (1971, 1973), fieldwork was necessary in order to prevent a reduction of geography to natural regions and visible landscapes: 'civilization is not in the landscape', but acts on it and therefore should be directly studied (Gourou 1971: 107; also Gallais 1976). Another important and often neglected contribution of the tropical school to social geography was its insistence on and approach to technology (a theme of Gourou's teaching in the Collège de France in 1968–9). Gourou not only explored a central mediation between society and space through this emphasis on technology, but also refused to separate the material dimensions of technology (artefacts) from the social ones (institutions, statistics). Once again, though, this geography remained exotic (in the different senses of the word) for mainstream geographers.

One of the reasons for the isolation of Rochefort and the marginality of the tropical school was probably the existence in France of a tacit contract between geographers and the state: geographers were given a strong position in the system of education (they were present for 12 years in public schools), but were 'asked' in return not to deal too much either with abstract matters of theory or sensitive social issues (Lévy 1999: 9). This contract between the French state and geographers took a slightly different form in the 1960s, in that teaching was complemented by the growing importance of applied geography. In this period, regional planning (*aménagement du territoire*) offered geographers new contracts and job opportunities, and applied geography, especially dealing with urban issues, developed spectacularly. Consequently, in relation to the 'needs' of the state, geographers ended up being not only the key players in effecting a culturalist description of 'France's personality' (Vidal 1903), but also, with the developments somewhat unwittingly initiated by the Marxian George, in contributing useful research for economic and physical planning strategies. This new bond between the community of geographers and the state did not encourage critical research any more than had the bond of earlier years, even if geographers of the 1960s – beginning to operate as spatial scientists – probably started to investigate more than their predecessors had, such serious social issues as homelessness, poverty and the effects of immigration.

The social as a 'solid geometry': spatial social geographies

Hoke's modern-sounding definition of social geography as 'deal[ing] with the distribution in space of social phenomena' (Hoke 1907: 64) paved the way for the development of a determinedly spatial-scientific social geography from the 1950s through to the 1970s. This was the period when regional geography came under serious attack, and when Hartshorne's 'exceptionalist' thesis, positioning geography (with history) as a discipline concerned with the idiographic recovery of (areal) differences, was seriously criticized by those who wished to return geography to the fold of 'nomothetic' sciences concerned with finding and applying supposedly general laws (Burton 1963; Haggett 1965; Harvey 1969; Schaefer 1953). This was a transition which connected geography to wider currents of thinking in the natural and social sciences, as well as opening the door to a range of positivist and functionalist forms of explanation which had previously enjoyed only a shadowy presence within the discipline.

It was a passage of disciplinary history that certainly impacted upon social geography, and it might be said that regional social geographies were usurped by spatial social geographies, wherein the principal aim was to map out the spatial distributions of social phenomena with a view to establishing the basic laws (or at least regularities and trends) underlying the 'geometry' of these distributions. This exercise might go no further than specifying apparently fundamental spatial laws, such as the tendency of a particular phenomena to cluster or disperse; it might try to relate one spatial distribution (e.g. outbreaks of tuberculosis) to another (e.g. poor quality housing), maybe inferring a causal relationship whereby the one phenomena (and its patterns) determines the other (and its patterns); it might speculate about the mechanisms at work in such causal relationships, at which point more sociological notions regarding the interlocking elements of the social (e.g. illness, poverty, housing) could be mobilized; or it might even hint at still deeper processes and forces in operation, at which point more social-theoretical notions regarding the social, its systems, structures and articulations with economy, politics and culture could be invoked. Various conceptions of the social began to filter into the spatial social geographies, but in practice few studies reached far beyond the first two steps noted here, and consequently left their understandings of the social (and their borrowings from sociology and social theory) largely unspoken. In the words of Gregory (1982), the spatial analysis of the social often remained confined to the description of a 'solid geometry' expressing the supposedly autonomous laws of space. For these geographers the social was a solidified form and not a continuously evolving process. The problem with this hypothesis of the 'separateness' of society and space was, as Gunnar Olsson (1980) observed, that different processes can generate the same form and that such an analysis consequently says little about the underlying dynamics of social geographies.

It would be possible to reference any number of specific studies which might be cast as spatial social geographies, notably Frederick Boal's important research on the territoriality of religious groupings around the Shankhill-Falls divide in Belfast, Northern Ireland (Boal 1969), but the most obvious body of work was that termed 'spatial sociology' by Ceri Peach (1975a), which sought to detect, enumerate and draw conclusions about the spatial patterns of residence associated with different 'ethnic' groupings in the city. Two such studies are D. Doeppers' (1967) reconstruction of the ethnic geographies of Denver's Globesville neighbourhood, tracing different patterns of residence at different time periods, involving a diversity of European immigrants and their descendants, and John Western's (1973) reconstruction of the spatially restricted lives led by French Cajuns in the city of Houma, Louisiana, exploring both static residential patterns and more dynamic activity networks. Both studies underlined that geographical research on ethnicity should not only focus upon people with 'darker' skin pigmentation (too often it has been assumed that black people, in particular, have 'ethnicity' while white people do not), but it is the case that much research conducted in this vein has latched on to the 'problems' of 'the black ghetto', usually but not exclusively in the USA, and has looked to the obvious polarization of 'black' and 'white' as expressed spatially (Morrill 1965). Doeppers and Western also demonstrated a sensitivity to matters of culture and local politics which was absent from more extreme versions of spatial sociology, notably those that became fixated on using statistical 'indices of segregation' to measure the degrees of spatial (dis)similarity in the residential distributions of different ethnic groupings (see many of the chapters in Peach 1975b; Peach, Robinson and Smith 1981). As Peter Jackson reflected, work in this vein was 'describing the spatial patterns of minority group concentration, with gestures towards an explanation in terms of "choice" and "constraint"', assessing thereby the balance between forces pushing groupings into being segregated (poverty, housing markets, discrimination) and decisions consciously made by groupings to segregate (to preserve identity, religion and language, maybe for safety). As he continued, though, such work 'rais[ed] few questions about the meaning or significance of segregation' and was arguably 'guilty of "narrow empiricism" at best and "socio-cultural apologism for racial segregation" at worst' (Jackson 1987: 4). The good thing about such studies was that they enlarged the realm of social matters brought into geographical purview – sensitizing geographers to the differing social groups making up society, their socio-spatial interrelations and, by implication, their enmeshing in a spatialized politics of identity – but there was scant attempt to bring on board deeper senses of the social, to think more deeply about ethnicity and race (let alone class and gender) and their very constitution in and through space (S. J. Smith 1989). The likes of Ceri Peach (1996, 1999) have continued to produce high quality spatial sociology, adding in elements which somewhat mute the purchase of the thumbnail criticisms just outlined, but these spatial social geographies – certainly in their original guises – should probably be treated with caution.

Crucial in all this was the debt which spatial social geographers owed to the Chicago school sociologists of the 1920s and 1930s, whose research into the society and spaces of early twentieth-century Chicago was taken up as a possible template for much that these later geographers were looking to achieve. (It should also be mentioned that in the sub-discipline known as urban geography the influence of the Chicago school is most obvious and acknowledged.) Robert Park's penchant for suggesting that social relations ('social distances') could be read off from spatial patterns ('physical distances') – as discussed by Jackson and Smith (1984: 66–86) – was taken as a grounding statement by these geographers, while E. W. Burgess's well-known maps showing the 'rings' (basically of class) and the 'zones' (basically of ethnicity) of Chicago have become staples of social geography textbooks (Burgess 1924). Burgess's own claims about how these urban distributions reflect underlying laws of social (dis)organization in a rapidly growing metropolis are now rarely cited, however, and this observation keys into a broader argument about the partiality of what the spatial social geographers borrowed from the Chicago school. It is obvious that they were inspired by the statistical manipulations and mapping procedures of the Chicago 'human ecologists', and that, refracted in part through E. Shevky and W. Bell's well-known 'social area analysis' of Los Angeles (Shevky and Bell 1955), they developed a battery of statistical-mapping devices for conducting 'factorial ecologies' on huge arrays of urban social data (Carter 1976: chapters 9 and 11; Herbert 1972: chapter 6). Their results clearly revealed dimensions of the city's social geography which are potentially interesting, teasing out deeper 'structures' within the numerical data which probably can tell us something about certain regularities in (if not laws about) how social phenomena are interrelated across urban space. Yet such exercises remained little more than elaborate descriptions, efforts in taxonomy – what do we call the 'factors' or 'components'? – rather than engaging with theory (Carter 1976: 271), and the often dubious nature of the statistical 'wizardry' involved meant that many were sceptical of the regularities and apparent interrelations uncovered.

More importantly, these exercises lost touch with the theoretical coordinates that had energized the Chicago sociologists, thereby abandoning the rich veins of thought which had enabled the likes of Burgess, Park and many others to reflect on both the political economy of urban society and its everyday lived dimensions (a claim central to Jackson and Smith 1984: chapter 4). The geographers failed to grasp the diversity of ideas about the social that had excited Burgess *et al.*, and, if anything, the only baggage that the geographers retained from the Chicago sociologists was the simplistic concept that the social life of the city was regulated by principles similar to those governing the distributions (invasions and successions) of plant and animal communities. They kept in sight only the more literally 'ecological' claims of the Chicago sociologists, and their own theoretical moments thereby tended to focus on '*sub*-social ecological forces of competition' (Carter 1976: 175, emphasis added, also 189–90) rather than exploring more obvious and arguably pressing social forces (for summaries see Grafmeyer and Joseph 1979 and Chapoulie 2001). The further risk for these geographers, as for any social scientists who were seduced by ecological thinking, was that they

> . . . turned city life into an unalterable and naturalistic destiny in which human beings are mechanically caught up, much as the planets are mechanically caught up in their motions around the sun. In this way, then, urban poverty, slums, racial segregation, etc. are seen not as *socially imposed* (and therefore mutable) phenomena, but as the inescapable expression of the self-engendered environment of the metropolis.
>
> (Scott 1980: 71, emphasis added)

It might be claimed that there was a continuing reluctance to engage with the immaterial relations binding and fracturing the social world, the likes of class, power, race and prejudice, and that the preference was to 'materialize' this world into more manageable, less threatening forms, such as statistics and maps, or through treating the city as an ecological assemblage akin to the plants and animals of the forest. As such, and notwithstanding gains already noted, the versions of social geography enacted at this time continued to internalize a rather limited sense of the social.

Spatial analysis was indeed embraced later and with less enthusiasm by French-speaking, German and other European geographers than it was by Anglo-American and Scandinavian academics. The hegemony of the classical school, the fact that spatial analysis only really developed in the 1970s, and the interest that many of the actors in this 'reform' had in philosophy and epistemology all explain why French geographers were more cautious about the potential of the so-called 'new geography'. As often happens, this development was accompanied by the creation of a new journal, *L'Espace géographique*, founded in 1972. Marking its difference from Vidal's definition of geography (a 'spirit' or 'fold of the intelligence'), the editorial of the first issue affirmed that geography was 'a well defined scientific field and not an art of describing or way of seeing' (*L'Espace géographique*: vol. 6). In French social geography, factorial ecology became an important and 'trendy' instrument for the study of socio-economic differentiation at this time, and Jean-Bernard Racine's (1973) thesis on Montreal was one of the most ambitious contributions to this first attempt at writing spatial geographies of the social. His analysis identified the structure of relations between the social and physical variables characterizing suburban Montreal and foreshadowed a series of social geographies of the city in French-speaking countries that focused on intra-urban structures. These contributions unearthed the subtle differentiations within urban milieus after a long period of regional studies in which the (external) relations between cities had been privileged. In the mid-1980s, together with the Geneva geographer, Claude Raffestin, Racine himself developed a trenchant critique of such spatial social geographies, arguing that spatial analysis had often uncritically adopted the categories of the official census, 'a "social" constructed by power' (Racine and Raffestin 1983: 309).

Despite such critiques, spatial analyses of the social have grown in importance since the 1960s and 1970s, and even today constitute an important part of French-speaking geographical production. Increasingly sophisticated models, inspired by René Thom's chaos theory, Ilya Prigogine's 'bifurcations' and Benoît Mandelbrot's 'fractals', have been introduced in a continuous search for spatial ordering principles underlying the social. The group PARIS (Pour l'avancement des recherches sur l'interaction spatiale), in Paris, around Denis Pumain and Thérèse Saint-Julien, and the Maison de la Géographie, created in Montpellier by Roger Brunet, became, in the 1980s and 1990s, the most important centres of theoretical innovation and careful empirical work (Brunet 1990–6; Pumain and Saint-Julien 1978; Pumain *et al.* 1989), even if the former has adopted a rather sectarian and dogmatic outlook on the creation of geographic knowledge. These developments, including models inspired by contemporary biology and physics, have enriched a formerly predominantly geometrical imagination: they have rendered the social more fluid, processual and malleable (see Doreen Massey's comparable claims about developments in Anglo-American geography, 1992, 1999). However, this approach to social geography has continued to naturalize the social, being reluctant to envisage its human, messy, 'subjective' characteristics. As a consequence, the social has remained something of a black box here, which explains why these spatial geographies of the social are still the target of critique by geographers more interested in many different facets to the immateriality of the social.

IMMATERIAL SOCIAL GEOGRAPHIES: IN THE 1970s, 1980s AND BEYOND

Social geography from the 1970s through to the 1980s and beyond can be cast as work on 'immaterial social geographies', those preoccupied with unequal structurings, lived experiences and the agency-structure intersections bound up in a much wider range of social phenomena than had been considered previously. The geographers concerned have enlarged greatly their sense of the social, adopting an alertness to society's internal relations, the subjectivities of social groups, the connections between such relations and subjectivities and the implicated nature of space at every turn. These manoeuvres have occurred principally in Anglo-American geography, but important adaptations, inflections and independent inventions have figured in continental European geography as well. In Italy, France and Switzerland, for instance, different groups of geographers began dealing with perception and then with representations of space. 'L'espace vécu' (Frémont 1976), the hidden world of ordinary people, as theorized by Henri Lefebvre (1974) or Michel de Certeau (1984), has become a major preoccupation (Bertrand 1978).

The social as structure and difference: radical social geographies

As the 1960s came to a close, a number of geographers became increasingly vocal in criticizing the failures of spatial science to tackle issues of social inequality and social injustice, objecting to its emphasis on material things (ones that can be readily identified, counted, measured, blocked on graphs, dotted on maps) and attendant reluctance to consider immaterial relations, powers, structures and the like. There was a desire to render the discipline more socially aware and socially relevant, and one index of this development was the mood of the annual meeting of the Association of American Geographers held in Boston in 1971, when professional geographers *en masse* began to accept a much more inclusive 'social' agenda than ever before. David Smith, a British geographer at this meeting, neatly summarized this shift to what he called 'an emerging "radical" geography and an embryonic "revolution of social responsibility"', suggesting that atlases of the USA, for instance, needed to supplement their maps showing the locations of 'turkeys, chickens and hogs' with ones showing a diversity of 'social conditions' (Smith 1971: 153, 155). Smith's repeated reference to the *social* realm is instructive, since his prime goal, reflecting that of many others at the Boston meeting, was to nourish a much expanded sense of the social throughout human geography:

> However we define geography . . . there are now (and probably always have been) sound logical reasons for studying many *social* phenomena that we have traditionally tended to ignore. These would include such matters as racial segregation, poverty, hunger, infant mortality, morbidity, drug addiction, mental illness, suicide, illegitimacy, sexual deviance, welfare services, medical care, crime, justice, the incidence of areas or regions of social deprivation, and so on. Many of these phenomena show more extreme areal variation, and are stronger criteria of areal differentiation, than some of the physical and economic phenomena to which we have traditionally attached so much importance.
>
> (Smith 1971: 156, emphasis added)

In the latter part of this quote, Smith echoed Wreford Watson's reworking of Hartshorne by suggesting that immaterial social phenomena, rather than just physical and economic phenomena, might be important markers of difference from one region to the next. More significantly, though, the substantive breadth of what Smith included as elements of the social was remarkable, and we would identify here the bare bones of a new 'socialized' human geography, which inevitably put the sub-discipline of social geography much more squarely at the heart of the overall human-geographical project.

It would be possible to match every one of the social phenomena listed by Smith to subsequent studies of social geography investigating such phenomena in detail, and mention could be made of his own sterling efforts to create a 'welfare geography', documenting the uneven geography of societal 'goods' and 'bads', not only empirically but also theoretically through an appeal to welfare economics (Smith 1974, 1977, 1979, 1994a). Revealingly, Smith later reflected on the initial formulations of welfare geography:

> The early preoccupation with descriptive research in welfare geography has now given way to more process-orientated work on the question of *how* inequality arises. The abstract formulation of welfare problems based in neoclassical economics has been found impotent as a basis for explanatory analysis, and alternatives such as Marxian economics have become useful sources of guidance.
>
> (Smith 1994b: 526)

Smith's identification of a shift to a body of Marxian theory is illuminating, because the chief occurrence in this radicalization of human geography, and more specifically of social geography, was the insertion of explicitly Marxist and, more indirectly, Marxian (political-economic) insights capable of explaining how (under capitalism, at least) social inequalities are systematically imprinted on the spaces of society. In the Anglophone world of geography, this amounted to a rediscovery of what French geographers such as George and Chatelain had already discovered more than 20 years before. As a result, geographers took on board a host of concepts – to do with class, class struggle, capital and labour, social relations under capitalism, the appropriation of surplus value and the like – which added to Smith's substantive social agenda an attempt to scissor conceptually into the innermost workings of the social (as inescapably linked to the economic and the political).

A significant person here was David Harvey, a British geographer who has worked in North America, whose intellectual biography saw him break decisively with his earlier incarnation as a spatial scientist (Harvey 1969) in turning to a hard-edged Marxist geography with revolutionary ambitions both intellectually and politically. Much has been written elsewhere about Harvey's enormous contribution, and we wish only to underline the extent to which his Marxism impacted upon, and was forged through reference to, his interest in the grounded social geographies of oppression and conflict. For instance, in his groundbreaking 1972 paper, which was arguably the first shot at a developed Marxist geography in the English-speaking literature, he declared:

> Th[e] immediate task is nothing more nor less than the self-conscious and aware construction of a new paradigm for *social* geographic thought through a deep and profound critique of our existing analytical constructs. . . . Our task is therefore to mobilise our powers of thought to formulate concepts and categories, theories and arguments, which we can apply in the process of bringing about a humanizing social change.
>
> (Harvey 1972: 10–11, emphasis added)

While Harvey may have meant 'social geographic' to be interchangeable with 'human geographic' in this sentence, thus repeating that oft-made elision noted earlier, it is likely that his thinking was also directly influenced by his great concern for the plight of marginalized social groups within western cities (and hence with a focal point of distinctively social-geographical interest). In the 1972 paper, as well as introducing the key concept of surplus value from the Marxist lexicon, he also attacked ecological explanations of 'ghetto formation' by appealing to the class-based account that Engels (Marx's collaborator) provided of inner-city poverty in 1840s Manchester. Using Engels' own words, Harvey conjured up the social geography of this heavy-industrial city, recording how shops lining the main thoroughfares 'suffice to conceal from the eyes of the wealthy men and women of strong stomachs and weak nerves the misery and the grime which form the complement of their wealth' (Harvey 1972: 7). As Harvey's use of this phrase from Engels indicated, a Marxist theorization of nineteenth-century Manchester, or any western city, should be about excavating the 'structural' relationships, the unequal social relations binding together 'wealth' and 'misery', which are arguably endemic to the machinations of a capitalist society. Here was Harvey's platform for building into a progressively deeper engagement between geography and Marxism, commencing with his famous book *Social Justice and the City* (1973; this includes a minor reworking of the 1972 paper), itself as much a specific charter for social geography as a general call to arms for all human geography, and continuing with a sequence of books (Harvey 1982, 1985a and b, 1989, 1996), which have all returned at one point or another to the unequal social geographies of capitalist cities and regions.

It would be easy to mention numerous Marxist or Marxian inquiries into the social geographies of class, poverty and oppression. Richard Peet's (1975) attempts to found a 'Marxist-geographic theory' of poverty could be listed, as could Neil Smith's sustained attention to the churnings of capital, class, gentrification and homelessness out of which '[a] new social geography of the city is being born' (Smith 1996: 29, 1979b, 1982, 1987b), or Richard Harris's (1984, 1989) attempts to put a 'Marxist synthesis' into 'practice' when researching the conditions, politics and residential patterns of city neighbourhoods and communities. It would also be appropriate to mention the diversity of input to radical social geographies coming from different versions of Marxism, political economy, anarchism and William Bunge's 'advocacy geography' on the streets of Detroit and Toronto, but it is perhaps most pertinent to emphasize the exceptionally important contribution that has been made here by the dawning of a feminist perspective within academic geography (and note the references to the importance of feminist arguments to developments surveyed throughout other chapters in this volume). We cannot say much about the tangled theories and politics written into the rise of feminist geography from the early 1970s onwards (McDowell 1999; Rose 1993), but it is appropriate to reference the efforts of someone like Jacquie Tivers, whose 1978 paper, 'How the other half lives', provided an early feminist statement of why women *as women* should be taken much more seriously than hitherto in substantive geographical work. Tivers was clear that she wished to plug a glaring hole in social geography by rescuing from invisibility women's occupation, utilization and experience of social spaces, and in 1981 she remarked quite explicitly that '[i]t is the impact of feminist ideas on *social* geography which I have myself studied' (Tivers 1981: emphasis added). She conducted an in-depth study of 400 women with children under the age of full-time schooling in the London borough of Merton, using questionnaire and diary techniques to excavate what she believed to be a certain 'poverty' to these women's spatial worlds: a constrained geography entailing a complex juggling act in time-space as the women sought to cope with managing young children, part-time work and household, shopping and health care chores, usually without the use of a car (Tivers 1985, 1988). Moreover this was also a geography which afforded scant opportunity for these women to hold down employment with any kind of career prospects, or to access recreational, educational and other services. Tivers explained this limited geography as bound up with a conventional 'gender role ideology', which predetermines the tasks to be performed by, and hence spaces available to, many women in less well-off situations, particularly in contrast to the roles and spaces allotted to their male partners, if present.

Tivers arguably deserves to be better remembered as a pioneer of feminist social geography, as does Suzanne Mackenzie (1988, 1989), a Canadian geographer whose sustained efforts to render 'visible' the 'histories' of women living in post-war Brighton, England, were exemplary. That said, their 'geography of women' approach was itself built upon – and sometimes critiqued by – a more thoroughgoing feminist geography which, with the publication in 1984 of the landmark text, *Geography and Gender*, started to insist on 'a geography which explicitly takes into account the socially-created gender structure of society' (WGSG 1984: 21). Hence gender became the focus, or rather it was the systematic structuring of unequal gender relations within a 'patriarchal' social order, and the aim became an exploration of how inequalities between women and men in terms of power, status, resources and control over the means of production and reproduction are translated into – and then reinforced by – a gendered arrangement of space (from the scale of the home to the scale of the city, the region and the nation state). Linda McDowell's (1983) influential paper on the 'gender division of urban space' argued that the division of public and private spheres was a deeply gendered affair, with men being regarded as 'natural' inhabitants of the former and women the 'natural' inhabitants of the latter, and went on to show that such a division was inextricably implicated in the spatial divisions of the western city between districts of salaried full-time labour, public duty and political involvement and districts of residences, schools, health clinics, parks and other extensions of home and garden. As with any 'model', McDowell could offer only a partial picture, glossing over such late twentieth-century realities as many women in full-time employment away from the home while many men experienced unemployment and enforced time at home, but this was still a significant pointer to a feminist form of radical social geography, which greatly expanded our sense of society by highlighting fundamental gender dimensions previously left wholly unexamined. Furthermore feminist ideas also began to alert geographers to a host of issues to do with the role of space and place in the constitution of identities (Keith and Pile 1993), the conditioning and performances of bodies (Kenworthy Tether 1999), the fostering and practice of heterosexuality, homosexuality and bisexuality (Bell and Valentine 1995), the variability of 'femininities' (Laurie *et al.* 1999) and the dominance of a 'masculinist' knowledge, gaze and power throughout all walks of life, from the garden to the academy (Rose 1993), to name but a few possibilities; all these issues have had dramatic implications for both social geography and the overall terrain of human geography.

It is more difficult to talk of radical social geographies arising in French-speaking areas. For obvious reasons, during the 1970s – May 1968, the economic crisis, the rise of critical discourse in the social sciences – there was a return to and a reframing of Marxian social geography, and in this context the social was described increasingly in terms of 'structures', which effectively lie in between the material and the immaterial. George had already used this term in the 1940s, but in a very concrete sense, whereas 30 years later the term became 'loaded' by French structuralism, and in particular by the specifications of Louis Althusser's structural Marxism (Castells 1973). In this process, structure began to be regarded as something more abstract, an ordering principle that split society into different 'spheres' of production, circulation and consumption. Marxian social geographers duly sought to identify spatial divisions within a given country, region or city that corresponded in some manner to these structural spheres; the historical geography of Thailand proposed by Michel Bruneau, Alain Durand-Lasserve and Marie Moline (1977) embodied certain of these attempts to develop a social geography within a structural Marxist framework. The description and genetic explanation of spatial differentiation in terms of domination through unequal exchange was the prime objective of their analysis, and one result was a complex table where each of seven delimited sets of spaces was characterized in terms of: 'conditions of production and exchange', 'relations of production and exchange', 'present superstructures (political, ideological, cultural, legal)', 'present spatial expression' and so on (Bruneau *et al.* 1977: 189). The term 'spatial expression' succinctly summarized the basic logic to this research in that the geography of Thailand was portrayed as the reflection of its social formation, a historical social product, the imprint of the succession of different modes of production over time. Material traces for Bruneau *et al.* were not just a 'solid geometry', but the surface outcome of underlying structures, just as the organization of the Bororo village studied by Claude Lévi-Strauss (1958) was seen as the signature of a social and symbolic organization.

There were many reactions to this renewal of Marxian geography in post-1968 France. It was a period of intense turmoil in the academy, and polemical debates of the mid-1970s were characterized by the entanglements of academic issues (territorial claims by a new generation of geographers), political ones (the classic left/right opposition) and theoretical ones (liberalism versus Marxism). In 1976, the 'established geographer' Maurice Le Lannou wrote an article in *Le Monde*, 'Geographers against geography', to criticize the iconoclasm of the young founders of the journal *EspacesTemps*. One month later, the reply from Christian Grataloup and Jacques Lévy in the same newspaper was tellingly entitled 'Geographers for another geography'. Paul Claval, one of the dominant figures of post-war French geography, played an important role in these debates (Claval 1967, 1977, 1987), since he developed a critique of Marxian approaches and proposed an alternative version of social geography. For Claval, Marxian geographies too often reduced their analysis to a 'mechanics of class' and relied too heavily on an untenable economic reductionism, and this critique was integral to his outline for a refounded social geography. In a dense theoretical essay of 1973, he called for a general theory of the relations between space and society, positioning social geography as one of the two main orientations of human geography, the other being ecological geography (*grosso modo* the Vidalian legacy). Thus social geography was for Claval a humpty-dumpty sub-discipline reassembling existing economic, political, cultural and, of course, aspects of social geography. The main innovation was the introduction of behaviour and representations – Claval called himself a 'neo-humanist' – grounded on an extensive reading of behavioural research in English-speaking geography. While other French geographers of the period were usually satisfied with rather loose and all-embracing definitions of the social, he also strove to define and articulate different dimensions of the social: the 'architecture of the social', 'social systems' and 'societal relations'. The study of 'social architecture' (the morphology of social groups and the representations that individuals have of these groups) was taken as the first task of social geographers: it was through this analysis that they could delve into the deeper dimensions of society and there discover the 'links [of social morphology] to ways of living, feeling, thinking' (Claval 1973a: 256). Interestingly, it might be said that Claval was looking for an alternative (non-Marxist) totalizing theory which would hold together what we would call today structure and agency (see chapter 2). Claval's contribution built on the interest for psychology and *mentalités* within the French school, echoing Brunhes, but it also announced an interpretive turn that would come into its own a decade or so later (if it ever really took place in French-speaking geography at all).

The most substantial theoretical contribution to non-Anglophone social geography in the 1970s and 1980s, however, was to be found in the work of the Swiss geographer, Claude Raffestin. Being rather idiosyncratic, his social geography was difficult to categorize in the neat boxes traditionally used to describe English-speaking geography (terms such as spatial analysis, humanistic geography and radical geography). During the late 1970s and early 1980s, Raffestin elaborated a personal, original and influential theory of 'territoriality'. This theory used as its resources elements from a great variety of traditions: Michel Foucault's ('radical') theory of power, the semiotics school of Tartu (Lotman 1985), human ecology and also cultural anthropology (Raffestin and Bresso 1979; Raffestin 1981). Raffestin was one rare example of a French-speaking geographer active within and not outside the concert of the wider *sciences humaines*; indeed until very recently authors like Foucault, Deleuze, Baudrillard and Bourdieu have been ignored. It might be said that Raffestin was the author of a 'grand theory' – another rare thing in French-speaking geography of the twentieth century – the aim of which was to provide a general understanding of 'territorial ecogenesis': 'the how and why of territorialization, deterritorialization and reterritorialization' (Raffestin 1986: 91). This theory was based on 'the study of [our] relations with exteriority and alterity in the perspective of attaining the greatest possible autonomy compatible with the resources of the system' (Raffestin 1986: 92). Promoting the notions of 'territory' (appropriated, enacted space), 'territoriality' (the sum of relations between subjects, belonging to a collectivity, with the environment) and 'territorialization' (the process through which these relations are established), Raffestin redefined geography in opposition to both the Vidalian tradition and spatial analysis. Thanks to him and a few other authors, territory has emerged as an essential notion in recent (re)configurations of French-speaking social geography, and has been deployed critically by an important part of the French-speaking (and also Italian) research community to move geography out of its 'solid geometries' and into approaches focused on human action. Territory has thereby come to reference a non-Newtonian, non-Kantian definition of space, encapsulating what the term *espace* arguably does not (ensembles of action, appropriation, representations and so on), and it is intriguing to note that the same theoretical shifts in English-speaking countries have not necessitated the same lexical change. Territory hence comprised a second important 'transitional' notion in the 'French tradition', in the sense that it has been, and still is, a rallying point for geographers critical of spatial analysis: working under the banner of *territoire* has commonly meant being sensitive to radical and humanistic positions. Raffestin's own 'radicality' has been of a traditional type, it might be said – i.e. inspired mainly by German philosophy (from Karl Marx to Georg Simmel and Martin Heidegger) – paralleling that of many other French-speaking intellectuals of his generation. As a consequence, both reification (of human life) and commodification (of society) have been continuous background narratives to Raffestin's geography (Raffestin 1994).

The social as personal and intersubjective: humanistic social geographies

Running alongside the emergence of a radical critique of spatial science from the late 1960s, another chorus of geographical voices began to criticize the failures of spatial science when it came to tackling the lived experiences of people as feeling, thinking and acting beings in the world (not merely as 'atoms' whizzing around in response to spatial laws operating 'behind their backs'). The upshot was an approach sometimes called 'humanistic geography', and studies under this rubric commonly concentrated on so-called 'senses of place' (Relph 1976), the aim being to excavate the intimate relations – sometimes loving, sometimes hating, sometimes indifferent – which always grow up, if often unremarked upon, between people and the many places (from the buildings to the countries) where they live, work, play and travel (Tuan 1974, 1980). This was another angle introducing immaterial aspects into the discipline, and it quickly began to draw inspiration from various 'philosophies of meaning' (Ley 1981), such as phenomenology, existentialism and variants of the two (Cloke *et al.* 1991: chapter 3). This is not the occasion to review the broader critique of humanistic geography and its philosophical underpinnings (Entrikin 1976; Ley 1981), but it is necessary to point out that this was not an approach which initially promised much for social geography. The reason for this was that the geographers involved tended to think either in terms of the 'universal Person' (with a capital 'P') or the 'individual person' (with a small 'p'), and in neither case did anything particularly *social* intrude into the scene. The impetus in the first instance was towards supposing that at some foundational level all people, whatever their background and capacities, are basically the same in terms of how they develop relations of involvement, dwelling, care and concern with respect to the places in their world. It was here that borrowings from Husserlian phenomenology and Heideggerian existentialism arguably diverted the attention of geographers away from the social contexts, including the social collectives, within which people live, foster and maybe reflect upon their 'senses of place'. The impetus in the second instance, as a mirror image of the first, was towards supposing that all people are so irretrievably different from one another, so totally unique in their personalities, biographies and viewpoints, that all we can do is celebrate the specificity of each individual's relations with the places in their world. Few studies ended up at this second extreme, although several (Rodaway 1988; Rowles 1978) came close in their angst about imposing generalizations of any kind upon the human subjects of their research, even where these included only a handful of seemingly quite similar people (elderly residents of a midwest US urban neighbourhood or residents of one small ex-mining village). Once again, though, the social dimensions of the situation in question rather receded from immediate consideration.

One scholar stood out as different in this respect, however, and this was David Ley, a British scholar who went to lecture in Canada and who was clearly endeavouring in the later 1970s to build bridges between the perspective of humanistic geography and the practice of social geography. Acknowledged as an expert on the theory of humanistic geography (Ley 1980, 1981; Ley and Samuels 1978), Ley stressed that he was also very much a social geographer, and his classic papers of 1977 and 1978 both had 'social geography' in their titles. His humanistic version of social geography arose from his doctoral research in the early 1970s (Ley 1974; see also Ley 1988), in the course of which he adopted the stance of an 'explorer' on an 'expedition' to inner-city Philadelphia, striving to discover something of the lives led by everyday people struggling to 'get by' in this run-down, often fearful place. In particular, he built up a picture of the 'existential space' (Ley 1974: 219) inherent to street gangs, their sense of belonging and security as attached to given 'turfs' covering specific city blocks, and he noted how acts such as spraying 'graffiti obscenities' at the margins of gang territories, and also more aggressive acts too, commonly tied into an identification with and defence of given turfs. Leading from this social geography of the inner city, and notably of Philadelphia street gangs, Ley strove to blend what he found 'on the streets' with the often abstract and obtuse claims of the philosophies of meaning. In outline, it was evident to him that he could not stop at the level of the unique individual, but nor could he jump to the universalizing claims of phenomenology and existentialism in their excavation of mental and even bodily realms far removed from the more everyday 'stuff' in people's heads (their everyday assumptions, notions, hopes and fears). He thus consulted the 'constitutive phenomenology' of Alfred Schutz, a philosopher who was unhappy with Edmund Husserl's search for the buried 'essences' of phenomena in the realm of transcendental reflection, and who thereby 'objected to Husserl's almost obsessive and at times exclusive concern with uncovering the "essences" of social phenomena, and proposed instead to investigate the way in which they were concealed by skeins of intersubjectively woven social meanings' (Gregory 1978: 126). Schutz concentrated on the meanings which really do drive human thoughts and actions, as constructed (or 'constituted') in the everyday routines, interactions, conversations and practices of people living, working and playing in *social* groups; in so doing, the emphasis of research shifted from singular subjectivities to plural intersubjectivities. For Ley, this meant examining the coming together of the subjectivities possessed by different members of identifiable groups, a process which facilitated the coalescence of shared meanings (Schutz talked of shared 'structures of meaning') as a storehouse of resources available to all group members in their own activities. These meanings may not be particularly recognized or reflected upon in a self-conscious fashion, and Ley (and Schutz) accented their 'taken-for-granted' character – another term in the title of one of Ley's papers from the late 1970s (Ley 1977). He then added the element of place to the picture, a simple but all-important acknowledgement that social groups such as gangs do not exist in some curious ether, but must always exist in a manner anchored to specific worldly places, as with gangs in their local turfs. These places serve both as material supports for social groups, the sites within which routine interactions occur, and as more immaterial reference points within the identities of groups and their members, as 'homes', centres of spiritual rest, nourishment, loathing and so on. Such a vision allowed for conflicts between different groups over the same places, with such groups clashing over using these places and over the symbolisms then attached to them, which meant that Ley's position was hardly a 'whimsical' geography devoid of attention to social groups, actions and conflicts. Furthermore it should be apparent that Ley's work introduced a fresh slant on geographers' conceptualizations of the social, calling on us to embrace the more subjective, experiential and even imaginative 'life-worlds' which cross-cut within, and sometimes fragment, the spaces of society.

Jackson and Smith's important 1984 text, *Exploring Social Geography*, engaged with the literature of humanistic geography when calling for a 'hermeneutic revival' in social geography, hermeneutics being the interpretation of meaning: 'a hermeneutic revival in which social geography re-emerges as an exploration of understanding to offer an *interpretation* of human experience in its social and spatial setting' (Jackson and Smith 1984: 20). By 'revival' they principally meant a return to aspects of Chicago school sociology, not the ecological models but the more engaged ethnographic research which some of these sociologists had conducted on the streets of Chicago, encountering communities and neighbourhoods which were the 'meaningful' reference points for local people in their everyday lives, experiences and grounded 'definitions of the situation' (Jackson and Smith 1984: chapter 4; Jackson 1984, 1985, 1988). Ley, too, had been influenced by the Chicago school ethnographies, and here we see social geography connected back to traditions of intensive qualitative research (participant observation, in-depth interviewing, even sensitive questionnaire survey work) in a manner which has since proved vital in shaping most of the sub-discipline's methodological practices at the close of the twentieth century (Cook and Crang 1995; Eyles and Smith 1988). At the same time, this call for an interpretative moment within social geography, echoed by David Smith (1988) and Ley (1988) himself, also entailed an adoption of 'semiotic' insights – in particular, drawing on the cultural ('interpretative') anthropology of Clifford Geertz (1973, 1983) – attentive to the 'webs of meaning' which are woven through any given social situation, creating a 'thick' layering of situated interpretations held by the participants and informing how they can then 'go on' in their dealings with the world. Furthermore such a move has prompted much more interest in the realm of culture, understood in the Geertzian sense 'as a series of signs and symbols which convey meaning' (Jackson and Smith 1984: 38), and here are the origins of that fusion between social geography and cultural geography which – beginning in Britain, where cultural geography has never possessed the distinct identity that it acquired in North America (see chapter 5) – can be seen now to have fostered a broader 'cultural turn' throughout all of human geography. We will return to this development in our closing remarks, but it is important to note here that this hybrid social-cultural geography, built out of humanistic geography through the contributions of Ley, Jackson and Smith and others (Cloke *et al.* 1991: 88–92), has elaborated our conceptions of the social enormously: clarifying that the social is also shot through with (immaterial) intersubjective cultural elements, meanings, understandings and interpretations which permeate into the relations, systems, structures and inequalities of the social as stressed in the radical social geographies.

The early 1980s in France corresponded to a self-conscious and organized attempt to institutionalize the sub-discipline of social geography, an attempt in which humanistic perspectives were central. The creation of two journals in the 1970s – apart from the already mentioned *L'Espace géographique* – signalled the aspiration of many French-speaking geographers to situate the discipline within the social sciences. Both established in 1976, *EspacesTemps* (founded by Jacques Lévy) redefined the object of geography as being '*l'espace social*', or social space, while *Hérodote* (founded by Yves Lacoste), in its first issue, suggested that to understand space was to understand power. The group around *EspacesTemps* proposed to ground a rethinking of geography around two elements: the first was a Marxian political economy, but the second was an alertness to the relations between objective and 'subjective, lived, conceived space'. Social space (*l'espace social*) (Alvarenga and Matcheff 1980) and 'lived space' (*l'espace vécu*) were the two key concepts for this blend of humanistic and radical geography as it took shape in the early 1980s. The relative popularity of the first notion (already used by Sorre in the 1950s) throughout intellectual circles of that period was the sign of a renewed concern for space in French sociology, crystallizing around the interdisciplinary journal, *Espaces et sociétés* (founded by Henri Lefebvre and Anatole Kopp in 1970), and featured in the work of authors like Raymond Ledrut (1977) and Jean Remy and Liliane Voyé (1974). The latter term was coined by Armand Frémont (1976) and the group of social geographers around him: '*L'espace vécu*' here referred to the dimensions of practice, social relations, perception and representation (Frémont 1980). It entailed – and here again his influence was very clear – what Lefebvre called, in his now nearly too famous distinction, 'spaces of representation' as opposed to 'representations of space' (which indexes a 'thingified', reductionist and objectivist *conception* of space).

This group of social geographers – Robert Hérin, Jacques Chevalier, Armand Frémont, André Vant and Guy Burgel – met their goal in that they finally succeeded in institutionalizing social geography as a sub-discipline in French geography. This was the result of a long process which included, first, the creation in 1973 of an interdisciplinary research group, Espaces vécus et civilisations, which pursued transcultural studies on the experience of space and place, and second, a research programme on social change launched at the end of the 1970s by the Centre National de Recherche Scientifique. An important conference in Lyon in 1982, a common book (Frémont *et al.* 1984) and a second conference in 1984 (Collectif français de géographie sociale et urbaine 1984) were additional initiatives that, despite the sarcasm of 'traditional geographers', managed to install social geography firmly on the French academic map. 'For the first time', wrote Frémont in 1984, 'at the end of this process social geography becomes a collective endeavour' (Frémont *et al.* 1984: 10). The importance of the theoretical contribution made by these social geographers is perhaps more disputable, as Robert Hérin observed, because 'as is often the case in French human geography, the practice of research precedes theoretical reflection, which remains implicit' (Hérin 1984: 23).

Questions must be asked, therefore, about the substance of this collectively defined social geography. According to Frémont *et al.*, social geographers should explore four dimensions of the human world: social indicators, social questions, social groups and socio-spatial combinations (Frémont *et al.* 1984: 121); and social geography was thus defined as: 'The exploration of the interrelations existing between social relations [relations between individuals] and spatial relations [relations between individuals and places] and more generally between societies and spaces' (Frémont *et al.* 1984: 90). The social and the spatial were envisioned as two distinct spheres entertaining 'dialectical relations'. The study of the first was the domain of sociology, that of the second was geography, and social geography was situated at their intersection. This approach, therefore, was yet another version of 'spatial separatism': instead of viewing space as a constitutive dimension of society, it revamped the spatial fetishism of spatial analysis. Such a vision of society and space in much of French-speaking social geography in the 1980s, and the conception of social geography that it implies, was symptomatic of the difficulty of addressing fundamental theoretical questions such as: what do we talk about when we use the notions of space, society, action? Is space not a constitutive part of society? In the 'lived space' school, for instance, there was surprisingly little discussion of the notion of 'life-world' as elaborated by German phenomenology. It is also significant that the important contribution to a phenomenology of space by Eric Dardel in 1952, *L'homme et la terre*, was only rediscovered and discussed in the late 1980s. In other words, there was no French-speaking equivalent to the 'philosophical turn' observable in Anglo-American geography from the mid-1970s into the 1980s, and the result is that categories of social theory – power, interaction, sociability – tended to be used throughout the 1980s in a loose and often unconvincing way (although whether this was really any different to what happened in Anglophone literature is another matter).

DISSOLVING SOCIAL GEOGRAPHIES AND 'CULTURALLY TURNED' SOCIAL GEOGRAPHIES

The landscape of human geography in the 1990s became a turbulent one in many ways; it was stimulating, to be sure, but it was also a landscape in which the multiplicity of theoretical possibilities, methodological innovations and substantive interests created a head-spinning mix for anyone attempting to delineate even its boldest contours (see also chapter 1). The radical impulses of the 1970s spawned a diversity of offshoots, curving towards all manner of debates over classical Marxism, structural Marxism and its variants, non-essentialist Marxism, regulation theory, regime theory and visions of radical democracy. Many of the geographers who might tentatively be framed as part of this 'post-Marxist geography' (Corbridge 1993) have been battling with what is for them the spectre of a theoretically, politically and ethically vacuous postmodernism, which sells out any sense of totality and coherence in favour of a relativistic 'anything goes' mentality (Harvey 1989). Others, though, have been seeking to reach an accommodation which aims to be constructive in enriching a radical perspective with insights from the postmodern critique concerning the irreducibility of difference, notably social difference. Recent strands within feminist geography have been prominent in suggesting ways of reaching a *rapprochement* between studies maintaining a highly political-ethical commitment attuned to both structural iniquities (under capitalism, heteropatriarchy and the heirs of 'orientalism') and contextual particularities (bound up with specific peoples, places, hopes and fears), and the writings of Doreen Massey must be cited as inspirational in this respect (Massey 1994; Gibson-Graham 1996; McDowell 1999). The humanistic impulses of the 1970s have similarly spawned a diversity of offshoots, with often fierce debates over identity politics, psychoanalysis, embodiment, performance and the constitution of the subject. Many of the geographers who might tentatively be framed as part of this 'post-humanistic geography' (Barnes and Gregory 1997: 359–60) have actually adopted a post-structural (and maybe an 'actor-network') stance, veering towards an *anti*-humanism, suspicious of claims about the pre-given sovereignty of the human subject and preferring instead to regard human beings as contingent socio-spatial achievements sitting at the intersection of multiple planes of identity, and also questioning the extent to which humans are so different from other beings in the world (Hinchliffe 1999; Laurier and Philo 1999; Wilbert 1999). All sorts of further questions are emerging for such geographers about the geographies wrapped up in the everyday nature of interactions and practices, as in the turn of some to so-called 'non-representational' theories and an interest in the routine acts of being, doing and saying which enable people to get by on a daily basis. Nigel Thrift and his students at Bristol are at the forefront of such developments with respect to the being and doing components (Thrift 1996, 1997, 1999a and b), while interest in the saying can be found in various studies by Lorenza Mondada, a Swiss linguist and quasi-geographer, together with one of the authors of this chapter, in the course of several interactionist studies of cities and urban planning (Mondada and Söderström 1993a and b; Söderström 1994). These authors have described the interpretative strategies of urban actors using conversational analysis, an offspring of ethnomethodology, and their work can be bracketed together with an English-speaking parallel in the work of Eric Laurier (1996, 1999).

All the positions mentioned by name (and more besides) have implications for understanding the social, conceptualizing how the social and the geographical intersect and, more narrowly, for the ideas and practices of social geography. It would be feasible to trace all these implications in systematic fashion, but to do so would necessitate a much longer chapter (indeed probably several books) and cleverer authors. Nonetheless we will draw the chapter to a close by rehearsing one particular line of argument that has begun to be voiced about the fate of social geography in the 1990s, as connected to that broader move throughout human geography now widely labelled the 'cultural turn' (Barnett 1998b and c). While this phrase has sometimes been used loosely in lumping together many of the above-mentioned *fin-de-siècle* currents (Johnston 1997: chapter 8), a narrower account would suggest that such a turn encompasses attempts within geography to take seriously the cultural 'stuff' of human life, not only phenomena routinely designated as cultural (e.g. 'highbrow' arts and 'lowbrow' media), but also the complete panorama of meaning systems, both collective (e.g. religions and nationalisms) and more individual (residing in personal psychic worlds). (A more sustained discussion of culture, cultural phenomena and cultural geography is to be found in chapter 5.) In Britain, an early index of this development was an 'initiative' pursued in 1990–1 by the Social and Cultural Geography Study Group of the Institute of British Geographers, the prompt for which was an emerging sense that it was time to rethink the relations of the social and the cultural. Following a conference and a publication (Philo 1991b), it became apparent that there was 'something happening' within social geography, paralleling and contributing to a wider move throughout human geography, the crux of which appeared to be the inserting of a cultural sensibility into the heart of both the sub-discipline and the parent discipline. While we are probably being too simplistic here, a few commentators, including ourselves, have become concerned that this 'enculturing' of social geography – while clearly having many significant gains – is also now posing certain threats to treatments of the social by geographers generally and also to social geography. In stressing the importance of the cultural as understood by cultural theorists and cultural anthropologists, as 'webs of meaning' saturated with representations, significations and imaginations, these 'culturally turned' geographies risk becoming too immaterial in their emphases and, thereby, too divorced from terrains that would be regarded more conventionally as social. There are dangers here of a *dematerializing* of human geography which at the same time amounts to a *desocializing* of human geography (Philo 2000).

In an introduction to the writings from the 1990–1 initiative mentioned above, one of the present authors did worry 'that a process originating in rethinking "the social" had ended up (ironically enough) spawning a "cultural turn" in which "the social" itself becomes completely deconstructed' (Philo 1991a: 3). Similarly, when reflecting on this initiative, Nicky Gregson (1993: 528–9) declared that, '[r]ather than rethinking the social, then, it is the social itself which is being deconstructed in the current reflexive phase'. Moreover, she expressed her concern about the geographers involved slipping into an 'in-house dialogue', couched almost solely in abstracted realms of theory and representational politics, and with them 'redefining their project so as to exclude empirical social worlds and the others who are seen to constitute them' (Gregson 1993: 529). These are strong claims, which may need some qualification, particularly given the rich vein of ongoing social-geographical research on a whole range of 'other peoples' and their 'other worlds', but Gregson's concern about losing a more substantive grip on the constitution, conflicts and comprehension of everyday 'empirical social worlds' is one with which we do have some sympathy. Intriguingly, this would be a loss, reversing what various different social geographers have argued for over the years, in which case, a measure of coherence can be detected after all in the diverse contributions of Vidal, Gilbert and Steel, Wreford Watson, D. M. Smith, Harvey, Ley, Jackson and S. J. Smith and countless others, all of whom have at some point anchored their inquiries in everyday 'empirical social worlds' (however they might then have theorized them). Pamela Shurmer-Smith (1996: v) has echoed such criticisms when introducing a collection of postgraduate essays in social and cultural geography with the objection that 'there seemed to be so much *culture* and so little *society*' in the essays, and when lamenting that '[t]here is remarkably little solid sociological work going on in cultural geography today'. Yet her concerns in this respect were also tempered with a strong belief that new advances can still be made, new meetings between the social and the cultural forged in the production of high quality and worthwhile human geography, provided that postgraduate students – and by extension all scholars – keep talking to each other:

> . . . perhaps, if we can make sure that there is more genuine sharing of ideas between young researchers, these problems will solve themselves. It is too much solitary work that leads to academic sterility and the best ideas always occur in dialogue.
>
> (Shurmer-Smith 1996: vi)

This vision may return us to Kimble's clamour of geographical voices, admittedly not always speaking 'in unison or in harmony' (Kimble 1951: 151), but social geography will probably only be saved from dissolving itself by the many partial and even fractious dialogues, provided that they are not too 'in-house', which we fully expect to continue echoing into the new century.

Conclusion, or an introduction to human geography in the 21st century

Georges Benko and Ulf Strohmayer

This conclusion is conceived not as the traditional summary but as an opening of sorts: arbitrary though centennial divides undoubtedly are, geographers everywhere at the beginning of the twenty-first century have embarked upon novel ways of interpreting the world that wed many elements of bygone days to newly coined concepts, ideas and forms of organizing knowledge. What is more, the beginning of the new century denotes an enviable position for human geographers: if arguably many periods in the twentieth century were characterized by a one-sided form of knowledge transfer from cognate disciplines to human geography, today's sociology, economics and cultural studies all employ insights and concepts originally developed by geographers.

Although this development has yet to create a more widespread positive appreciation of geography as a discipline, the positions occupied and the concepts coined by geographers have attracted commentaries in many places. The 'spatial turn' that followed in postmodern footsteps has clearly become a sign of its time, and a welcome one for anyone working in geography. Any of the lists of defining concepts, ideas and problems that litter the contemporary intellectual and political landscape will give more than a passing flavour of this recognition of 'space' as a key to many present-day debates: from globalization to the revival of ethnic and cultural conflicts, from global ecological debates to unfettered processes of urbanization, there is a renewed geographical awareness that characterizes the flow of knowledge and networks of power – geography is more present than ever in these debates due to the development of spatial 'reflexes' across the social and human sciences and the accompanying opening up of geographic discourses towards neighbouring disciplines. Compared with the inward-looking perspective that – however indirectly – led to the closure of key departments in the USA during the second half of the twentieth century, this is a most welcome development.

Crucially, the recent recognition of geography as an intellectually vibrant discipline was hindered neither by methodological eclecticism nor by the lack of a unified and recognizable focus; the presence of important topics, the coining of relevant concepts and perhaps the occurrence of heated theoretical debates did suffice to rectify a none too glowing image of the discipline at large. In light of the above observation, however, it would be all too simplistic to attribute the changing fortunes of a particular way of thinking to changes in the conceptual apparatus developed and employed by its practitioners. Even though the use and suitability of concepts is at least partly driven by changes in intellectual fashion, concepts themselves never really come to a standstill either: they derive their explanatory power to a large extent from the context that surrounds them – and if this latter changes, concepts change too. A 'landscape', to use a common enough conceptual warhorse in geographic analyses throughout the twentieth century, can be a descriptive concept, can denote drawn-out geographical processes or point to the constructed nature of our mostly visual forms of knowledge. But whatever concepts geographical curiosities adopt, their history is always already there – unless one were to pin one's hopes to the mast of neologisms and continuously invest in the creation of new concepts (and run the risks associated with solipsism instead).

Deprived of similarly short-lived conceptual revolutions, human geographers thus can only profit from being critically aware of their own history. If nothing else, such an awareness will enlarge the scope for future insights and hence contribute to more nuanced insights. While we see little to be gained from speculating about the concrete shape of this future, we notice encouraging signs everywhere, of which the renewed acceptance of geographical thinking in academia, the media and political circles is but the metaphorical icing on the cake. We should like to conclude this book with a cursory glance at some recent developments, which in our opinion support an optimistic interpretation of any future human geography.

To begin with, the twentieth century witnessed a dramatic broadening of the field of geographic research. This expansion has accelerated even more, especially during the last 30 years, and continues unabatedly. It is true that similar expansions in disciplinary scope have characterized most human and social sciences throughout the last century. Geography is different, however, in that it never really had a core identity beyond its rather vague and amorphous spatial concern. To claim that geography 'was about space' in the same way that history 'was about time' was never to say very much; once the colonial use-value attached to the institutionally formative years of the discipline had retreated into the background, this lack of a clear legitimation for the 'synthetic' character of geography could lead to despair or liberation. It is largely due to the creativity of its practitioners that geography has come to where it is today: opting for breadth over a narrowly defined turf, geographers the world over managed to retain a particular spatial angle, even while no topic was immune to geographical analysis. While some lament the non-specialized characteristics of many resultant insights, others celebrate the survival of 'renaissance' forms of knowledge. But whatever one's taste, since the world has become an increasingly complex and interrelated structure, the need for a synthesizing discipline like geography is now more urgently felt across and beyond academia. If geography is indeed 'everywhere', as geographers commonly believe and assert, it is virtually impossible reasonably to eliminate anything from the realm of the geographically relevant. It goes without saying that even a celebration of any resultant synthesis rarely ever marks the work of one woman or man, with teamwork having become more of a norm these days. At the same time, we need to acknowledge the help and influence of technologies in the representation and analyses of an expanded geographical domain: data storage facilities, extended forms of photographic memory or GIS possibilities all contribute to an increase in the scope of geographical knowledge production.

Hand-in-hand with this very pronounced expansion in scope and aspirations went a literal explosion in the field of methods. If nineteenth-century geography was chiefly characterized by often detailed forms of description, and the twentieth century witnessed a prolonged move towards analysis, the beginning of the twenty-first century has seen a shift towards interpretation across the discipline. The ensuing effort to incorporate qualitative, ethnographic and visual methodologies into the already established canon of narrative and quantitative methods added considerable scope to the possibilities of writing geographies. The key here was less the acknowledgement that different methods were practised within geography than the often merely implicit (but no less powerful) justification of different methods occupying a level playing field. As a result, anyone embarking upon a new research project today – from the comparatively humble M.Phil. to any externally financed, large-scale comparative project – faces a plethora of choices in the methodological realm; choices, we should stress, which often refer not to mutually exclusive goals, but rather complement one another. It almost seems that the more we know about the context-dependency of knowledge, the less we are satisfied by any 'one size fits all' type of methodological approach.

Chief among the more specific changes we take to be the outspoken acknowledgment of the *complexity* of geographic phenomena. Largely gone are the days where the reduction towards unified principles, the selection of a priori concepts or mechanized models of human behaviour dictated preferences amongst geographers. The rise of 'culturally' inspired modes of analysis, the assimilation of 'actor-network' theories or the development of notions like 'social nature' (just to mention some of the more central of recent acknowledgements of 'complexity' that have been discussed in human geography), all share an aversion to reductionism of any kind. As a result, the discipline has witnessed a decline in the number of bold and simple debates, which gave way to more subtle and involved discussions. While this development is welcomed by most geographical practitioners, we are tempted to note that 'complexity' can become a mantra of sorts: where everything is held to be 'complex' as a matter of principle, we stand to lose sight of the possibility even of non-complex forms of determination. However, the fact that geographers have begun to think about complex structures and open-ended systems is more than merely encouraging: it facilitates the kind of discussion that is urgently required in a world that is suffering still from the consequences of reductionist forms of science on a grand scale.

Mention of complexity conveniently allows us to introduce a fourth key change that encourages confidence in the future within the geographical community. This adjustment concerns the rigid distinction between theory and practice, which has been eroded gradually by developments since (and including) the quantitative revolution of the 1960s. This has had far-reaching consequences, not merely for the role of theory in geographical practice, but also in terms of how it has affected distinctions across the board of the discipline. From the time-honoured differentiation between idiographic and nomothetic approaches to the less prominent but equally important delineation between nature and culture, geographers today see little to be gained from separating empirical matter from theoretical concerns or interests. On the contrary, establishing links is increasingly seen to be a mutually beneficial affair; the discipline is richer as a result of these cross-fertilizations.

A fifth development addresses a marked shift in how the *relevance* of geographical knowledge is established. Used as an external criterion that more often than not came down like a sledgehammer to evaluate the social use-value of knowledge after it had been produced, 'relevance' in the twenty-first century appears to be more akin to implementation and praxis. The retreat from the ivory towers of old has led to a renewed emphasis on questions of democracy, governance and citizenship across the geographic community. In this context, the inclusion of hitherto excluded topics such as geographies of gender, sexuality, homelessness and mobility (to name but a few) has certainly contributed to the increased importance and application of geographical knowledge to contemporary societies. 'Relevance', in other words, is no longer regarded as a criterion external to the construction of scientific knowledge, but evolves from within concrete existing scientific practices.

Finally, we see our sense of optimism being founded by a fairly recent but marked shift away from establishing necessarily partial claims of objectivity towards embodied and positioned forms of geographical knowledge. We are encouraged by these developments because they help to reposition scientific responsibility where it belongs: with the researcher instead of a set of external components, be they methodological, theoretical or topological. While the accompanying danger of a self-absorbed, indeed solipsist, form of science is quite real and has been noted by some, we see no alternative to the paths now taken: especially within a science that is itself positioned a notch 'above' the intimacy provided by more specialized forms of scientific practice, the danger of usurping a position in no man's land appears to us be far greater than the occasional forms of self-indulgence. Acknowledging one's partialities and becoming aware of the context surrounding and permeating one's production of knowledge also brings with it the welcome erosion of previously accepted positions of power: rather than relying on externally established yardsticks (academic rank, size of grants or the prestige of institutions, to name but a few), the validity of any claim to knowledge now has to be worked through and constituted by its own produced contextuality.

Taken together, these recent developments in the world of human geography – which also attach to the world of geography at large – may well represent a unique set of conditions for future advances. Not all will be welcomed and not every advance will be recognized in its own time, but we are reassured in the sense that many interesting developments have taken place already and will continue to emanate from the discipline of geography. We look forward to such changes.

BIBLIOGRAPHY

Abler, R., 1999, 'Geography then and now', *Annals of the Association of American Geographers*, vol. 89, no. 1, 144–5.

Abler, R., Adams, J. S. and Gould, P., 1971, *Spatial Organization: the geographer's view of the world*, Englewood Cliffs, NJ: Prentice-Hall.

Ackerman, E. A., 1958, 'Geography as fundamental research discipline', University of Chicago, Department of Geography Research Paper no. 53.

Agnew, J., 1997, 'Places and the politics of identities', in Agnew, J. (ed.), *Political Geography: a reader*, New York: Arnold, 249–55.

Agnew, J., 1997, *Political Geography: a reader*, London: Arnold.

Agnew, J., 1998, *Geopolitics: revisioning world politics*, London: Routledge.

Agnew, J. and Brusa, C., 1999, 'New rules for national identity? The Northern League and political identity in contemporary Northern Italy', *National Identities*, vol. 1, 117–33.

Agnew, J. and Corbridge, S., 1995, *Mastering Space: hegemony, territory and international political economy*, London: Routledge.

Ajo, R., 1953, *Contributions to 'Social Physics': a programme sketch with special regard to national planning*, Lund: Gleerups, Lund Studies in Geography, Series B (Human Geography).

Ajo, R., 1955, *An Analysis of Automobile Frequencies in a Human Geographic Continuum*, Lund: Gleerups, Lund Studies in Geography, Series B (Human Geography).

Alegria, M. F., Garcia, J. C. and Relaño, F., 1998, 'Cartografia e viagens', in Bethancourt, F. and Chaudhuri, K. (eds.), *História da expansão portuguesa*, Lisbon: Círculo de Leitores, 26–61.

Alexander, J., 1990, 'Analytic debates: understanding the relative autonomy of culture', in Alexander, J. and Seidman, S. (eds.), *Culture and Society: contemporary debates*, Cambridge: Cambridge University Press, 1–27.

Alonso, W., 1965, *Location and Land Use: toward a general theory of land rent*, Cambridge, MA: Harvard University Press.

Alvarenga, A. and Malcheff, J., 1980, 'L'espace social, nouveau paradigme?', *Espaces et sociétés*, vols. 34–5, 47–74.

Amin, S., 1973, *Le Développement inégal; essai sur les formations sociales du capitalisme périphérique*, Paris: Les Éditions de Minuit.

Anderson, K., 1993, *Vancouver's Chinatown: racial discourse in Canada 1875–1980*, Montreal: McGill-Queens University Press.

Anderson, K. and Gale, F. (eds.), 1992, *Inventing Places: studies in cultural geography*, Melbourne: Longman Cheshire.

Anon., 1963, 'An A is an A', *Time Magazine*, 22 February, 24.

Aydalot, P., 1985, *Économie régionale et urbaine*, Paris: Economica.

Aydalot, P., 1986, *Milieux innovateurs en Europe*, Paris: GREMI, 345–61.

Bagnasco, A., 1977, *Tre Italie: la Problematica Territoriale dello Sviluppo Italiano*, Bolgna: Il Mulino.

Bailey, T. C. and Gatrell, A. C., 1995, *Interactive Spatial Data Analysis*, London: Addison-Wesley Longman.

Bailly, A., 1975, *L'Organisation urbaine*, Paris: Centre de Recherche Urbaine.

Bailly, A., 1981, *Percevoir l'espace: vers une géographie de l'espace vécu. Actes de la Table Ronde de géographie de la perception*, Geneva: Université de Genève, Département de géographie.

Baker, A. R. H., 1972, 'Rethinking historical geography', in Baker, A. R. H. (ed.), *Progress in Historical Geography*, Newton Abbott: David & Charles, 11–28.

Baker, A. R. H., 1992, 'Introduction: on ideology and landscape', in Baker, A. R. H. and Biger, G. (eds.), *Ideology and Landscape in Historical Perspective*, Cambridge: Cambridge University Press, 1–14.

Balchin, W., 1987, 'United Kingdom geographers in the Second World War', *Geographical Journal*, vol. 153, 159–80.

Baltensperger, B. H., 1992, 'Plains boomers and the creation of the Great American Desert' *Journal of Historical Geography*, vol. 18, 59–73.

Bancroft Library Archives, Correspondence between Carl Sauer, John Leighly and Richard Hartshorne.

Barlow, I. M., 1991, *Metropolitan Government*, London: Routledge.

Barnes, T. J., 1984, 'Theories of agricultural rent within the surplus approach', *International Review of Regional Science*, 9, 125–40.

Barnes, T., 1994, 'Probable writing: Derrida, deconstruction and the quantitative revolution in human geography', *Environment and Planning A*, vol. 26, 7–35.

Barnes, T. J., 2000, 'Inventing Anglo-American economic geography, 1889–1960', in Sheppard, E. and Barnes, T. J. (eds.), *A Companion to Economic Geography*, Oxford: Blackwell, 11–26.

Barnes, T. and Duncan, J., 1992, 'Introduction: writing worlds', in Barnes, T. and Duncan, J. (eds.), *Writing Worlds: discourse, text and metaphor in the representation of landscape*, London: Routledge, 1–17.

Barnes, T. J. and Duncan, J. S. (eds.), 1992, *Writing Worlds: discourse, text, and metaphor in the representation of landscape*, London: Routledge.

Barnes, T. and Gregory, D. (eds.), 1997, *Reading Human Geography: the poetics and politics of inquiry*, London: Edward Arnold.

Barnes, T. J. and Sheppard, E., 1984, 'Technical choice and reswitching in space economies', *Regional Science and Urban Economics*, 14, 345–62.

Barnett, C., 1997, '"Sing along with the common people": politics, postcolonialism and other figures', *Environment and Planning D: Society and Space*, vol. 15, 137–54.

Barnett, C., 1998a, 'Impure and worldly geography: the Africanist discourse of the Royal Geographical Society, 1831–1871', *Transactions of the Institute of British Geographers*, vol. 23, 239–51.

Barnett, C., 1998b, 'The cultural worm turns: fashion or progress in human geography', *Antipode*, vol. 30, 379–94.

Barnett, C., 1998c, 'Cultural twists and turns', *Environment and Planning D: Society and Space*, vol. 16, 631–4.

Barnett, C., 2001, 'Cultural geography and the arts of government', *Environment and Planning D: Society and Space*, vol. 19, no. 1, 7–24.

Barrell, J., 1980, *The Dark Side of the Landscape*, Cambridge: Cambridge University Press.

Barrows, H. H., 1923, 'Geography as human ecology', *Annals of the Association of American Geographers*, vol. 13, 1–14.

Bartels, D., 1969, 'Der Harmoniebegriff', *Die Erde*, vol. 100, 124–37.

Bassin, M., 1987a, 'Friedrich Ratzel', *Geographers: bio-bibliographical studies*, vol. 11, 123–32.

Bassin, M., 1987b, 'Race contra space. The conflict between German Geopolitik and National Socialism', *Political Geography Quarterly*, vol. 6, 115–34.

Bassin, M., 1991a, 'Inventing Siberia: visions of the Russian east in the early 19th century', *American Historical Review*, vol. 96, 763–94.

Bassin, M., 1991b, 'Russia between Europe and Asia: the ideological construction of geographical space', *Slavic Review*, vol. 50, 1–17.

Bassin, M., 1992, 'Geographical determinism in *fin-de-siècle* Marxism: Georgii Plekhanov and the environmental basis of Russian history', *Annals of the Association of American Geographers*, vol. 82, 3–22.

Bassin, M., 1993, 'Turner, Solov'ev, and the "Frontier Hypothesis": the nationalist signification of open spaces', *Journal of Modern History*, vol. 65, 473–511.

Bassin, M., 1996, 'Nature, geopolitics and Marxism: ecological contestations in Weimar Germany', *Transactions of the Institute of British Geographers*, vol. 21(NS), 315–41.

Bassin, M., 1999, *Imperial Visions: nationalist imagination and geographical expansion in the Russian Far East 1840–1865*, Cambridge: Cambridge University Press.

Bassin, M., 2000, '"I object to rain that is cheerless": landscape art and the Stalinist aesthetic imagination', *Ecumene*, vol. 7, 253–76.

Battersbury, S. *et al.*, 1997, 'Environmental transformations in developing countries: hybrid research and democratic practices', *Geographical Journal*, vol. 163, 126–32.

Beaujeu-Garnier, J., 1980, *Géographie urbaine*, Paris: Armand Colin.

Beaujeu-Garnier, J., 1983, 'Autobiographical essay', in Buttimer, A. (ed.), *The Practice of Geography*, London: Longman, 141–52.

Becattini, G., 1987, *Mercato e forze locali: il distretto industriale*, Bologna: Il Mulino.

Becker, B. K. and Miranda, M. (eds.), 1997, *A geografica politica do desenvolvimento sustentavel*, Rio de Janeiro: Editora UFRJ.

Bell, D. and Valentine, G., 1995, *Mapping Desire: geographies of sexualities*, London: Routledge.

Bell, D. and Valentine, G., 1997, *Consuming Geographies: we are where we eat*, London: Routledge.

Ben-Artzi, Y., 1992, 'Religious ideology and landscape formation: the case of the German Templars in Eretz-Israel', in Baker, A. R. H. and Biger, G. (eds.), *Ideology and Landscape in Historical Perspective*, Cambridge: Cambridge University Press, 83–106.

Benko, G., 1991, *Géographie des technopôles*, Paris: Masson.

Benko, G. B., 1997, 'Introduction: modernity, postmodernity and the social sciences', in Benko, G. B. and Strohmayer, U. (eds.), *Space and Social Theory*, Oxford: Blackwell, 1–48.

Benko, G. and Lipietz, A. (eds.), 1992, *Les Régions qui gagnent. Districts et réseaux: les nouveaux paradigmes de la géographie économique*, Paris: Presses Universitaires de France.

Benko, G. and Lipietz, A., 1995, 'De la régulation des espaces aux espaces de la régulation', in Boyer, R. and Saillard, Y. (eds.), *Théorie de la régulation: l'état des savoirs*, Paris: La Découverte, 293–303.

Berdoulay, V., 1981, [Editions du CTHS] *La Formation de l'école française de géographie (1870–1914)*, Paris: Bibliothèque nationale.

Berdoulay, V., 1988, *Des Mots et des lieux. La dynamique du discours géographique*, Paris: CNRS Éditions.

Berdoulay, V., 1993, 'La géographie vidalienne: entre texte et contexte', in Claval, P. (ed.), *Autour de Vidal*, Paris: CNRS Éditions, 19–26.

Berdoulay, V., [1981] 1995a, *La Formation de l'école française de géographie (1870–1914)*, Paris: Editions du CTHS.

Berdoulay, V. (ed.), 1995b, *Les Pyrénées, lieux d'interaction des savoirs (XIXe–début XXe siècles)*, Paris: Editions du CTHS.

Berdoulay, V., 1999, 'Géographie culturelle et liberté', in Pitte, J.-R. and Sanguin, A.-L. (eds.), *Géographie et liberté*, Paris: L'Harmattan, 567–73.

Berdoulay, V., 2000, 'Le retour du refoulé, ou les avatars modernes du récit géographique', in Lévy, J. and Lussault, M. (eds.), *Logique de l'espace, esprit des lieux*, Paris: Belin, 111–26.

Berdoulay, V. and Bielza de Ory, V., 2000, 'Pour une relecture de l'urbanisme médiéval: processus transpyrénéens d'innovation et de diffusion', *Sud-ouest européen*, vol. 8, 75–81.

Berdoulay, V. and Entrikin, J. N., 1998, 'Lieu et sujet. Perspectives théoriques', *L'Espace géographique*, vol. 27, 111–21.

Berdoulay, V. and Gomez Mendoza, J. (eds.), 1998, *Travel, Circulation, and Transfer of Ideas (19th–20th c.)*, special issue of *Finisterra*, Lisbon.

Berdoulay, V. and Sénécal, G., 1993, 'Pensée aménagiste et discours de la colonisation au Québec', *Géographe canadien (Canadian Geographer)*, vol. 37, 28–40.

Berdoulay, V., Sénécal, G. and Soubeyran, O., 1996, 'Colonisation, aménagement et géographie: convergences franco-québécoises (1850–1920)', in Berdoulay, V. and Ginkel, J. A. van (eds.), *Geography and Professional Practice*, Utrecht: Nederlandse Geografische Studies, 153–69.

Berdoulay V. and Soubeyran O., 1991, 'Lamarck, Darwin et Vidal: aux fondements naturalistes de la géographie', *Annales de géographie*, vol. 100, 617–34.

Berdoulay, V. and Soubeyran, O., 2000, *Milieu, colonisation et développement durable. Perspectives géographiques sur l'aménagement*, Paris: L'Harmattan.

Bergman, E. F., 1975, *Modern Political Geography*, Dubuque, IA: William Brown.

Berlin, I., 1999, *The Roots of Romanticism*, Princeton, NJ: Princeton University Press.

Bermingham, A., 1986, *Landscape and Ideology: the English rustic tradition*, Berkeley, CA: University of California Press.

Berque, A., 1990, *Médiance: de milieux en paysage*, Montpellier: RECLUS.

Berry, B., 1966, 'Essays on commodity flow and the spatial structure of the Indian economy', University of Chicago, Department of Geography Research Paper no. 3.

Berry, B., 1967, *Geography of Market Centers and Retail Distribution*, Englewood Cliffs, NJ: Prentice-Hall.

Berry, B. 1969, 'Review of Russett, B. M. international regions and the international system', *Geographical Review*, vol. 59, 450–1.

Berry, B. and Garrison, W. L., 1958a, 'Functional bases of the central place hierarchy', *Economic Geography*, 34, 145–54.

Berry, B. and Garrison, W. L., 1958b, 'Recent development of central place theory', *Papers and Proceedings of the Regional Science Association*, 4, 107–20.

Berry, B. and Garrison, W. L., 1958c, 'A note on central place theory and the range of a good', *Economic Geography*, vol. 34, 304–11.

Bertrand, M.-J., 1978, *Pratique de la ville*, Paris: Masson.

Bertrand, J.-R. and Chevalier, J. (eds.), 1998, *Logement et habitat dans les villes européennes*, Paris: L'Harmattan.

Biger, G., 1992, 'Ideology and the landscape of British Palestine', in Baker, A. R. H. and Biger, G. (eds.), *Ideology and Landscape in Historical Perspective*, Cambridge: Cambridge University Press, 173–96.

Billinge, M., 1977, 'In search of negativism: phenomenology and historical geography', *Journal of Historical Geography*, vol. 3, 55–68.

Billinge, M., Gregory, D. and Martin, R. (eds.), 1984, *Recollections of a Revolution*, London: Macmillan.

Bingham, N., 1996, 'Object-ions: from technological determinism towards geographies of relations', *Environment and Planning D: Society and Space*, vol. 14, 635–58.

Blache, J., 1934, *L'Homme et la montagne*, Paris: Gallimard.

Blanchard, R., 1912, *Grenoble, étude de géographie urbaine*, Paris: Armand Colin.

Blanchard, R., 1934, *La Géographie de l'industrie*, Montreal: Editions Beauchemin.

Blij, H. J. de, 1967, *Systematic Political Geography*, New York: Wiley.

Bloch, M., 1931, *Les Caractères originaux de l'histoire rurale française*, Oslo: Institut pour l'Étude comparée des Civilisations.

Blomley, N., 1994, *Law, Space and the Geographies of Power*, New York: Guilford Press.

Blouet, B. W. and Lawson, M. P. (eds.), 1975, *Images of the Plains: the role of human nature in settlement*, Lincoln, NE: University of Nebraska Press.

Boal, F., 1969, 'Territoriality on the Shankhill-Falls divide, Belfast', *Irish Geography*, vol. 6, 30–50.

Boaz, F., 1928, *Anthropology and Modern Life*, New York: Norton.

Bobeck, H., 1948, 'Stellung und Bedeutung der Sozialgeographie', *Erdkunde*, vol. 2, 118–25.

Bondi, L., 1995, 'Locating identity politics', in Keith, M. and Pile, S., *Place and the Politics of Identity*, London: Routledge.

Bondi, L. and Domosh, M., 1992, 'Other figures in other landscapes: on feminism, postmodernism and geography', *Environment and Planning D: Society and Space*, vol. 10, 199–213.

Borchert, J., 1961, 'The Twin Cities urbanised area: past, present and future', *Geographical Review*, vol. 51, 47–70.

Bordo, S., 1990, 'Feminism, post-modernism and gender scepticism', in Nicholson, L. (ed.), *Feminism/Postmodernism*, London: Routledge.

Borts, G. and Stein, J., 1964, *Economic Growth in a Free Market*, New York: Columbia University Press.

Boudeville, J.-R. and Antoine, S., 1968, *L'Espace et les pôles de croissance, recherches et textes fondamentaux*, Paris: Presses Universitaires de France.

Bourdieu, P., 1972, *Esquisse d'une théorie de la pratique*, Geneva: Librairie Droz.

Bousquet-Bressolier, C. (ed.), 1995, *L'Oeil du cartographe et la représentation du Moyen Age à nos jours*, Paris: Editions du CTHS.

Bowden, M. J., 1969, 'The perception of the western interior of the United States, 1800–1870: a problem in historical geosophy', *Proceedings, Association of American Geographers*, vol. 1, 267–76.

Bowden, M. J., 1975, 'The Great American Desert in the American mind: the historiography of a geographical notion', in Lowenthal, D. and Bowden, M. J. (eds.), *Geographies of the Mind: essays in historical geosophy in honor of John Kirkland Wright*, New York: Oxford University Press, 119–48.

Bowman, I., 1922, *The New World. Problems in political geography*, New York: World Book Company.

Boyer, R., 1986, *La Théorie de la régulation: une analyse critique*, Paris: Algalma.

Braudel, F., 1951, 'La géographie face aux sciences humaines', *Annales économies, sociétés et civilisations*, vol. 16, 485–92.

Braudel, F., 1967, *Civilisation matérielle et capitalisme*, Paris: Armand Colin.

Braudel, F., 1969, *Écrits sur l'histoire*, Paris: Flammarion.

Braudel, F., 1979, *Civilisation materielle, économie, et capitalisme, XVe–XVIIIe siècle*, 3 vols., Paris: Armand Colin.

Brewer, C. (ed.), 1999, 'The state of U.S. cartography', *Journal of the American Congress of Surveying and Mapping*, vol. 26, no. 3.

Brewer, C. and McMaster, R., 1999, 'The state of academic geography', in Brewer, C. (ed.), *Journal of the American Congress on Surveying and Mapping*, vol. 26, no. 3, 215–34.

Broek, J., 1932, *The Santa Clara Valley, California: a study in landscape changes*, Utrecht: A. Oosthoeck.

Brook, C. H. R., 1995, 'The drive to global regions', in Anderson, J., Brook, C. and Cochrane, A. (eds.), *A Global World? Re-ordering political space*, Oxford: Oxford University Press, 113–65.

Brown, R. H., 1943, *Mirror for Americans. Likeness of the Eastern Seaboard, 1810*, New York: American Geographical Society.

Bruneau, M. and Dory, D. (eds.), 1994, *Géographies de la colonisation, XVe–XXe siècles*, Paris: L'Harmattan.

Bruneau, M., Durand-Lasserve, A. and Moline, M., 1977, 'La Thaïlande. Analyse d'un espace national', *L'Espace géographique*, vol. 3, 179–94.

Brunet, R., 1990–6, *Géographie universelle*, Montpellier: Hachette.

Brunhes, J., 1904, *L'Irrigation. Ses conditions géographiques, ses modes et son organisation*, Paris: Masson.

Brunhes, J., 1906, 'Une géographie nouvelle. La géographie humaine', *Revue des deux mondes*, vol. 33, 541–74.

Brunhes, J., 1909, *La Géographie humaine*, 3 vols., Paris: Félix Alcan.

Brunhes, J., 1910, *La Géographie humaine: essai de classification positive: principes et exemples*, Paris: Félix Alcan; (trans.) 1920, *Human Geography: an attempt at a positive classification – principles and examples*, London: Harrap & Co.

Brunhes, J., 1913, 'Du caractère propre et du caractère complexe des faits de géographie humaine', *Annales de géographie*, vol. 22, 1–40.

Brunhes, J., 1956, *La Géographie humaine*, Paris: Presses Universitaires de France.

Brunhes, J. and Vallaux, C., 1921, *La Géographie de l'histoire. Géographie de la paix et de la guerre sur terre et sur mer*, Paris: Félix Alcan.

Brusco, S., 1982, 'The Emilian model: productive decentralization and social integration', *Cambridge Journal of Economics*, 6, 167–80.

Buckle, H. T., 1857–61, *History of Civilization in England*, London: J. W. Parker.

Bunge, W., 1962, 'Theoretical Geography', Lund: Department of Geography research paper.

Bunge, W., 1971, *Fitzgerald: the geography of a revolution*, Cambridge, MA: Schenkman.

Burgess, E. W., 1924, 'The growth of the city: an introduction to a research project', *Publications of the American Sociological Society*, vol. 18, 85–97.

Burghardt, A. F., 1969, 'The core concept in political geography: a definition of terms', *Canadian Geographer*, vol. 63, 349–53.

Burghardt, A. F., 1973, 'The bases of territorial claims', *Geographical Review*, vol. 63, 225–45.

Burnett, A. D. and Taylor, P. J. (eds.), 1981, *Political Studies from Spatial Perspectives*, New York: Wiley.

Burton, I., 1963, 'The quantitative revolution and theoretical geography', *Canadian Geographer*, vol. 7, 151–62.

Buttimer, A., 1971, *Society and Milieu in the French Geographical Tradition*, Chicago, IL: Randy McNally.

Buttimer, A., 1974, *Values in Geography*, Washington, D.C.: Association of American Geographers, Resource Paper 24.

Buttimer, A. (ed.), 1992, *History of Geographical Thought*, special issue of *GeoJournal*, vol. 26.

Buttimer, A., 1993, *Geography and the Human Spirit*, Baltimore, MD: Johns Hopkins University Press.

Buttimer, A., Brunn, S. and Wardenga, U. (eds.), 1998, *Text and Image. Social construction of regional knowledges*, Leipzig: Institut für Länderkunde (Beitäge zur Regionalen Geographie, 48).

Butzer, K., 1994, 'Toward a cultural curriculum for the future: a first approximation', in Foote, K., Hugill, P., Mathewson, K. and Smith, J. (eds.), *Re-reading Cultural Geography*, Austin, TX: University of Texas Press, 409–28.

Butzer, K., 2002, 'A random walk in *terra incognita*', in Gould, P. and Pitts, F. (eds.), *Geographical Voices*, Syracuse, NY: Syracuse University Press.

Büttmann, G., 1977, *Friedrich Ratzel. Leben und Werk eines deutschen Geographen 1844–1904*, Stuttgart: Wissenschaftliche Verlagsgesellschaft MBH.

Camena d'Almeida, P., 1893, *Les Pyrénées, développement de la connaissance géographique de la chaîne*, Paris: Armand Colin.

Campbell, J. and Livingstone, D., 1983, 'Neo-Lamarckianism and the development of geography in the United States and Britain', *Transactions of the Institute of British Geographers*, vol. 8, 267–94.

Capel, H., 1983, *Filosofía y ciencia en la geografía contemporánea: (una introducción a la geografía)*, 2nd edn., Barcelona: Barcanova.

Capel, H., 1994, *Las tres chimeneas*, 3 vols., Barcelona: FECSA.

Capot-Rey, R., 1934, *La Région industrielle sarroise: territoire de la Sarre et bassin houiller de la Moselle*, Paris: Berger-Levrault.

Carlstein, T., Parks, D. and Thrift, N. (eds.), 1978, *Timing Space and Spacing Time*, 2 vols., London: Arnold.

Carter, H., 1976, *The Study of Urban Geography*, London: Edward Arnold.

Carter, P., 1988, *The Road to Botany Bay: an exploration of landscape and history*, Chicago, IL: University of Chicago Press.

Castells, M., 1972, *La Question urbaine*, Paris: Maspero.

Castells, M., 1973, *Luttes urbaines et pouvoir politique*, Paris: Maspero.

Casti, E., 1998, *L'Ordine del mondo e la sua rappresentazione. Semiosi cartografica e autoreferenza*, Milan: Unicopli.

Castree, N., 2003, 'A post-environmental ethics?', *Ethics, Place and Environment*, vol. 6, no. 1, 3–12.

Chapman, J. and Harris, T. M., 1982, 'The accuracy of the enclosure estimates: some evidence from Northern England', *Journal of Historical Geography*, vol. 8, 261–4.

Chapoulie, J.-M., 2001, *La Tradition sociologique de Chicago, 1892–1961*, Paris: Seuil.

Chapuis, R., 1984, 'Le système socio-spatial', in *Collectif français de géographie sociale et urbaine. Sens et non-sens de l'espace*, Paris: Corlet, 43–53.

Chardak, H., 1997, *Elisée Reclus. L'homme qui aimait la terre*, Paris: Stock.

Chatelain, A., 1946, 'Cette nouvelle venue: la géographie sociale', *Annales, économies, sociétés, civilisations*, vol. 3, 266–70.

Chatelain, A., 1956, 'Géographie sociale des villes françaises', *Revue de géographie de Lyon*, vol. 31, 119–27.

Chisholm, G., 1889, *Handbook of Commercial Geography*, London: Longman.

Chisholm, M., 1982, *Modern World Development: a geographical perspective*, London: Hutchinson.

Chivallon, C., 1995, 'Space and identity in Martinique: towards a new reading of the spatial history of peasantry', *Environment and Planning D: Society and Space*, vol. 13, 289–309.

Chorley, R., 1995, 'Haggett's Cambridge: 1957–1966', in Cliff, A., Gould, P., Hoare, A. and Thrift, N. (eds.), *Diffusing Geography: essays for Peter Haggett*, Oxford: Blackwell, 354–74.

Chorley, R. J. and Haggett, P. (eds.), 1967, *Models in Geography*, London: Methuen.

Chouinard, V., 1989, 'Transformations in the capitalist state: the development of legal aid clinics in Canada', *Transactions of the Institute of British Geographers*, vol. 14, no. 3, 329–49.

Chouinard, V., 1997, 'Structure and agency: contested concepts in human geography', *Canadian Geographer*, vol. 41, 363–77.

Christaller, W., 1933, *Die zentralen Orte in Süddeutschland*, Jena: Gustav Fischer.

Christaller, W., [1933] 1966, *Central Places in Southern Germany*, C. W. Baskin (trans.), Englewood Cliffs, NJ: Prentice Hall.

Clark, A. H., 1949, *The Invasion of New Zealand by People, Plants and Animals*, New Brunswick, NJ: Rutgers University Press.

Clark, G. L., 1981, 'The employment relation and spatial division of labor', *Annals of the Assocation of American Geographers*, 71, 412–24.

Clark, G. L., Gertler, M. S. and Whiteman, J., 1986, *Regional Dynamics: studies in adjustment theory*, Boston, MA: Allen and Unwin.

Claval, P., 1962, *Géographie générale des marchés*, Paris: Les Belles Lettres.

Claval, P., 1967, 'Géographie et profondeur sociale', *Annales, économies, sociétés, civilisations*, vol. 7, 173–99.

Claval, P., 1968, *Régions, nations, grands espaces*, Paris: Editions Génin.

Claval, P., 1973a, *Principes de géographie sociale*, Paris: Editions M.-Th. Génin.

Claval, P., 1973b, 'Problèmes théoriques en géographie sociale', *Le Géographe Canadien*, vol. 18, 103–12.

Claval, P., 1976, *Eléments de géographie économique*, Paris: Editions Génin.

Claval, P., 1977, 'Le marxisme et l'espace', *L'Espace géographique*, vol. 6, 145–64.

Claval, P., 1980, 'Epistemology and the history of geographic thought', *Progress in Human Geography*, vol. 4, 371–84.

Claval, P., 1981, *La Logique des villes*, Paris: Litec.

Claval, P., 1984, 'The coherence of political geography', in Taylor, P. J. and House, J. W. (eds.), *Political Geography: recent advances and future directions*, London: Croom Helm, 8–24.

Claval, P., 1986, 'Social geography in France', in Eyles, J. (ed.), *Social Geography in International Perspective*, London: Croom Helm, 13–29.

Claval, P., 1987, 'Le néo-marxisme et l'espace', *L'Espace géographique*, vol. 16, 161–6.

Claval, P., 1988, 'Les géographes français et le monde méditerranéen', *Annales de géographie*, vol. 97, 385–403.

Claval, P., 1990, *La Conquête de l'espace américain*, Paris: Flammarion.

Claval, P., 1992a, 'Champ et perspectives de la géographie culturelle', *Géographie et cultures*, vol. 1, 7–38.

Claval, P., 1992b, 'Postmodernisme et géographie', *Géographie et cultures*, vol. 4, 3–24.

Claval, P., 1994, *Géopolitique et géostratégie. La pensée politique, l'espace et le territoire au 20e siècle*, Paris: Nathan.

Claval, P., 1995, *La Géographie culturelle*, Paris: Nathan.

Claval, P., 1998, *Histoire de la géographie française de 1870 à nos jours*, Paris: Nathan.

Claval, P., 1999, 'Qu'apporte l'approche culturelle à la géographie?', *Géographie et cultures*, vol. 31, 5–24.

Claval, P. and Singaravélou (eds.), 1995, *Ethnogéographies*, Paris: L'Harmattan.

Claval, P. and Sanguin, A.-L. (eds.), 1997, *Metropolisation et politique*, Paris: L'Harmattan.

Cliff, A. and Ord, K., 1973, *Spatial Autocorrelation*, New York: Methuen.

Cliff, A. D., Haggett, P., Ord, J. K. and Versey, G. R., 1981, *Spatial Diffusion. An historical geography in an island community*, Cambridge: Cambridge University Press.

Cliff, A. D., Haggett, P. and Graham, R., 1983, 'Reconstruction of diffusion processes at local scales: the 1846, 1882, and 1904 measles epidemics in northwest Iceland', *Journal of Historical Geography*, vol. 9, 347–74.

Cloke, P., Philo, C. and Sadler, D., 1991, *Approaching Human Geography: an introduction to contemporary human geography*, London: Paul Chapman.

Cohen, S. B. and Rosenthal, L. D., 1971, 'A geographical model for political systems analysis', *Geographical Review*, vol. 61, 5–31.

Collectif Français de Géographie Sociale et Urbaine, 1984, *De la Géographie urbaine à la géographie sociale. Sens et non-sens de l'espace*, 25th congress of the IGU, Paris.

Conzen, M. P., 1990, 'Ethnicity on the land', in Conzen, M. P. (ed.), *The Making of the American Landscape*, London: HarperCollins Academic, 221–48.

Cook, I. and Crang, M., 1995, *Doing Ethnographies*, Norwich: Geo Books.

Cooke, P., 1989, *Localities: the changing face of urban Britain*, London: Unwin Hyman.

Corbridge, S., 1993, 'Marxisms, modernities and moralities: development praxis and the claims of distant strangers', *Environment and Planning D: Society and Space*, vol. 11, 449–72.

Cornish, V., 1923, *The Great Capitals*, London: Methuen.

Cosgrove, D., 1984, *Social Formation and Symbolic Landscape*, London: Croom Helm.

Cosgrove, D., 1993, 'Commentary', *Annals of the Association of American Geographers*, vol. 83, 515–16.

Cosgrove, D., 2001, *Apollo's Eye: a cartographic genealogy of the earth in the western imagination*, Baltimore, MD: Johns Hopkins University Press.

Cosgrove, D. and Jackson, P., 1987, 'New directions in cultural geography', *Area*, vol. 19, 95–101.

Cosgrove, D. and Daniels, S. (eds.), 1988, *The Iconography of Landscape: essays on the symbolic representation, design, and use of past environments*, Cambridge: Cambridge University Press.

Cox, K. R., 1969, 'The voting decision in spatial context', *Progress in Human Geography*, vol. 1, 81–117.

Cox, K. R., 1972, *Man, Location, and Behavior: an introduction to human geography*, New York: Wiley.

Cox, K. R., 1973, *Conflict, Power and Politics in the City*, New York: McGraw-Hill.

Cox, K. R., 1978, *Urbanization and Conflict in Market Societies*, Chicago, IL: Maaroufa.

Cox, K. R., 1979, *Location and Public Problems: a political geography of the contemporary world*, Chicago, IL: Maaroufa.

Cox, K. R., Reynolds, D. R. and Rokkan, S. (eds.), 1974, *Locational Approaches to Power and Conflict*, New York: Wiley.

Crang, P., 1994, 'It's showtime: on the workplace geographies of display in a restaurant in South East England', *Environment and Planning D: Society and Space*, vol. 12, 675–704.

Crang, P., 1996, 'Displacements: geographies of consumption', *Environment and Planning A*, vol. 28, no. 1, 47–68.

Crang, P., 1997, 'Cultural turns and the (re)-constitution of economic geography: introduction to section one', in Lee, R. and Wills, J. (eds.), *Geographies of Economies*, 3–15.

Credner, W., 1926, 'Arbeitsmethoden und Problemen der Wirtschaftsgeographie', *Abhandlungen des Deutschengeographentag*, Breslau: Hirt.

Cresswell, T., 1996, *In Place/Out of Place: geography, ideology and transgression*, Minneapolis, MN: University of Minnesota Press.

Crush, J., 1994, 'Post-colonialism, de-colonialization and geography', in Godlewska, A. and Smith, N. (eds.), *Geography and Empire*, Oxford: Blackwell, 333–50.

Curry, L., 1966, 'Chance and landscape', in *Northern Geographical Essays in Honour of G. H. J. Daysh*, Newcastle-upon-Tyne: Oriel, 40–5.

Curry, L., 1998, *The Random Spatial Economy and its Evolution*, Aldershot: Ashgate.

Curry, M., 1996, *The Work in the World. Geographical practice and the written word*, Minneapolis, MN: University of Minnesota Press.

Curry, M., 1998, *Digital Places: living with geographic information technologies*, London: Routledge.

Da Costa Gomes, P. C., 1996, *Geografia e modernidade*, Rio de Janeiro: Bertrand Brasil.

Dainville, F. de, 1964, *Le Language des géographes*, Paris: Picard.

Dalby, S., 1990, *Creating the Second Cold War*, London: Pinter.

Dalby, S., Routledge, P. and O'Tuathail, G., 1998, *Rethinking Geopolitics*, London: Routledge.

Daniels, S., 1985, 'Arguments for a humanistic geography', in Johnston, R. J. (ed.), *The Future of Geography*, New York: Methuen, 143–58.

Daniels, S., 1986, 'The implications of industry: Turner and Leeds', *Turner Studies*, vol. 6, 10–17.

Daniels, S., 1988, 'The political iconography of woodland in later Georgian England', in Cosgrove, D. and Daniels, S. (eds.), *The Iconography of Landscape: essays on the symbolic representation, design, and use of past environments*, Cambridge: Cambridge University Press, 43–82.

Daniels, S., 1993, *Fields of Vision: landscape imagery and national identity in England and the United States*, Cambridge: Polity Press.

Daniels, S., 1998, 'Mapping national identities: the culture of cartography, with particular reference to the Ordnance Survey', in Cubitt, G. (ed.), *Imagining Nations*, Manchester: Manchester University Press, 112–31.

Darby, H. C., 1932, 'The medieval sea state', *Scottish Geographical Magazine*, vol. 48, 136–9.

Darby, H. C. (ed.), 1936, *An Historical Geography of England before AD 1800*, Cambridge: Cambridge University Press.

Darby, H. C., 1953, 'On the relations of geography and history', *Transactions of the Institute of British Geographers*, vol. 19, 2–11.

Darby, H. C., 1962, 'Historical geography', in Finberg, H. P. R. (ed.), *Approaches to History. A symposium*, London: Routledge and Kegan Paul, 127–56.

Darby, H. C. (ed.), 1973, *A New Historical Geography of England*, Cambridge: Cambridge University Press.

Darby, H. C. and Versey, G. R., 1952–77, *Domesday Geography of England*, 7 vols., Cambridge: Cambridge University Press.

Dardel, E., 1952, *L'Homme et la terre*, Paris: Presses Universitaires de France.

Dardel, E., [1952] 1990, *L'Homme et la terre: nature de la réalité géographique*, Paris: Editions du CTHS.

De Certeau, M., 1984, *The Practice of Everyday Life*, Los Angeles, CA: University of California Press.

Dear, M., 1986, 'Theory and object in political geography', *Political Geography Quarterly*, vol. 5, 295–7.

Dear, M., 1988, 'The postmodern challenge: reconstructing human geography', *Transactions of the Institute of British Geographers*, vol. 13, 262–74.

Dear, M. and Flusty, S., 1998, 'Postmodern urbanism', *Annals of the Association of American Geographers*, vol. 88, no. 1, 50–72.

Debarbieux, B., 1995, 'Le lieu, le territoire et trois figures de rhétorique', *L'Espace géographique*, vol. 2, 97–112.

Deffontaines, P., 1948, *Géographie des religions*, Paris: Gallimard.

Deffontaines, P., 1957, *L'Homme et l'hiver au Canada*, Paris: Gallimard.

Demangeon, A., 1923, *L'Empire britannique. Étude de géographie coloniale*, Paris: Armand Colin.

Dematteis, G., 1985, *Le metafore della terra*, Milan: Feltrinelli.

Demeritt, D., 1994, 'Ecology, objectivity and critique in writings on nature and human societies', *Journal of Historical Geography*, vol. 20, 20–37.

Demeritt, D., 2000, 'Social theory and the reconstruction of science and geography', *Transactions of the Institute of British Geographers*, vol. 21, 484–503.

Demolins, E., 1901, *Les Grandes Routes des peuples. Essai de géographie sociale*, Paris: Librairie de Paris.

Denecke, D., 1976, 'Innovation and diffusion of the potato in Central Europe in the 17th and 18th centuries', in Buchanan, R. H. *et al.* (eds.), *Fields, Farms, and Settlement in Europe*, Holywood, Co. Down: Ulster Folk and Transport Museum, 60–96.

Denecke, D., 1992, 'Ideology in the planned order upon the land: the example of Germany', in Baker, A. R. H. and Biger, G. (eds.), *Ideology and Landscape in Historical Perspective*, Cambridge: Cambridge University Press, 303–29.

Dennis, R., 1984, *English Industrial Cities in the 19th Century: a social geography*, Cambridge: Cambridge University Press.

Dennis, R., 1994, 'At the intersection of time and space', in Monkkonen, E. H. (ed.), *Engaging the Past: the uses of history across the social sciences*, Durham, NC: Duke University Press, 154–88.

Derycke, P.-H., 1979, *Économie et planification urbaines*, Paris: Presses Universitaires de France.

Desrosières, A., 1993, *La Politique des grands nombres. Histoire de la raison statistique*, Paris: La Découverte.

D. G. [Gregory, Derek], 1981, 'Cross-section', in Johnston, R. J. (ed.), *Dictionary of Human Geography*, Oxford: Blackwell, 62–3.

Dickenson, R. E., 1943, *The German Lebensraum*, Harmondsworth: Penguin.

Dijkink, G., 1997, *National Identities and Geopolitical Visions*, London: Routledge.

Dikshit, R. D., 1997, *Developments in Political Geography. A century of progress*, New York: Sage.

Dion, R., 1934, *Essai sur la formation du paysage rural français*, Tours: Arrault.

Dion, R., 1959, *Histoire de la vigne et du vin en France, des origines au XIXe siècle*, Paris: self-published.

Dion, R., 1977, *Aspects politiques de la géographie antique*, Paris: Les Belles Lettres.

Dixon, D. P. and Jones, J. P., III, 1998, 'My dinner with Derrida, or spatial analysis and poststructuralism do lunch', *Environment and Planning A*, vol. 30, no. 2, 247–60.

Dockès, P., 1969, *L'Espace dans la pensée économique du XVIe au XVIIe siècle*, Paris: Flammarion.

Dodge, S. D., 1932, 'Bureau and the Princeton community', *Annals of the Association of American Geographers*, vol. 22, 159–209.

Doel, M., 1999, *Poststructuralist Geographies*, Edinburgh: University of Edinburgh Press.

Doeppers, D. F., 1967, 'The Globeville neighbourhood in Denver', *Geographical Review*, vol. 57, 506–22.

Domosh, M., 1987, 'Imagining New York's first skyscrapers, 1875–1910', *Journal of Historical Geography*, vol. 13, 233–48.

Domosh, M., 1990, 'Those sudden peaks that scrape the sky: the changing imagery of New York's first skyscrapers', in Zonn, L. (ed.), *Place Images in Media: portrayal, experience, and meaning*, Totowa, NJ: Rowman & Littlefield, 9–30.

Domosh, M., 1996, *Invented Cities: the creation of landscape in nineteenth-century, New York and Boston*, New Haven, CT: Yale University Press.

Drake, C. and Horton, J., 1983, 'Comment on editorial essay: sexist bias in political geography', *Political Geography Quarterly*, vol. 2, 329–37.

Driver, F., 1988, 'The historicity of human geography', *Progress in Human Geography*, vol. 12, 497–506.

Driver, F., 1998, 'Heart of empire? Landscape, space and performance in imperial London', *Environment and Planning D: Society and Space*, vol. 16, 11–28.

Driver, F., 2001, *Geography: militant cultures of exploration and empire*, Oxford: Blackwell.

Droulers, M., 2001, *Brésil: une géohistoire*, Paris: P.U.F.

Dugin, A. G., 1999, *Osnovy geopolitiki. Geopoliticheskoe budutchee Rossii* ('The Basics of Geopolitics. The geopolitical future of Russia'), Moscow: Arctogea-center.

Dunbar, G., 1977, 'Some early occurrences of the term "social geography"', *Scottish Geographical Magazine*, vol. 93, 15–20.

Duncan, J. S., 1980, 'The Superorganic in American Cultural Geography', *Annals of the Association of American Geographers*, vol. 70, no. 2, 181–98.

Duncan, J. S., 1985, 'Individual action and political power: a structuration perspective', in Johnston, R. J. (ed.), *The Future of Geography*, London: Methuen, 174–89.

Duncan, J. S., 1990, *The City as Text: the politics of landscape interpretation in the Kandyan Kingdom*, Cambridge: Cambridge University Press.

Duncan, J. S., 1993, 'Commentary', *Annals of the Association of American Geographers*, vol. 83, 517–18.

Duncan, J. S., 1994, 'After the civil war: reconstructing cultural geography as heterotopia', in Foote, K., Hugill, P., Mathewson, K. and Smith, J. (eds.), *Re-reading Cultural Geography*, Austin, TX: University of Texas, 401–8.

Duncan, N. and Sharp, J., 1993, 'Confronting representation(s)', *Environment and Planning D: Society and Space*, vol. 11, 473–86.

Durand, M. F., Lévy, J. and Retaille, D., 1993, *Le Monde: espaces et systèmes*, Paris: Presses de la fondation nationale des sciences politiques and Dalloz.

Durkheim, E., 1893, *La Division du travail social*, Paris.

Durkheim, E. (ed.), 1898, *L'Année sociologique*, vol. 1, 533–9.

Durkheim, E., 1909, 'Sociologie et sciences sociales', in *De la Méthode dans les sciences*, Paris: Félix Alcan.

Dyck, I., 1990, 'Space, time and renegotiating motherhood: an exploration of the domestic workplace', *Environment and Planning D: Society and Space*, vol. 8, 459–83.

East, W. G., 1933, 'A note on historical geography', *Geography*, vol. 102, no. 18, 282–92.

Easton, D., 1963, *Systems Analysis of Political Life*, New York: Wiley.

Editorial Board, 1982a, 'Editorial essay: political geography – research agendas for the 1980s', *Political Geography Quarterly*, vol. 1, 1–18.

Editorial Board, 1982b, 'Research agendas for the 1980s: comments, additions and critiques', *Political Geography Quarterly*, vol. 1, 167–80.

Edney, M. H., 1997, *Mapping an Empire. The geographical construction of British India*, Chicago, IL: University of Chicago Press.

Eisel, U., 1980, *Die Entwicklung der Anthropogeographie von einer Raumwissenschaft zur Gesellschaftwissenschaft*, Kassel: Kasseler Schriftung zur Geographie und Plannung.

Emmanuel, A., 1969, *L'Échange inégal*, Paris: Maspero.

England, K., 1993, 'Suburban pink collar ghettos: the spatial entrapment of women', *Annals of the Association of American Geographers*, vol. 83, 225–42.

England, K., 2003, 'Towards a feminist political geography?', *Political Geography*, vol. 22, no. 6, 611–16.

Enjalbert, H., 1975, *Histoire de la vigne et du vin. L'avénement de la qualité*, Paris: Bordas.

Entrikin, J. N., 1976, 'Contemporary humanism in geography', *Annals of the Association of American Geographers*, vol. 66, 615–32.

Entrikin, J. N., 1988, 'Diffusion research in the context of the naturalism debate in twentieth-century social thought', in Hugill, P. and Dickson, D. B. (eds.), *The Transfer and Transformation of Ideas and Material Culture*, College Station: Texas A&M University Press, 165–78.

Entrikin, J. N., 1991, *The Betweennness of Place: towards a geography of modernity*, Baltimore, MD: Johns Hopkins University Press.

Entrikin, J. N., 1997, 'Lieu, culture, et démocratie', *Cahiers de géographie du Québec*, vol. 41, 349–56.

Entrikin, J. N., 1999, 'Political community, identity and cosmopolitan place', *International Sociology*, vol. 14, 269–82.

Errani, P. L., 1984, 'Introduzione', in Reclus, E., *L'Homme. Geografia sociale*, Milan: Franco Angeli.

Ewald, F., 1986, *L'État providence*, Paris: Grasset.

Eyles, J. and Smith, D. M. (eds.), 1988, *Qualitative Methods in Human Geography*, Cambridge: Polity Press.

Fairgrieve, J., 1915, *Geography and World Power*, London: University of London Press.

Falah, G. and Newman, D., 1995, 'The manifestation of threat: Israelis and Palestinians seek a "good" border', *Political Geography*, vol. 14, 689–706.

Fawcett, H., 1919, *The Provinces of England*, London: Hutchinson.

Febvre, L., 1922, *La Terre et l'évolution humaine. Introduction géographique à l'histoire*, Paris: Albin Michel.

Fellmann, J. D., 1986, 'Myth and reality in the origin of American economic geography', *Annals of the Assocation of American Geographers*, 76, 313–30.

Fisher, A. and Mackenzie, W., 1922, 'The correlation of weekly rainfall', *Quarterly Journal of the Royal Meteorological Society*, vol. 48, 234–45.

Fisher, P., 1993, 'Visualizing uncertainty in soil maps by animation', *Cartographica*, vol. 30, nos. 2 and 3, 20–7.

Fisher, P. and Wishart, J., 1930, 'The arrangement of field experiments and the statistical reduction of results', *The Imperial Bureau of Soil Science: technical communication*, vol. 10.

Fisher, R., 1958, *Statistical Methods for Research Workers*, New York: Hefner.

Fisher, R. and Eden, T., 1929, 'Studies in crop variation. V1 experiments on the response of the potato to potash and nitrogen', *Journal of Agricultural Science*, vol. 19, 201–13.

Fitzgerald, W., 1945, 'The geographer as humanist', *Nature*, vol. 156, 355–7.

Fitzgerald, W., 1946, 'Geography and its components (correspondence)', *Geographical Journal*, vol. 107 (January–June), 272–3.

Fitzsimmons, M., 1989, 'The matter of nature', *Antipode*, vol. 21, 106–20.

Flatres, P. (ed.), 1979, *Paysages ruraux européens*, Rennes: Université de Haute-Bretagne.

Fleure, H. J., 1947, *Some Problems of Society and Environment*, London: George Philip & Son.

Flint, C. and Shelley, F. M., 1996, 'Structure, agency and context: the contributions of geography to world-systems analysis', *Sociological Inquiry*, vol. 66, 496–508.

Foote, K., Hugill, P., Mathewson, K. and Smith, J. (eds.), 1994, *Re-reading Cultural Geography*, Austin, TX: University of Texas Press.

Forest, B., 1995, 'West Hollywood as a symbol: the significance of place in the construction of gay identity', *Environment and Planning D: Society and Space*, vol. 13, 133–57.

Foucault, M., 1976, 'Questions à Michel Foucault sur la géographie', *Hérodote*, vol. 1, 71–85.

Frank, G. A., 1968, *Capitalisme et sous-développement en Amérique latine*, Paris: Maspero.

Freeman, T. W., 1946, 'Geography and its components (correspondence)', *Geographical Journal*, vol. 108 (July–December), 276–7.

Friedman, S., 1996, *Marc Bloch, Sociology and Geography. Encountering social disciplines*, Cambridge: Cambridge University Press.

Friedrich, E., 1904, 'Wesen und geographisches Verbreitung der Raubwirtschaft', *Pettermanns Mitteilungen*, 50, 3, 68–79 and 50, 4, 92–5.

Friis, H., 1940, *A Series of Population Maps of the Colonies and the United States, 1625–1790*, New York: AGS Publication no. 3.

Frémont, A., 1976, *La Région, espace vécu*, Paris: PUF.

Frémont, A., 1980, 'L'espace vécu et la notion de région', *Travaux de l'Institut de Géographie de Reims*, vols. 41–2, 47–58.

Frémont, A., Chevalier, J., Hérin, R. and Rénard, J., 1984, *Géographie sociale*, Paris: Masson.

Fröbel, F., Heinrichs, J. and Kreye, O., 1980, *The New International Division of Labour*, Cambridge: Cambridge University Press.

Gale, S. and Olsson, G. (eds.), 1979, *Philosophy in Geography*, London: Reidel.

Gallais, J., 1976, 'Espace vécu et sociétés tropicales', *L'Espace géographique*, vol. 1, 5–10.

Gallois, L., 1908, *Régions naturelles et noms de pays. Étude sur la région parisienne*, Paris: Armand Colin.

Gandy, M., 1997, 'Contradictory modernities: conceptions of nature in the art of Joseph Beuys and Gerhard Richter', *Annals of the Association of American Geographers*, vol. 87, 636–59.

Garrison, W., 1999, letter to P. Gould, 19 May.

Gauthier, H., 1968, 'Transportation and the growth of the Sâo Paulo economy', *Journal of Regional Science*, vol. 8, 77–94.

Geertz, C., 1973, *The Interpretation of Cultures: selected essays*, New York: Basic Books.

Geertz, C., 1983, *Local Knowledge: further essays in interpretive anthropology*, New York: Basic Books.

Géneau de Lamarlière, I. and Staszak, J.-F., 2000, *Principes de géographie économique*, Paris: Bréal.

George, P., 1938, *Géographie économique et sociale de la France*, Paris: Editions sociales.

George, P., 1946, *Géographie sociale du monde*, Paris: PUF.

George, P., 1956, *Précis de géographie économique*, Paris: Presses Universitaires de France.

George, P., 1961, *Les Grands Marchés du monde*, Paris: Presses Universitaires de France.

George, P., 1966, *Sociologie et géographie*, Paris: PUF.

Gibson-Graham, J. K., 1996, *The End of Capitalism (As We Knew It): a feminist critique of political economy*, Oxford: Blackwell.

Giddens, A., 1979, *Central Problems in Social Theory: action, structure and contradiction in social analysis*, Berkeley, CA: University of California Press.

Giddens, A., 1991, *Modernity and Self-Identity. Self and society in the late modern age*, Stanford, CA: Stanford University Press.

Gilbert, E. W., 1932, 'What is historical geography?', *Scottish Geographical Magazine*, vol. 48, 129–36 (reprinted in Green 1991: 10–16).

Gilbert, E. W. and Steel, R. W., 1945, 'Social geography and its place in colonial studies', *Geographical Journal*, vol. 106, 118–31.

Glacken, C. J., 1956, 'Changing ideas of the habitable world', in Thomas, W. L. (ed.), *Man's Role in Changing the Face of the Earth*, Chicago, IL: University of Chicago Press, 70–92.

Glacken, C. J., 1967, *Traces on the Rhodian Shore*, Berkeley, CA: University of California Press.

Glasscock, R. E., 1975, *The Lay Subsidy of 1334. British Academy records of social and economic history*, vol. 2 (NS), London: British Academy.

Godlewska, A. and Smith, N. (eds.), 1994, *Geography and Empire*, Oxford: Blackwell.

Godlund, S., 1956a, *Bus Service in Sweden*, Lund: Gleerups, Lund Studies in Geography, Series B (Human Geography) no. 17.

Godlund, S., 1956b, *The Function and Growth of Bus Traffic within the Sphere of Urban Influence*, Lund: Gleerups, Lund Studies in Geography, Series B (Human Geography), no. 18.

Gómez Mendoza, J., 1992, *Ciencia y política de los montes españoles*, Madrid: ICONA.

Goodman, N., 1988, 'On capturing cities', in Teyssot, G. (ed.), *World Cities and the Future of the Metropolis*, Milan: Electa, 69–72.

Gottmann, J., 1951, 'Geography and international relations', *World Politics*, vol. 3, 153–73.

Gottmann, J., 1952a, *La Géographie des états et leur géographie*, Paris: Flammarion.

Gottmann, J., 1952b, 'The political partitioning of our world', *World Politics*, vol. 4, 512–19.

Götz, W., 1882, 'Die Aufgabe der wirtschaftlichen Geographie', *Zeifschrift der Gesellschaft zur Erdkunde zu Berlin*, 17, 354–88.

Gould, P., 1970, 'Is *Statistix Inferens* the geographical name for a wild goose?', *Economic Geography*, vol. 46, 439–48.

Gould, P., 1979, 'Geography in the Augean Period', *Annals of the Association of American Geographers*, vol. 69, 139–51.

Gould, P., 1999a, *Becoming a Geographer*, Syracuse, NY: Syracuse University Press.

Gould, P., 1999b, 'Do Foraminifera assemblages exist – at least in the Persian Gulf?', in *Becoming a Geographer*, Syracuse, NY: Syracuse University Press, 289–99.

Gould, P. and Pitts, F., 2001, *Geographical Voices*, Syracuse, NY: Syracuse University Press.

Gould, P. and White, R., [1974] 1986, *Mental Maps*, 2nd edn., London: Allen and Unwin.

Gourou, P., 1936, *Les Paysans du delta tonkinois. Étude de géographie humaine*, Paris: Editions d'Art et d'Histoire.

Gourou, P., 1970, *L'Afrique*, Paris: Hachette.

Gourou, P., 1971, *Leçons de géographie tropicale*, Paris: Mouton.

Gourou, P., 1973, *Pour une géographie humaine*, Paris: Flammarion.

Gradmann, R., 1901, 'Das mitteleuropäische Landschaftsbild nach seiner geschichtlichen Entwicklung', *Geographische Zeitschrift*, vol. 7, 361–77, 435–47.

Gradmann, R., 1931, *Süddeutschland*, 2 vols., Stuttgart: J. Engelhorn.

Grafmeyer, Y. and Joseph, I. (eds.), 1979, *L'École de Chicago*, Paris: Aubier.

Granelle, J. J., 1969, *Espace urbain et prix du sol*, Paris: Sirey.

Grant, R., 1998, 'Japan. A foreign aid super power', in Grant, R. and Nijman, J. (eds.), *The Global Crisis in Foreign Aid*, Syracuse, NY: Syracuse University Press, 44–60.

Grant, R. and Agnew, J., 1996, 'Representing Africa: the geography of Africa in world trade, 1960–1992', *Annals of the Association of American Geographers*, vol. 86, no. 4, 729–44.

Grataloup, C. and Lévy, J., 1976, 'Des géographes pour une autre géographie', *Le Monde*, 14–15 March.

Gray, H. L., 1915, *The English Field System*, Cambridge, MA: Harvard University Press.

Green, D. B. (ed.), 1991, *Historical Geography: a methodological portrayal*, Savage, MD: Rowman & Littlefield.

Gregory, D., 1978a, *Ideology, Science and Human Geography*, London: Macmillan.

Gregory, D., 1978b, 'The discourse of the past: phenomenology, structuralism and historical geography', *Journal of Historical Geography*, vol. 4, 161–73.

Gregory, D., 1981, 'Human agency and human geography', *Transactions of the Institute of British Geographers*, vol. 6 (NS), 1–18.

Gregory, D., 1982, 'Solid geometry: notes on the recovery of spatial structure', in Gould, P. and Olsson, G. (eds.), *A Search for Common Ground*, London: Pion, 187–219.

Gregory, D., 1984, *Regional Transformation and Industrial Revolution*, London: Macmillan.

Gregory, D., 1994, *Geographical Imaginations*, Oxford: Blackwell.

Gregory, D., 1995a, 'Between the book and the lamp: imaginative geographies of Egypt', *Transactions of the Institute of British Geographers*, vol. 20 (NS), 29–57.

Gregory, D., 1995b, 'Imaginative geographies', *Progress in Human Geography*, vol. 19, 447–85.

Gregson, N., 1993, '"The initiative": delimiting or deconstructing social geography', *Progress in Human Geography*, vol. 17, 525–30.

Guelke, L., 1997, 'The relations between geography and history reconsidered', *History and Theory*, vol. 36, 216–34.

Guerin, J.-P. and Gumuchian, H., 1985, *Les Représentations en actes: actes du colloque de Lescheraines*, Grenoble: Institut de géographie alpine.

Haack, S., 1998, *Manifesto of a Passionate Moderate: unfashionable essays*, Chicago, IL: University of Chicago Press.

Habermas, J., 1998, 'Kant's idea of perpetual peace: At two hundred years' historical remove', in Cronin, C. and De Greiff, P. (eds.), *The Inclusion of the Other: studies in political theory*, Cambridge, MA: MIT Press, 165–201.

Hägerstrand, T., 1949, 'Flyttningarna till och från Simrishamn under 1900-talet', in Helge Nelson *et al.*, *Simrishamn med omland*, Lund: Ehrnberg & Sons Läderfabrik.

Hägerstrand, T., 1952, *The Propagation of Innovation Waves*, Lund: Gleerups, Lund Studies in Geography, no. 4.

Hägerstrand, T., 1953, *Innovationsforloppet ur Korologisk Synpunkt*, Lund: Gleerups, Meddelanden från Lunds universitets geografiska institution, 25. In Allan Pred (trans.), 1967, *Innovation Diffusion as a Spatial Process*, Chicago, IL: University of Chicago Press.

Hägerstrand, T., 1982, 'Diorama, path, and project', *Tijdshrift voor Economische en Sociale Geographie*, vol. 73, 323–39.

Hägerstrand, T., 1983, 'In search for the sources of concepts', in Buttimer, A. (ed.), *The Practice of Geography*, London: Longman, 238–56.

Haggett, P., 1965, *Locational Analysis in Human Geography*, London: Arnold.

Hahn, E., 1896a, *Die Haustiere und ihre Beziehungen zur Wirtschaft des Menschens*, Leipzig: Duncker und Humblot.

Hahn, E., 1896b, *Demeter und Baubo. Versuch einder Theorie der Entstehung unseres Ackerbau*, Lübeck.

Hahn, E., 1914, *Von der Hacke zum Pfluge*, Leipzig: Quelle and Meyer.

Hall, P., 1988, *Cities of Tomorrow. An intellectual history of urban planning and design in the 20th century*, Oxford: Blackwell.

Hall, S., 1993, *Mapping the Next Millennium: how computer-driven cartography is revolutionizing the face of science*, New York: Routledge.

Hamshere, J. D., 1987, 'Data sources in historical geography', in Pacione, M. (ed.), *Historical Geography: progress and prospect*, London: Croom Helm, 46–69.

Hannah, M., 1997, 'Imperfect panopticism: envisioning the construction of normal lives, in Benko, G. and Strohmayer, U. (eds.), *Space and Social Theory*, Oxford: Blackwell, 344–59.

Hannah, M. and Strohmayer, U., 1991, 'Ornamentalism: geography and the labor of language in structuration theory', *Environment and Planning D: Society and Space*, vol. 9, 309–27.

Hannah, M. and Strohmayer, U., 1992, 'Domesticating postmodernism', in *Antipode*, vol. 24, no. 1, 29–55.

Hannah, M. and Strohmayer, U., 1995, 'The artifice of conviction, or, towards an internal geography of responsibility', in *Geographical Analysis*, vol. 27, no. 4, 339–59.

Hanson, S., 1999, 'Isms and schisms: healing the rift between the nature-society and space-society traditions in human geography', *Annals of the Association of American Geographers*, vol. 89, no. 1, 133–43.

Haraway, D., 1991, *Simians, Cyborgs and Women. The reinvention of nature*, London: Free Association Books.

Hard, G., 1970, *Die 'Landschaft' der Sprache und die 'Landschaft' der Geographen*, Bonn: Demmlers.

Harding, S., 1986, *The Science Question in Feminism*, Milton Keynes: Open University Press.

Harley, J. B., 1988, 'Maps, knowledge, and power', in Cosgrove, D. and Daniels, D. (eds.), *The Iconography of Landscape. Essays on the symbolic representation, design, and use of past environments*, Cambridge: Cambridge University Press, 277–312.

Harley, J. B., 1989, 'Deconstructing the map', *Cartographica*, vol. 26, no. 2, 1–20. Reprinted in: Barnes, T. J. and Duncan, J. (eds.), 1992, *Writing Worlds. Discourse, text, and metaphor in the representation of landscape*, London: Routledge, 231–47.

Harley, J. B., 1990, 'Cartography, ethics and social theory', *Cartographica*, vol. 27, no. 2, 1–23.

Harley, J. B. and Woodward, D. (eds.), 1992–4, *History of Cartography*, 2 vols., Chicago, IL: University of Chicago Press.

Harley, J. B., 1992, 'Deconstructing the map', in Barnes, T. J. and Duncan, J. (eds.), *Writing Worlds. Discourse, text, and metaphor in the representation of landscape*, London: Routledge, 231–47.

Harris, B., 1956, 'Projecting industrial growth of urban regions', *Papers and Proceedings of the Regional Science Association*, 2, 239–49.

Harris, R. C., 1971, 'Theory and synthesis in historical geography', *Canadian Geographer*, vol. 15, no. 3, 157–72.

Harris, R. C., 1978, 'The historical mind and the practice of geography', in Ley, D. and Samuels, M. (eds.), *Humanistic Geography: problems and prospects*, London: Croom Helm, 123–37.

Harris, R. C., 1984, 'Residential segregation and class formation in the capitalist city', *Progress in Human Geography*, vol. 8, 26–49.

Harris, R. C., 1989, 'Synthesis in human geography: a demonstration of historical materialism', in Kobayashi, A. and Mackenzie, S. (eds.), *Remaking Human Geography*, London: Unwin Hyman, 78–94.

Harris, R. C., 1991, 'Power, modernity and historical geography', *Annals of the Association of American Geographers*, vol. 81, 671–83.

Harrisson, T., 1946, 'Geography and its components (correspondence)', *Geographical Journal*, vol. 108 (July–December), 126.

Hartke, W., 1956, 'Die "Sozialbrache" als Phänomen der geographischen Differenzierung der Landschaft', *Erdkunde*, vol. 10, 257–69.

Hartshorne, R., 1937, 'A survey of the boundaries problems of Europe', in Colby, C. C. (ed.), *Geographic Aspects of International Relations*, New York: Books for Libraries Press, 163–216.

Hartshorne, R., 1939, *The Nature of Geography*, Lancaster, PA: Association of American Geographers.

Hartshorne, R., 1950, 'The functional approach in political geography', *Annals of the American Association of Geographers*, vol. 40, 95–130.

Hartshorne, R., 1954, 'Political geography', in James, P. E. and Jones, C. F. (eds.), *American Geography: inventory and prospect*, Syracuse, NY: Syracuse University Press.

Hartshorne, R., 1959, *Perspective on the Nature of Geography*, London: Rand McNally.

Harvey, D., 1969, *Explanation in Geography*, London: Edward Arnold.

Harvey, D., 1972, 'Revolutionary and counter-revolutionary theory in geography and the problem of ghetto formation', *Antipode*, vol. 4, no. 2, 1–13.

Harvey, D., 1973, *Social Justice and the City*, London: Edward Arnold.

Harvey, D., 1982, *The Limits to Capital*, Oxford: Blackwell.

Harvey, D., 1984, 'On the history and present condition of geography', *The Professional Geographer*, vol. 36, 1–11.

Harvey, D., 1985a, *Consciousness and the Urban Experience: studies in the history and theory of capitalist urbanisation*, vol. 1, Oxford: Blackwell.

Harvey, D., 1985b, *The Urbanisation of Capital: studies in the history and theory of capitalist urbanisation*, vol. 2, Oxford: Blackwell.

Harvey, D., 1989, *The Condition of Postmodernity: an enquiry into the origins of cultural change*, Oxford: Blackwell.

Harvey, D., 1996, *Justice, Nature and the Geography of Difference*, Oxford: Blackwell.

Harvey, D., 1996a, 'The domination of nature and its discontents', *Justice, Nature and the Geography of Difference*, Oxford: Blackwell, 120–49.

Harvey, D., 1996b, 'Class relations, social justice, and the political geography of difference', *Justice, Nature and the Geography of Difference*, Oxford: Blackwell, 334–65.

Harvey, D., 2000, 'Cosmopolitanism and the banality of geographical evils', *Public Culture*, vol. 2, 529–64.

Haudricourt, A.-G., 1987, *La Technologie, science humaine*, Paris: Maison des Sciences de l'Homme.

Haudricourt, A.-G. and Jean-Brunhes Delamarre, M., 1955, *L'Homme et la charrue à travers le monde*, Paris: Gallimard.

Hauner, M., 1992, *What Is Asia to Us Today? Russia's Asian heartland yesterday and today*, London: Routledge.

Hauser, H., 1905, *L'Impérialisme américain*, Paris: Pages Libres.

Hauser, H., 1915, *Les Méthodes allemandes d'expansion économique*, Paris: Armand Colin.

Hauser, H., 1947, 'Esquisse d'une philosophie de l'histoire de la géographie économique', *Revue Historique*, No.1, 1–22.

Haushofer, K., 1931, *Geographie der Panideen*, Berlin: Zentral Verlag.

Hautreux, J. and Rochefort, M., 1963, *Le Niveau supérieur de l'armature urbaine française*, Paris: Commissariat Général du Plan.

Hayden, D., 1976, 'Communal idealism and the American landscape', *Landscape*, vol. 20, 20–32.

Heathcote, R. L., 1965, *Back of Bourke: A study of land appraisal in semi-arid Australia*, Carlton: Melbourne University Press.

Heffernan, M., 1995, 'For ever England: the Western Front and the politics of remembrance in Britain', *Ecumene*, vol. 2, 293–323.

Heffernan, M., 1998, *The Meaning of Europe. Geography and geopolitics*, London: Arnold.

Helmfrid, S., 1999, 'A hundred years of geography in Sweden', in Öhngren, B. (ed.), *Swedish Research in Human Geography*, Uppsala: Swedish Science Press, 19–54.

Henderson, G., 1994, 'Romancing the sand: constructions of capital and nature in arid America', *Ecumene*, vol. 1, 235–55.

Herb, G. H., 1997, *Under the Map of Germany. Nationalism and propaganda, 1918–1945*, London: Routledge.

Herbert, D., 1972, *Urban Geography: a social perspective*, Newton Abbott: David & Charles.

Hérin, R., 1983, 'Géographie humaine, géographie sociale, sciences sociales', in Noin, D. (ed.), *Géographie sociale. Actes du colloque de Lyon, 14–16 octobre 1982*, Paris: Centre de polycopie de l'Université de Paris I, 16–26.

Hérin, R., 1984, 'Le renouveau de la géographie sociale française', in Collectif français de géographie sociale et urbaine, *De la Géographie urbaine à la géographie sociale. Sens et non-sens de l'espace*, 25th congress of the IGU, Paris, 19–30.

Hérin, R. and Muller, C. (eds.), 1998, *Espaces et sociétés à la fin du XXe siècle: quelles géographies sociales?*, Caen: Maison de la recherche en sciences humaines de Caen Basse-Normandie.

Herskovits, M., 1962, *The Human Factor in Changing Africa*, New York: Alfred Knopf.

Hetter, A., 1927, *Die Geographie: Ihre Geschichte, ihr Wesen, und ihre Methoden*, Breslau: Hirt.

Higounet, C., 1975, *Paysages et villages neufs du Moyen Age*, Bordeaux: Fédération Historique du Sud-Ouest.

Hinchliffe, S., 1996, 'Technology, power and space – the means and ends of geographies of technology', *Environment and Planning D: Society and Space*, vol. 14, 659–82.

Hinchliffe, S., 1999, 'Entangled humans: specifying powers and their spatialities', in Sharp, J. P., Routledge, P., Philo, C. and Paddison, R. (eds.), *Entanglements of Power: geographies of domination/resistance*, London: Routledge, 219–37.

Hirsch, W. Z., 1959, 'An application of area input-output analysis', *Papers and Proceedings of the Regional Science Association*, 5, 79–92.

Hirschman, A. O., 1958, *The Strategy of Economic Development*, New Haven, CT: Yale University Press.

Hoefle, S. W., 1999, 'Débats épistémologiques dans la géographie culturelle anglo-américaine', *Géographie et cultures*, vol. 31, 25–47.

Hoke, G. W., 1907, 'The study of social geography', *Geographical Journal*, vol. 29, 64–7.

Holdar, S., 1992, 'The ideal state and the power of geography. The life work of Rudolf Kjellen', *Political Geography*, vol. 11, 307–23.

Holmes, J., 1944, *The Geographical Basis of Government*, Sydney: Angus & Robertson.

Hooson, D., 1981, 'Carl O. Sauer', in Blouet, B. W. (ed.), *The Origins of Academic Geography in the United States*, Hamden: Archon Books, 165–74.

Hooson, D. (ed.), 1994, *Geography and National Identity*, Oxford: Blackwell.

Hoover, E. M., 1937, *Location Theory and the Shoe and Leather Industries*, Cambridge, MA: Harvard University Press.

Hoppe, G. and Langton, J., 1986, 'Time-geography and economic development: the changing structure of livelihood positions on arable farms in 19th-century Sweden', *Geografiska Annaler*, vol. 68B, 115–37.

Hoskins, W. G., 1955, *The Making of the English Landscape*, London: Hodder and Stoughton.

Hotelling, H., 1929, 'Stability in competition', *Economic Journal*, 39, 41–57.

Humboldt, A. von, 1845, *Cosmos: sketch of a physical description of the universe*, London: Longman.

Isard, W., 1956, *Location and Space Economy*, Cambridge, MA: MIT Press.

Isard, W., Schooler, E. W. and Vietorisz, T., 1959, *Industrial Complex Analysis and Regional Development: a case study of refinery-petrochemical-synthetic fiber complexes and Puerto Rico*, Cambridge, MA: MIT Press.

Jackson, J. B., 1972, *American Space: the centennial years*, New York: Norton.

Jackson, J. B., 1979, 'The order of a landscape: reason and religion in Newtonian America', in Meinig, D. W. (ed.), *The Interpretation of Ordinary Landscapes: geographical essays*, New York: Oxford University Press, 153–63.

Jackson, J. B., 1984, *Discovering the Vernacular Landscape*, New Haven, CT: Yale University Press.

Jackson, P., 1983, 'Berkeley and beyond: broadening the horizons of cultural geography', *Annals of the Association of American Geographers*, vol. 83, 519–20.

Jackson, P., 1984, 'Social disorganisation and moral order in the city', *Transactions of the Institute of British Geographers*, vol. 9 (NS), 168–80.

Jackson, P., 1985, 'Urban ethnography', *Progress in Human Geography*, vol. 9, 157–76.

Jackson, P., 1987, 'The idea of "race" and the geography of racism', in Jackson, P. (ed.), *Race and Racism: essays in social geography*, London: Allen & Unwin, 3–21.

Jackson, P., 1988, 'Definitions of the situation: neighbourhood change and local politics in Chicago', in Eyles, J. and Smith, D. M. (eds.), *Qualitative Methods in Human Geography*, Cambridge: Polity Press, 49–74.

Jackson, P. and Smith, S. J., 1984, *Exploring Social Geography*, London: Allen & Unwin.

Jackson, R., 1978, 'Mormon perception and settlement', *Annals of the Association of American Geographers*, vol. 68, 317–34.

Jackson, W. A. D., 1964, *Politics and Geographic Relationships*, Englewood Cliffs, NJ: Prentice Hall.

Jacobs, J. and Nash, C., 2003, 'Too little, too much: cultural feminist geographies', *Gender, Place and Culture*, vol. 10, no. 3, 265–79.

James, Preston, 1931, 'Vicksburg, a study in urban geography', *Geographical Review*, vol. 21, 234–43.

Jean-Brunhes Delamarre, M., 1975, 'Jean Brunhes (1869–1930)', in *Les Géographes français*, Paris: Bibliothèque Nationale, 49–80.

Johnson, J. H. and Pooley, C. G. (eds.), 1982, *The Structure of 19th-Century Cities*, London: Croom Helm.

Johnson, N. C., 1992, 'Nation-building, language and education: the geography of teacher recruitment in Ireland, 1925–1955', *Political Geography Quarterly*, vol. 11, 170–89.

Johnston, R. J., 1979, *Political, Electoral and Spatial Systems*, London: Oxford University Press.

Johnston, R. J., 1997, *Geography and Geographers: Anglo-American human geography since 1945*, 5th edn., London: Edward Arnold.

Johnston, R. J., Pattie, C. J. and Alsopp, J. G., 1988, *A Nation Dividing? The electoral map of Great Britain, 1979–1987*, London: Longman.

Jones, J. P., III, 1995, 'Making geography objectively: ocularity, representation, and *The Nature of Geography*', in Natter, W., Schatzki, T. R. and Jones, J. P., III (eds.), *Objectivity and its Other*, London: Guilford Press, 67–92.

Jones, S. B., 1954, 'A unified field theory of political geography', *Annals of the American Association of Geographers*, vol. 44, 111–23.

Juillard, E., 1953, *La Vie rurale dans la plaine de Basse-Alsace. Essai de géographie sociale*, Paris-Strasbourg: Le Roux.

Kalaora, B. and Savoye, A., 1989, *Les Inventeurs oubliés. Le Play et ses continuateurs aux origines des sciences sociales*, Seyssel: Champ Vallon.

Kant, E., 1951, *Studies in Rural-Urban Interaction*, Lund: Gleerups, Lund Studies in Geography, Series B (Human Geography) no. 3.

Kant, I., 1970, 'Perpetual peace', in *Kant's Political Writings*, Cambridge: Cambridge University Press (also in *Werke XI*, Frankfurt am Main: Suhrkamp, 1977).

Kashani-Sabet, F., 1998, 'Picturing the homeland: geography and national identity in late 19th–early 20th-century Iran', *Journal of Historical Geography*, vol. 24, 413–30.

Kasperson, R. E. and Minghi, J. V. (eds.), 1969, *The Structure of Political Geography*, Chicago, IL: Aldine.

Katz, C., 1992, 'All the world is staged: intellectuals and the projects of ethnography', *Environment and Planning D: Society and Space*, vol. 10, 495–510.

Kay, J., 1991, 'Landscapes of women and men: rethinking the regional historical geography of the United States and Canada', *Journal of Historical Geography*, vol. 17, 435–52.

Kearns, G., 1985, *Urban Epidemics and Historical Geography: cholera in London, 1848–9*, Historical Geography Research Series, Norwich: Geo Books.

Keith, M. and Pile, S. (eds.), 1993, *Place and the Politics of Identity*, London: Routledge.

Kenworthy Tether, E. (ed.), 1999, *Embodied Geographies: spaces, bodies and rites of passage*, London: Routledge.

Kimble, G. H. T., 1951, 'The inadequacy of the regional concept', in Stamp, L. D. and Wooldridge, S. W. (eds.), *London Essays in Geography: Rodwell Jones Memorial Volume*, London: Longmans, Green & Co., 151–74.

Kinda, A., 1997, 'Some traditions and methodologies of Japanese historical geography', *Journal of Historical Geography*, vol. 23, 62–75.

Knox, P. L. and Taylor, P. J. (eds.), 1995, *World Cities in a World-System*, New York: Cambridge University Press.

Knüll, B., 1903, *Historische Geographie Deutschlands im Mittelalter*, Breslau: Ferdinand Hirt.

Kolossov, V. A. (ed.), 2000, *Geopoliticheskoe polozhenie Rossii: predstavlenija i realnost* ('The geopolitical position of Russia. Perceptions and reality'), Moscow: Art-courier.

Konrad, V., 1986, 'Focus: nationalism in the landscape of Canada and the United States', *Canadian Geographer*, vol. 30, 167–80.

Koopmans, T. and Beckmann, M., 1957, 'Assignment problems and the location of economic activities', in Koopmans, T., *Three Essays on the State of Economic Science*, New York: McGraw-Hill, 165–220.

Korinman, M., 1990, *Quand l'Allemagne pensait le monde. Grandeur et décadence d'une géopolitique*, Paris: Fayard.

Kost, K., 1999, 'Anti-Semitism in German geography 1900–1945', *GeoJournal*, vol. 46, 285–91.

Kretschmer, K., 1904, *Historische Geographie von Mitteleuropa*, Munich.

Krim, A. J., 1969, 'Coney Island of the mind and related urban districts', *Monadnock*, vol. 43, 8–24.

Kristof, L. K. D., 1994, 'The image and vision of the fatherland: the case of Poland in comparative perspective', in Hooson, D. (ed.), *Geography and National Identity*, Oxford: Blackwell, 221–32.

Krugman, P., 1991, *Geography and Trade*, Leuven, Belgium: Leuven University Press.

Krugman, P., 1996, *Development, Geography, and Economic Theory*, Cambridge, MA: MIT Press.

Kuhn, T. S., 1962, *The Structure of Scientific Revolutions*, Chicago, IL: University of Chicago Press.

Kuklinski, A. and Petrella, R., 1972, *Growth Poles and Regional Policies, A Seminar*, The Hague: Mouton.

Lacoste, Y., 1977, *La Géographie, ça sert, d'abord, à faire la guerre*, Paris: Maspero.

Lacoste, Y., 1993, 'Préambule', in *Dictionnaire de géopolitique*, Paris: Flammarion, 1–35.

Latour, B., 1990, *Science in Action. How to follow scientist and engineers through society*, Cambridge, MA: Harvard University Press.

Latour, B., 1999, *Politiques de la nature. Comment faire entrer les sciences en démocratie*, Paris: La Découverte.

Laurie, N., Dwyer, C., Holloway, S. and Smith, F. M., 1999, *Geographies of New Femininities*, Harlow: Pearson Education.

Laurier, E., 1996, 'City of Glas/z', University of Wales, Lampeter: unpublished Ph.D. thesis.

Laurier, E., 1999, 'Geographies of talk: "Max left a message for you"', *Area*, vol. 31, 36–45.

Laurier, E. and Philo, C., 1999, 'X-morphising: review essay of Bruno Latour's *Aramis, or the Love of Technology*', *Environment and Planning A*, 1047–71.

Le Lannou, M., 1976, 'Des géographes contre la géographie', *Le Monde*, 8–9 February.

Ledrut, R., 1977, *L'Espace en question*, Paris: Anthropos.

Lefebvre, H., 1974, *La Production de l'espace*, Paris: Anthropos.

Leighly, J., 1976, 'Carl Ortwin Sauer, 1889–1975', in Freeman, T. W. and Pinchemel, P. H. (eds.), *Geographers*, 99–108.

Leith, C. K., 1931, *World Minerals and World Politics*, New York: McGraw-Hill.

Leroi-Gourhan, A., 1943–5, *Évolution et techniques*, 2 vols., *L'Homme et la matière*, *Milieu et techniques*, Paris: Albin Michel.

Levainville, J., 1913, *Rouen. Étude d'une agglomération urbaine*, Paris: Armand Colin.

Lévi-Strauss, C., 1958, *Anthropologie structurale*, Paris: Plon.

Lévy, J., 1994, *L'Espace légitime: sur la dimension géographique de la fonction politique*, Paris: Presses de la fondation nationale des sciences politiques.

Lévy, J., 1996, 'Une nouvelle géographie vient au monde', *Le Débat*, vol. 92, 43–57.

Lévy, J., 1997, *Europe. Une géographie*, Paris: Hachette.

Lévy, J., 1999a, *Le Tournant géographique: penser l'espace pour lire le monde*, Paris: Belin.

Lévy, J., 1999b, 'L'esprit des lieux', in Lévy, J. and Lussault, M. (eds.), *Logiques de l'espace, esprit des lieux* (textes préparatoires au colloque de Cerisy, 21–26 septembre 1999), 1–31.

Lewis, M. and Wigen, K., 1997, *Myth of Continents: a critique of metacartography*, Los Angeles, CA: University of California Press.

Ley, D., 1974, *The Black Inner City as Frontier Outpost: images and behavior of a Philadelphia neighborhood*, Washington, D.C.: Association of American Geographers Monograph Series no. 7.

Ley, D., 1977, 'Social geography and the taken-for-granted world', *Transactions of the Institute of British Geographers*, vol. 2 (NS), 498–512.

Ley, D., 1978, 'Social geography and social action', in Ley, D. and Samuels, M. S. (eds.), *Humanistic Geography: prospects and problems*, London: Croom Helm, 41–57.

Ley, D., 1980, 'Geography without man: a humanistic critique', University of Oxford: School of Geography Research Paper no. 24.

Ley, D., 1981, 'Behavioural geography and the philosophies of meaning', in Cox, K. and Golledge, R. G. (eds.), *Behavioural Problems in Geography Revisited*, London: Methuen, 209–30.

Ley, D., 1988, 'Interpretative social research in the inner city', in Eyles, J. (ed.), *Research in Human Geography: introduction and investigations*, Oxford: Blackwell, 121–38.

Ley, D., 2003, 'Forgetting postmodernism? Recuperating a social history of local knowledge', *Progress in Human Geography*, vol. 27, no. 5, 537–60.

Ley, D. and Samuels, M. (eds.), 1978, *Humanistic Geography: problems and prospects*, London: Croom Helm.

Lézy, E., 2000, *Guyane, Guyanes*, Paris: Belin.

Lipietz, A., 1974, *Le Tribut foncier urbain*, Paris: Maspero.

Lipietz, A., 1986, 'New tendencies in the international division of labor: regimes of accumulation and modes of social regulation', in Scott, A. J. and Storper, M. (eds.), *Production, Work, Territory: the anatomy of industrial capitalism*, Boston: Allen and Unwin, 16–40.

Lipset, S. M. and Rokkan, S., 1967, 'Cleavage structures, party systems and voter alignments: an introduction', in Lipset, S. M. and Rokkan, S. (eds.), *Party Systems and Voter Alignments*, New York: The Free Press, 3–64.

Livingston, D., 1992, *The Geographical Tradition. Episodes in the history of a contested enterprise*, Oxford: Blackwell.

Lloyd, P. E. and Dicken, P., 1972, *Location in Space: a theoretical approach to economic geography*, New York: Harper & Row.

Lösch, A., 1940, *Die räumliche Ordnung der Wirtschaft*, Jena: Gustav Fischer. Translated in Lösch, A., [1941] 1954, *The Economics of Location*, New Haven, CT: Yale University Press.

Lotman, J., 1985, *La Semiosfera: l'asimmetria e il dialogo nelle strutture pensanti*, Venice: Marsilio.

Lovering, J., 1999, 'Theory led by policy: the inadequacies of the new regionalism', *International Journal of Urban and Regional Research*, 23, 379–95.

Lowenthal, D., 1961, 'Geography, experience and imagination: towards a geographical epistemology', *Annals of the Association of American Geographers*, vol. 51, 241–60.

Lowenthal, D., 1975, 'The place of the past in the American landscape', in Lowenthal, D. and Bowden, M. J. (eds.), *Geographies of the Mind: essays in historical geosophy in honor of John Kirkland Wright*, New York: Oxford University Press, 89–118.

Lowenthal, D., 1994, 'European and English landscapes as national symbols', in Hooson, D. (ed.), *Geography and National Identity*, Oxford: Blackwell, 14–38.

Lowenthal, D. and Prince, H., 1965, 'English landscape tastes', *Geographical Review*, vol. 55, 186–222.

Lukermann, F., 1983, 'Edited roundtable discussion', in Buttimer, A. (ed.), *The Practice of Geography*, London: Longman, 196–208.

Lukermann, F., 1989, 'The Nature of Geography: *post hoc, ergo propter hoc?*', in Entrikin, J. N. and Brunn, S. (eds.), *Reflections of Richard Hartshorne's 'The Nature of Geography'*, Washington, D.C.: Association of American Geographers.

Lussault, M., 1993, *Tours: image de la ville et politique urbaine*, Tours: Collection Sciences de La Ville 3.

Lussault, M., 1997, 'Des récits et des lieux: le registre identitaire dans l'action urbaine', *Annales de géographie*, vol. 597, 522–30.

McCarty, H. H. and Lindberg, J. B., 1966, *A Preface to Economic Geography*, Englewood Cliffs, NJ: Prentice-Hall.

McDowell, L., 1983, 'Towards an understanding of the gender division of urban space', *Environment and Planning D: Society and Space*, vol. 1, 59–72.

McDowell, L., 1992, 'Doing gender: feminism, feminists and research methods in human geography', *Transactions of the Institute of British Geographers*, vol. 17, 399–416.

McDowell, L., 1994, 'The transformation of cultural geography', in Gregory, D., Martin, R. and Smith, G. (eds.), *Human Geography: society, space, and social science*, New York: Macmillan, 146–73.

McDowell, L., 1997, *Capital Culture: gender at work in the city*, Oxford: Blackwell.

McDowell, L., 1999, *Gender, Identity and Place: understanding feminist geographies*, Cambridge: Polity Press.

McDowell, L. and Court, G., 1994, 'Performing work: bodily representations in merchant banks', *Environment and Planning D: Society and Space*, vol. 12, 727–50.

McDowell, L. and Massey, D., 1984, 'A woman's place?', in Massey, D. and Allen, J. (eds.), *Geography Matters!*, Cambridge: Cambridge University Press.

McEwan, C., 1996, 'Paradise or pandemonium? West African landscapes in the travel accounts of Victorian Women', *Journal of Historical Geography*, vol. 22, 68–83.

McManis, D. R., 1964, 'The Initial Evaluation and Utilization of the Illinois Prairies, 1815–1840', Chicago, IL: University of Chicago, Department of Geography Research Paper no. 94.

MacEachren, A., 1994, 'Visualization in modern cartography: setting the agenda', in MacEachren, A. and Taylor, D. (eds.), *Visualization in Modern Cartography*, Tarrytown, NY: Elsevier Science, 1–12.

MacEachren, A. and Kraak, M.-J., 1997, 'Exploratory cartographic visualization: advancing the agenda', *Computers and Geosciences*, vol. 24, no. 3, 335–45.

MacIntyre, A., 1984, *After Virtue: a study in moral theory*, South Bend, IN: University of Notre Dame Press.

Macaulay, T. B., 1849, *The History of England from the Accession of James II*, London: Longman, Green and Co.

Mackenzie, S., 1988, 'Balancing our space and time: the impact of women's organisation on the British city, 1920–1980', in Little, J., Peake, L. and Richardson, P. (eds.), *Women in Cities: gender and the urban environment*, London: Macmillan, 41–60.

Mackenzie, S., 1989, *Visible Histories: women and environments in a postwar British city*, London: McGill-Queen's University Press.

Mackinder, H. J., 1904, 'The geographical pivot of history', *Geographical Journal*, vol. 23, 421–42.

Mackinder, H. J., 1919, *Democratic Ideals and Reality: a study in the politics of reconstruction*, London: Constable.

Mackinder, H. J., 1943, 'The round world and the winning of the peace', *Foreign Affairs*, vol. 21, 595–605.

Manshard, W., 1961, *Die geographischen Grundlagen der Wirtschaft Ghanas, unter besonderer Berücksichtigung der agrarischen Entwicklung*, Wiesbaden: F. Steiner.

Mantel, N., 1967, 'The detection of disease clustering using a generalised regression approach', *Cancer Research*, vol. 27, 209–20.

Marié, M., 1989, *Les Terres et les mots*, Paris: Klincksieck.

Marsh, G., 1864, *Man and Nature, or Physical Geography as Modified by Human Action*, New York: Scribner's.

Marsh, G., 1874, *The Earth as Modified by Human Action*, New York: Scribner's.

Marshall, A., 1890, *Principles of Economics*, London: Macmillan.

Marston, S., 2000, 'The social construction of scale', *Progress in Human Geography*, vol. 24, 219–42.

Martin, G., 1998, 'The emergence and development of geographic thought in New England', *Economic Geography*, 1–13.

Martin, R. and Sunley, P., 1996, 'Paul Krugman's geographical economics and its implications for regional development theory: a critical assessment', *Economic Geography*, 72, 259–92.

Massey, D., 1974, *Towards a Critique of Industrial Location Theory*, London: Centre for Environmental Studies, report no. 5.

Massey, D., 1984, *Spatial Division of Labour: social structures and the geography of production*, London: Macmillan.

Massey, D., 1992, 'Politics and space/time', *New Left Review*, vol. 196, 65–84.

Massey, D., 1994, *Space, Place and Gender*, Cambridge: Polity Press.

Massey, D., 1999, 'Spaces of politics', in Massey, D., Allen, J. and Sarre, P. (eds.), *Human Geography Today*, Cambridge: Polity Press, 279–94.

Massey, D. and Meegan, R. A., 1979, 'The geography of industrial reorganisation: the spatial effects of the restructuring of the electrical engineering sector under the Industrial Reorganisation Corporation', *Progress in Planning*, 10, 155–237.

Massey, D. and Meegan, R., 1982, *The Anatomy of Job Loss: the how, why and where of employment decline*, London: Methuen.

Matless, D., 1998, *Landscape and Englishness*, London: Reaktion.

Matless, D. and Philo, C., 1991, 'Nature's geographies: social and cultural perspectives', in Philo, C. (comp.), *New Words, New Worlds: reconceptualising social and cultural geography*, Lampeter: Social and Cultural Geography Study Group, 39–48.

Mattingly, D. J., and Falconer-Al-Hindi, K., 1995, 'Should women count? A context for the debate', *The Professional Geographer*, vol. 47, no. 4, 427–35.

Mauss, M., 1947, *Manuel d'ethnologie*, Paris: Payot.

Mauss, M. and Beuchat, H., 1906, 'Essai sur les variations saisonnières des sociétés eskimos. Études de morphologie sociale', *L'Année sociologique*, vol. 11, republished in Mauss, M., 1950, *Sociologie et anthropologie*, Paris: PUF, 393–4.

May, J., 1970, *Kant's Concept of Geography and its Relation to Recent Geographical Thought*, Toronto: Toronto University Press.

May, J., 1972, 'A reply to Professor Hartshorne', *Canadian Geographer*, vol. 16, 79–81.

Mayer, R., 1965, 'Prix du sol et prix du temps', *Bulletin de l'Association Professionelle des Ingénieurs des Ponts et Chaussées et des Mines*, 10, 9–37.

Meinig, D. (ed.), 1979, *Interpretation of Ordinary Landscapes*, New York: Oxford University Press.

Meinig, D. W., 1979a, 'Some idealizations of American communities', in Meinig, D. W. (ed.), *The Interpretation of Ordinary Landscapes: geographical essays*, New York: Oxford University Press, 164–92.

Meinig, D. W., 1979b, 'Reading the landscape: an appreciation of W. G. Hoskins and J. B. Jackson', in Meinig, D. W. (ed.), *The Interpretation of Ordinary Landscapes: geographical essays*, New York: Oxford University Press, 195–244.

Meitzen, A., 1895, *Siedlung und Agrarwesen der Westgermanen und Ostgermanen, der Kelten, Römer, Finnen und Slawen*, 4 vols., Berlin: Hertz.

Merlin, P., 1966, 'Modèle d'urbanisation spontanée', *Cahiers de l'Institut d'Aménagement et d'Urbanisme de la Région Parisienne*, 3.

Merrifield, A., 1993, 'Place and space: a Lefebvrian reconciliation', *Transactions of the Institute of British Geographers*, vol. 18 (NS), 516–31.

Merton, R. K., 1957, 'Manifest and latent functions', in Merton, R. K., *Social Theory and Social Structure*, Glencoe: The Free Press, 19–84.

Meynier, A., 1959, *Les Paysages agraires*, Paris: Armand Colin.

Meynier, A., 1969, *Histoire de la pensée géographique en France*, Paris: PUF.

Michelet, J., 1833, *Tableau de la France*, vol. 2, part 1 of *Histoire de France*, 2 vols., Paris: Hachette.

Mikesell, M. W., 1975, 'The rise and decline of "sequent occupance": a chapter in the history of American geography', in Lowenthal, D. and Bowden, M. J. (eds.), *Geographies of the Mind: essays in historical geosophy in honor of John Kirkland Wright*, New York: Oxford University Press, 149–70.

Mikesell, M., 1994, 'Afterword: new interests, unsolved problems, and persisting tasks', in Foote, K., Hugill, P., Mathewson, K. and Smith, J. (eds.), 1994, *Re-reading Cultural Geography*, Austin, TX: University of Texas Press, 437–44.

Miller, R., 1982, 'Household activity patterns in 19th-century suburbs: a time-geographic exploration', *Annals of the Association of American Geographers*, vol. 72, 355–71.

Mitchell, D., 1995, 'There's no such thing as culture: towards a reconceptualisation of the idea of culture in geography', *Transactions of the Institute of British Geographers*, vol. 20 (NS), 102–16.

Moellering, H., 1991, 'Whither analytical cartography', *Cartography and Geographic Information Systems*, vol. 18, no. 1, 7–9.

Mondada, L. and Söderström, O., 1993a, 'Du texte à l'interaction: parcours à travers la géographie culturelle contemporaine', *Géographie et cultures*, no. 8, 71–82.

Mondada, L. and Söderström, O., 1993b, 'Lorsque les objets sont instables (I): les faits culturels comme processus', *Géographie et cultures*, no. 8, 83–100.

Mondada, L. and Söderström, O., 1994, 'Lorsque les objets sont instables (II): des espaces urbains en composition', *Géographie et cultures*, no. 12, 87–108.

Mondada, L., Panese, F. and Söderström, O., 1992, *Paysage et crise de la lisibilité: de la beauté à l'ordre du monde: actes du colloque international de Lausanne*, Lausanne: Université de Lausanne.

Monk, J. and Hanson, S., 1982, 'On not excluding the other half from human geography', *The Professional Geographer*, vol. 32, 11–23.

Morissonneau, C., 1978, *La Terre promise: le mythe du Nord québécois*, Montreal: Hurtubise HMH.

Morrill, R. L., 1965, 'The Negro ghetto: problems and alternatives', *Geographical Review*, vol. 55, 339–61.

Morrill, R. L., 1965a, *Migration and the Spread and Growth of Urban Settlement*, Lund: Gleerups.

Morrill, R. L., 1965b, 'The negro ghetto: problems and alternatives', *Geographical Review*, vol. 55, 339–61.

Morrill, R. L., 1970a, *The Spatial Organization of Society*, Belmont, CA: Wadsworth.

Morrill, R. L., 1970b, 'The transportation problem and patient travel to physicians', *Annals of Regional Sciences*, vol. 5, 11–25.

Morris, M., 1997, 'Gardens "for ever England": landscape, identity, and the First World War British cemeteries on the Western Front', *Ecumene*, vol. 4, 410–34.

Mucchielli, L., 1998, *La Découverte du social. Naissance de la sociologie en France*, Paris: La Découverte.

Muir, R., 1975, *Modern Political Geography*, London: Macmillan.

Murdoch, J., 1997, 'Towards a geography of heterogeneous associations', *Progress in Human Geography*, vol. 21, 321–37.

Myrdal, G., 1959, *Economic Theory and Under-Developed Regions*, London: Gerald Duckworth & Co.

Nash, C., 1993, 'Embodying the nation: the west of Ireland landscape and Irish identity', in Cronin, M. and O'Connor, B. (eds.), *Tourism and Ireland: a critical analysis*, Cork: Cork University Press, 86–114.

Nast, H. and Pile, S. (eds.), 1998, *Places Through the Body*, London: Routledge.

National Aeronautics and Space Administration, 1966, *Spacecraft in Geographic Research*, Washington, D.C.: National Academy of Sciences National Research Council.

Newman, R., 1992, *Owen Lattimore and the 'Loss' of China*, Berkeley, CA: University of California Press.

Nierop, T., 1994, *Systems and Regions in Global Politics. An empirical study of diplomacy, international organization and trade 1950–1991*, Chichester: Wiley.

Nijman, J., 1993, *The Geopolitics of Power and Conflict: superpowers in the international system, 1945–1992*, Chichester: Wiley.

Nitz, H.-J., 1992, 'Planned temple towns and Brahmin villages as spatial expressions of the ritual politics of medieval kingdoms in South India', in Baker, A. R. H. and Biger, G. (eds.), *Ideology and Landscape in Historical Perspective*, Cambridge: Cambridge University Press, 107–24.

Nora, P. (ed.), 1984–92, *Les Lieux de mémoire*, Paris: Gallimard.

Norton, W., 1984, *Historical Analysis in Geography*, London: Longman.

Norwood, V. and Monk, J. (eds.), 1987, *The Desert Is No Lady: southwestern landscapes in women's writing and art*, New Haven, CT and London: Yale University Press.

Ogborn, M., 1998, *Spaces of Modernity: London's geographies, 1680–1780*, London: Guilford.

Olsson, G., 1980, *Birds in Egg/Eggs in Bird*, London: Pion.

Olsson, G., 1991, *Lines of Power, Limits of Language*, Minneapolis, MN: University of Minnesota Press.

Olwig, K., 1984, *Nature's Ideological Landscape*, London: Allen and Unwin.

Olwig, K., 1996, '"Nature": mapping the ghostly traces of a concept', in Earle, C., Mathewson, K. and Kenzer, M., *Concepts in Human Geography*, Savage, MD: Rowman & Littlefield, 63–96.

Openshaw, S. *et al.*, 1988, 'Investigation of leukemic clusters by use of a geographical analysis machine', *Lancet*, 272–3.

Osborne, B. S., 1988, 'The iconography of nationhood in Canadian art', in Cosgrove, D. and Daniels, S. (eds.), *The Iconography of Landscape: essays on the symbolic representation, design, and use of past environments*, Cambridge: Cambridge University Press, 162–78.

Osborne, B. S., 1992, 'Interpreting a nation's identity: artists as creators of national consciousness', in Baker, A. R. H. and Biger, G. (eds.), *Ideology and Landscape in Historical Perspective*, Cambridge: Cambridge University Press, 230–54.

Overton, M., 1984, 'Probate inventories and the reconstruction of agricultural landscapes', in Reed, M. (ed.), *Discovering Past Landscapes*, London: Croom Helm, 167–94.

Overton, M., 1985, 'The diffusion of agricultural innnovations in early modern England: turnips and clover in Norfolk and Suffolk 1580–1740', *Transactions of the Institute of British Geographers*, vol. 10 (NS), 205–22.

O'Loughlin, J. and Wusten, H. van der, 1990, 'The political geography of panregions', *Geographical Review*, vol. 80, 1–20.

O'Loughlin, J. and Wusten, H. van der (eds.), 1993, *A New Political Geography of Eastern Europe*, London: Belhaven.

O'Loughlin, J., Kolossov, V. and Vendina, O., 1997, 'The electoral geographies of a polarizing city: Moscow 1993–1996', *Post-Soviet Geography and Economics*, vol. 38, no. 10, 567–600.

O'Loughlin, J. *et al.*, 1998, 'The diffusion of democracy 1946–1994', *Annals of the Association of American Geographers*, vol. 88, 545–74.

O'Tuathail, G., 1996, *Critical Geopolitics*, Minneapolis, MN: University of Minnesota Press.

Paasi, A., 1996, *Territories, Boundaries, and Consciousness: the changing geographies of the Finnish–Russian border*, Chichester: Wiley.

Pahl, R., 1967, 'Sociological models in geography', in Chorley, R. J. and Haggett, P. (eds.), *Models in Geography*, London: Methuen, 217–42.

Painter, J., 1995, *Politics, Geography and 'Political Geography'*, London: Arnold.

Palander, T., 1935, *Beitrage zur Standortstheorie*, Uppsala: Almqvist and Wiksells.

Parker, G., 1982, *Mackinder. Geography as an aid to statecraft*, Oxford: Clarendon Press.

Parker, G., 1988, 'French geopolitical thought in the interwar years and the emergence of the European idea', *Political Geography Quarterly*, vol. 6, 145–50.

Parker, G., 2000, 'Ratzel, the French school and the birth of alternative geopolitics', *Political Geography*, vol. 19, 957–70.

Peach, C., 1975a, 'Introduction: the spatial analysis of ethnicity and class', in Peach, C. (ed.), *Urban Social Segregation*, London: Longman, 1–17.

Peach, C., 1975b, *Urban Social Segregation*, London: Longman.

Peach, C., 1996, 'Does Britain have ghettos?', *Transactions of the Institute of British Geographers*, vol. 21, 216–35.

Peach, C., 1999, 'Social geography', *Progress in Human Geography*, vol. 23, 282–8.

Peach, C., Robinson, V. and Smith, S. J. (eds.), 1981, *Ethnic Segregation in Cities*, London: Croom Helm.

Peet, R., 1975, 'Inequality and poverty: a Marxist-geographic theory', *Annals of the Association of American Geographers*, vol. 65, 564–71.

Peet, R., 1977, *Radical Geography: alternative viewpoints on contemporary social issues*, Chicago, IL: Maaroufa.

Peet, R., 1998, *Modern Geographical Thought*, Oxford: Blackwell.

Perrin, M., 1937, *Saint-Étienne et sa région économique: un type de la vie industrielle en France*, Tours: Arrault.

Perrot, M., 1972, *Enquêtes ouvrières au XIXe siècle*, Paris: Hachette.

Perroux, F., 1961, *L'Économie du XXe siècle*, Paris: Presses Universitaires de France.

Peters, E., 1997, 'Challenging the geographies of "indianness": the Batchewana case', *Urban Geography*, vol. 11, no. 6, 566–85.

Philo, C., 1991a, 'Introduction, acknowledgements and brief thoughts on older words and older worlds', in Philo, C. (comp.), *New Words, New Worlds: reconceptualising social and cultural geography*, Lampeter: Social and Cultural Geography Study Group, 1–13.

Philo, C. (comp.), 1991b, *New Words, New Worlds: reconceptualising social and cultural geography*, Lampeter: Social and Cultural Geography Study Group.

Philo, C., 2000, 'More words, more worlds: reflections on the "cultural turn" and human geography', in Cook, I., Crouch, D., Naylor, S. and Ryan, J. (eds.), *Cultural Turns/Geographical Turns*, London: Longman, 26–53.

Pickles, J., 1986, *Geography and Humanism*, CATMOG 44, Norwich: Geo Books.

Pickles, J. (ed.), 1995, *Ground Truth: the social implications of geographic information systems*, New York: Guilford Press.

Pickles, J., 1999, 'Cartography, digital transitions, and questions of history', *International Cartographic Association*, address at Ottawa in response to Michael Goodchild's keynote presentation.

Pijassou, R., 1980, *Un Grand vignoble de qualité, le Médoc*, 2 vols., Paris: Tallandier.

Pile, S. and Thrift, N., 1995, *Mapping the Subject: geographies of the cultural transformation*, London: Routledge.

Piolle, X., 1983, 'Géographie sociale et relations recherche-société', in Noin, D. (ed.), *Géographie sociale. Actes du colloque de Lyon, 14–16 octobre 1982*, Paris: Centre de polycopie de l'Université de Paris I, 56–65.

Pitte, J.-R., 1983, *Histoire du paysage français*, 2 vols., Paris: Tallandier.

Pitte, J.-R., 1986, *Terres de Castanide. Hommes et paysages du châtaigner de l'Antiquité à nos jours*, Paris: Fayard.

Pitte, J.-R., 1994, 'De la géographie historique', *Hérodote*, vol. 74, no. 75, 14–20.

Pitte, J.-R., 1995, 'Cultures régionales, culture universelle. Eloge de la diversité', *Géographie et cultures*, vol. 14, 3–8.

Piveteau, J.-L., 1995, *Temps du territoire*, Geneva: Editions Zoë.

Planhol, X. de, 1968, *Les Fondements géographiques de l'histoire de l'Islam*, Paris: Flammarion.

Planhol, X. de, 1972, 'Historical geography in France', in Baker, A. R. H. (ed.), *Progress in Historical Geography*, Newton Abbott: David & Charles, 29–44.

Planhol, X. de (with Claval, P.), 1988, *Géographie historique de la France*, Paris: Fayard.

Planhol, X. de, 1993, *Les Nations du Prophète. Manuel géographique de politique musulmane*, Paris: Fayard.

Platt, R., 1928, 'A detail of regional geography: Ellison Bay community as an industrial organism', *Annals of the Association of American Geographers*, vol. 18, 81–126.

Poche, B., 1996, *L'Espace fragmenté. Eléments pour une analyse sociologique de la territorialité*, Paris: L'Harmattan.

Pomian, K., 1986, 'L'heure des Annales', in Nora, P. (ed.), *Les Lieux de mémoire*, Paris: Gallimard, vol. 2, 377–429.

Ponsard, C., 1958, *Histoire des théories économiques spatiales*, Paris: Centre D'Études Économiques.

Popper, K., 1959, *The Logic of Scientific Discovery*, New York: Basic Books.

Pounds, N. J. G., 1963, *Political Geography*, New York: McGraw-Hill.

Pounds, N. J. G. and Ball, S. S., 1964, 'Core areas and the development of the European states system', *Annals of the American Association of Geographers*, vol. 54, 24–40.

Powell, J. M., 1971, 'Utopia, millennium, and the co-operative ideal: a behavioral matrix in the settlement process', *Australian Geographer*, vol. 9, 606–18.

Powell, J. M., 1977, *Mirrors of the New World: images and image-makers in the settlement process*, Folkestone: Wm Dawson & Son.

Powell, J., 1988, *An Historical Geography of Modern Australia: the restive fringe*, Cambridge: Cambridge University Press.

Pred, A., 1981, 'Production, family, and free-time project: a time-geographic perspective on the individual and societal change in 19th-century US cities', *Journal of Historical Geography*, vol. 7, 1–36.

Pred, A., 1981, 'Social reproduction and the time-geography of everyday life', *Geografiska Annaler*, vol. 63B, 5–22.

Pred, A., 1984, 'Place as historically contingent process: structuration and the time-geography of becoming places', *Annals of the Association of American Geographers*, vol. 74, 279–97.

Pred, A., 1986, *Place, Practice and Structure: social and spatial transformation in Southern Sweden 1750–1850*, Cambridge: Polity Press.

Pred, A., 1990, *Lost Words and Lost Worlds: modernity and the language of everyday life in late nineteenth-century Stockholm*, Cambridge: Cambridge University Press.

Pred, A., 1999, 'From living with/in the lines to lines of questioning', *Gender, Place and Culture*, vol. 6, 274–6.

Prevelakis, G. (ed.), 1996, *La Géographie des diasporas*, Paris: L'Harmattan.

Price, M. and Lewis, M., 1993a, 'The reinvention of cultural geography', *Annals of the Association of American Geographers*, vol. 83, 1–17.

Price, M. and Lewis, M., 1993b, '"Reply": on reading cultural geography', *Annals of the Association of American Geographers*, vol. 83, 520–2.

Prince, H., 1971, 'Real, imagined and abstract worlds of the past', *Progress in Geography*, vol. 3, 1–86.

Prince, H., 1988, 'Art and agrarian change, 1710–1815', in Cosgrove, D. and Daniels, S. (eds.), *The Iconography of Landscape: essays on the symbolic representation, design, and use of past environments*, Cambridge: Cambridge University Press, 98–118.

Proctor, J. and Smith, D., 1999, *Geography and Ethics: journeys in a moral terrain*, London: Routledge.

Pumain, D. and Saint-Julien, T., 1978, *Les Dimensions du changement urbain: évolution des structures socio-économiques du système urbain français de 1954 à 1975*, Paris: Ed. du centre national de la recherche scientifique.

Pumain, D., Sanders, L. and Saint-Julien, T., 1989, *Villes et auto-organisation*, Paris: Economica.

Rabinow, P., 1989, *French Modern: norms and forms of the social environment*, Cambridge, MA: MIT Press.

Racine, J.-B., 1971, 'Le modèle urbain américain. Le mot et les choses', *Annales de géographie*, vol. 80, 397–427.

Racine, J.-B., 1973, *Un Type nord-américain d'expansion métropolitaine: la couronne urbaine du Grand Montréal*, Université de Nice, thesis.

Racine, J.-B., 1986, 'Problématique pour une géograhie sociale des espaces sociaux en Suisse', *Geographica Helvetica*, vol. 41, 57–65.

Racine, J.-B. and Raffestin, C., 1983, 'Espace et société dans la géographie french-speaking: pour une approche critique du quotidien', in Paelinck, J. and Sallez, A. (eds.), *Espace et localisation. La redécouverte de l'espace dans la pensée scientifique de langue française*, Paris: Economica, 304–30.

Raffestin, C., 1981, *Pour une Géographie du pouvoir*, Paris: Litec.

Raffestin, C., 1983, 'Introduction à la géographie sociale des frontières', *Espace, populations, sociétés*, vol. 1, 87–8.

Raffestin, C., 1986, 'Territorialité: concept ou paradigme de la géograhie sociale?', *Geographica Helvetica*, vol. 41, 91–6.

Raffestin, C., 1994, 'Territoires, territorialités et argent', in Raffestin, C. and Piolle, X., *Fin des territoires ou diversification des territorialités*, Université de Pau, 10–11 octobre (unpublished).

Raffestin, C. and Bresso, M., 1979, *Travail, espace, pouvoir*, Lausanne: L'Age d'Homme.

Raivo, P., 1997, 'The limits of tolerance: the Orthodox milieu as an element in the Finnish cultural landscape', *Journal of Historical Geography*, vol. 23, 327–39.

Ratzel, F., 1881–91, *Anthropogeographie, oder Grundzüge der Anwendung der Erdkunde auf die Geschichte*, 2 vols., Stuttgart: Engleborn.

Ratzel, F., 1885–8, *Völkerkunde*, 3 vols., Leipzig: Bibliographisch Institut.

Ratzel, F., 1903, *Politische Geographie oder die Geographie der Staaten, des Verkehrs und des Krieges*, revised edn., Muenchen: Oldenbourg.

Ratzel, F., [1899] 1906a, 'Aleria. Historische Landscaft', *Kleine Schriften*, 2 vols., Munich/Berlin: Oldenbourg, vol. 1, 196–203.

Ratzel, F., [1896] 1906b, 'Die deutsche Landschaft', *Kleine Schriften*, 2 vols., Munich/Berlin: Oldenbourg, vol. 1, 127–50.

Raza, M., 1972, 'Geography as a social science', in The Indian Council of Social Science Research, *A Survey of Research in Geography*, Bombay: Popular Prakashan, xvii–xxi.

Reclus, E., 1876–94, *Nouvelle Géographie universelle*, 19 vols., Paris: Hachette.

Reilly, W. J., 1931, *The Law of Retail Gravitation*, New York, Knickerbocker Press.

Relph, E., 1976, *Place and Placelessness*, London: Pion.

Remy, J. and Voye, L., 1974, *La Ville et l'urbanisation: modalités d'analyse sociologique*, Gembloux: Duculot.

Reuber, P., 2000, 'Conflict studies and critical geopolitics – theoretical concepts and recent research in political geography', *GeoJournal*, vol. 50, no. 1, 37–43.

Reynaud, A., 1981, *Société, espace et justice: inégalités régionales et justice socio-spatiale*, Paris: PUF.

Reynaud, A., 1982, 'La géographie, science sociale', *Travaux de l'Institut de Géographie de Reims*, vols. 49–50, 1–164.

Reynolds, D. R., 1969, 'A spatial model for analysing voting behavior', *Acta Sociologica*, vol. 12, 122–30.

Reynolds, D. R., 1981, 'The geography of social choice', in Burnett, A. D. and Taylor, P. J. (eds.), *Political Studies from Spatial Perspectives*, New York: Wiley, 91–110.

Reynolds, D. R. and Knight, D. B., 1989, 'Political geography', in Gaile, G. L. and Willmott, A. (eds.), *Geography in America*, Columbus, GA: Merrill.

Ricoeur, P., 1992, *Oneself as Another*, K. Blamey (trans.), Chicago, IL: University of Chicago Press.

Ritter, C., 1862, *Allgemeine Erdkunde*, Berlin: Georg Reimer.

Robbins, J., 1999, 'High-tech camera sees what eye cannot', *New York Times*, 19 September, D5.

Roberts, M. C. and Rumage, K. W., 1965, 'The spatial variations in urban left-wing voting in England and Wales in 1951', *Annals of the American Association of Geographers*, vol. 55, 161–78.

Robic, M.-C., 1991, 'La stratégie épistémologique du mixte: le dossier vidalien', *EspacesTemps*, vols. 47–8, 53–66.

Rochefort, M., 1960, *L'Organisation urbaine de l'Alsace*, Strasbourg: Publications de la Faculté des Lettres de l'Université de Strasbourg.

Rochefort, R., 1961, *Travail et travaillerus en Sicile. Étude de géographie sociale*, Paris: PUF.

Rochefort, R., 1963, 'Géographie sociale et sciences humaines', *Bulletin de l'association de géographes français*, vols. 314–15, 18–32.

Rochefort, R., 1983, 'Réflexions liminaires sur la géographie sociale', in Noin, D. (ed.), *Géographie sociale. Actes du colloque de Lyon, 14–16 octobre 1982*, Paris: Centre de polycopie de l'Université de Paris I, 11–15.

Rocheleau, D., 1995, 'Maps, numbers, text and context: mixing methods in feminist political ecology', *The Professional Geographer*, vol. 47, 458–66.

Rodaway, P., 1988, 'Opening environmental experience', in Pocock, D. C. D. (ed.), *Humanistic Approaches in Geography*, University of Durham: Department of Geography Occasional Paper no. 22, 50–61.

Roger, J. (ed.), 1979, 'Les néolamarckiens français', *Revue de Synthèse*, vols. 95–6.

Rose, G., 1993, *Feminism and Geography: the limits of geographical knowledge*, Cambridge: Polity Press.

Rose, G., 1997, 'Situated knowledges: positionality, reflectivities and other tactics', *Progress in Human Geography*, vol. 21, 305–20.

Rossiter, D. J., Johnston, R. J. and Pattie, C. J., 1999, *The Boundary Commissions: redrawing the UK's map of parliamentary constituencies*, Manchester: Manchester University Press.

Roupnel, G., 1934, *Histoire de la campagne française*, Paris: Grasset.

Rowles, G., 1978, 'Reflections on experiential fieldwork', in Ley, D. and Samuels, M. S. (eds.), *Humanistic Geography: prospects and problems*, London: Croom Helm, 173–93.

Roxby, P. M., 1930, 'The scope and aims of human geography', *Scottish Geographical Magazine*, vol. 46, 276–90.

Rumley, D. and Minghi, J. V. (eds.), 1991, *The Geography of Border Landscapes*, London: Routledge.

Rumley, D., Chiba, T., Takagi, A. and Fukushima, Y. (eds.), 1996, *Global Geopolitical Change and the Asia-Pacific: a regional perspective*, London: Avebury.

Ryan, J. R., 1997, *Picturing Empire: photography and the visualization of the British Empire*, London: Reaktion.

Ryan, S., 1996, *The Cartographic Eye. How explorers saw Australia*, Cambridge: Cambridge University Press.

Saarinen, T., 1966, 'Perception of drought hazard on the Great Plains', University of Chicago, Department of Geography Research Paper no. 106.

Sack, R., 1997, *Homo-geographicus*, Baltimore, MD: Johns Hopkins University Press.

Said, E. W., 1978, *Orientalism*, London: Routledge.

Said, E. W., 1993, *Culture and Imperialism*, London: Chatto & Windus.

Sandner, G. and Rösler, M., 1994, 'Geography and Empire in Germany, 1871–1945', in *Geography and Empire*, Godlewska, A. and Smith, N. (eds.), Oxford: Blackwell.

Santos, M., 1974, 'Geography, Marxism and underdevelopment', *Antipode*, vol. 6, no. 3, 1–9.

Santos, M., 1977, 'Society and space: social formation as theory and method', *Antipode*, vol. 9, no. 1, 3–13.

Santos, M., 1979, *The Shared Space*, London: Methuen.

Sauer, C. O., 1925, 'The morphology of landscape', *University of California Publications in Geography*, vol. 2, no. 2, 19–54.

Sauer, C. O., 1927, 'Recent developments in cultural geography', in Hayes, E. C. (ed.), *Recent Developments in the Social Sciences*, Philadelphia, PA: Lippincott, 154–212.

Sauer, C. O., 1938, 'Theme of plant and animal destruction in economic history', *Journal of Farm Economics*, vol. 20, 765–75.

Sauer, C. O., 1941, 'Foreword to historical geography', *Annals of the Association of American Geographers*, vol. 31, 1–24.

Sauer, C. O., 1947, 'Early relations of man to plants', *Geographical Review*, vol. 37, 1–25.

Sauer, C. O., 1956, 'The education of a geographer', *Annals of the Association of American Geographers*, vol. 46, 287–99.

Sauer, C. O., [1925] 1963, 'The morphology of landscape', *Land and Life: a selection from the writings of Carl Ortwin Sauer*, Berkeley, CA: University of California Press.

Schaefer, F. K., 1953, 'Exceptionalism in geography: a methodological examination', *Annals of the Association of American Geographers*, 43, 226–49.

Schama, S., 1995, *Landscape and Memory*, New York: Knopf.

Schein, R., 1997, 'The place of landscape: a conceptual framework for interpreting an American scene', *Annals of the Association of American Geographers*, vol. 87, 660–80.

Schlüter, O., 1899, 'Bemerkungen zur Siedlungsgeographie', *Geographisch Zeitschrift*, vol. 5, 65–84.

Schlüter, O., 1906, *Die Ziele der Geographie des Menschen*, Munich and Berlin: Antrittsrede.

Schlüter, O., 1952–8, *Die Siedlungsräume Mitteleuropas in frühgeschichtlicher Zeit*, 3 vols., Hamburg: Remagen.

Schultz, H.-D., 1997, '"Deutschland? aber wo liegt es?" Zum Naturalismus im Weltbild der deutschen Nationalbewegung und der klassischen deutschen Geographie', in Ehlers, E. (ed.), *Deutschland und Europa: Historische, politische, und geographische Aspekte*, Bonn: F. Dümmler, 85–104.

Schultz, H.-D., 1998, 'Deutsches Land-deutsches Volk: Die Nation als geographischer Konstrukt', *Berichte zur deutschen Landeskunde*, vol. 72, 85–114.

Schuurman, N., 2000, 'Trouble in the heartland: GIS and its critics in the 1990s', *Progress in Human Geography*, vol. 24, no. 4, 569–90.

Scott, A. J., 1976, 'Land use and commodity production', *Regional Science and Urban Economics*, 6, 147–60.

Scott, A. J., 1980, *The Urban Land Nexus and the State*, London: Pion.

Scott, A. J., 1986, 'High technology industry and territorial development: the rise of the Orange County complex, 1955–1984', *Urban Geography*, 7, 3–45.

Scott, A. J., 1988a, *Metropolis: from the division of labor to urban form*, Berkeley, CA: University of California Press.

Scott, A. J., 1988b, *New Industrial Spaces: flexible production organization and regional development in North America and Western Europe*, London: Pion.

Scott, A. J., 1998, *Regions and the World Economy: the coming shape of global production, competition and political order*, Oxford: Oxford University Press.

Scott, A. J., 1999, 'The U.S. recorded music industry: on relations between organization, location, and creativity in the cultural economy', *Environment and Planning A*, vol. 31, 1965–84.

Scott, A. J., 2000, 'Economic geography: the great half-century', *Cambridge Journal of Economics*, 24, 483–504.

Seamon, D., 1979, *A Geography of the Lifeworld: movement, rest and encounter*, London: Croom Helm.

Semple, E., 1931, *The Geography of the Mediterranean Region. Its relation to ancient history*, New York: Holt.

Sharp, J. P., 2000, 'Towards a critical analysis of fictive geographies', *Area*, vol. 32, 327–34.

Shelley, F. M., Archer, J. C., Davidson, F. M. and Brunn, S. D., 1996, *Political Geography of the United States*, New York: Guilford.

Shevky, E. and Bell, W., 1955, *Social Area Analysis: theory, illustrative application and computational procedure*, Los Angeles, CA: University of California Press.

Short, J. R., 1982, *An Introduction to Political Geography*, London: Routledge.

Shurmer-Smith, P., 1996, 'Introduction', in Shurmer-Smith, P. (comp.), *All Over the Place: postgraduate work in social and cultural geography*, University of Portsmouth, Department of Geography Working Paper no. 36.

Sibley, D., 1981, *Outsiders in Urban Societies*, Oxford: Blackwell.

Sibley, D., 1995, *Geographies of Exclusion: society and difference in the West*, London: Routledge.

Sidaway, J. D., 2000, 'Postcolonial geographies: an exploratory essay', *Progress in Human Geography*, vol. 24, no. 4, 591–612.

Siegfried, A., 1913, *Tableau politique de la France de l'Ouest*, Paris: Armand Colin.

Simiand, F., 1910, 'Recension critique des thèses de A. Demangeon, R. Blanchard, C. Vallaux, A. Vacher et J. Sion', *L'Année sociologique*, vol. 11, 723–4.

Simonett, D., 1964, 'Possible uses of radar for geoscience purposes from orbiting spacecraft', Lawrence, KS: National Aeronautics and Space Administration, Report CRQ 61–2, 1–13.

Simonett, D. and Brown, D., 1965, 'Possible uses of radar on spacecraft in contributing to Antarctic mapping, crevasse, sea ice, and mass budget studies', Lawrence, KS: Center for Research in Engineering Science, Report 61–4, 1–18.

Sion, J., 1908, *Les Paysans de Normandie Orientale*, Paris: Armand Colin.

Sjaastad, L. A., 1960, 'The relationship between migration and income in the United States', *Papers and Proceedings of the Regional Science Association*, 6, 37–64.

Slater, D., 2000, 'Editorial statement: the process and prospect of political geography', *Political Geography*, vol. 19, 1–4.

Sluyter, A., 1997, 'On buried epistemologies: the politics of nature in (post)colonial British Columbia: on excavating and burying epistemologies', *Annals of the Association of American Geographers*, vol. 87, 700–2.

Smith, D. M., 1971, 'Radical geography: the next revolution?', *Area*, vol. 3, 153–7.

Smith, D. M., 1974, 'Who gets what where, and how: a welfare approach for human geography', *Geography*, vol. 59, 255–67.

Smith, D. M., 1977, *Human Geography: a welfare approach*, London: Edward Arnold.

Smith, D. M., 1979, *Where the Grass Is Greener: living in an unequal world*, London: Penguin.

Smith, D. M., 1994a, *Geography and Social Justice*, Oxford: Blackwell.

Smith, D. M., 1994b, 'Welfare geography', in Johnston, R. J., Gregory, D. and Smith, D. M. (eds.), *The Dictionary of Human Geography*, 3rd edn., Oxford: Blackwell, 674–6.

Smith, G. (ed.), 1995, *Federalism: the multiethnic challenge*, London: Longman.

Smith, G. A., 1894, *Historical Geography of the Holy Land*, London: Hodder & Stoughton.

Smith, J. R., 1913, *Industrial and Commercial Geography*, New York: Holt and Co.

Smith, N., 1979a, 'Geography, science and post-positivist modes of explanation', *Progress in Human Geography*, vol. 3, 356–83.

Smith, N., 1979b, 'Toward a theory of gentrification: a back to the city movement by capital not people', *Antipode*, vol. 11, no. 3, 24–35.

Smith, N., 1982, 'Gentrification and uneven development', *Economic Geography*, vol. 58, 139–55.

Smith, N., 1987a, 'Dangers of the empirical turn', *Antipode*, 19, 59–68.

Smith, N., 1987b, 'Gentrification and the rent gap', *Annals of the Association of American Geographers*, vol. 77, 462–5.

Smith, N., 1996, *The New Urban Frontier: gentrification and the revanchist city*, London: Routledge.

Smith, S. J., 1989, *The Politics of 'Race' and Residence: citizenship, segregation and white supremacy in Britain*, Cambridge: Polity Press.

Smith, W., 1949, *An Economic Geography of Great Britain*, London: Methuen.

Söderström, O., 1994, 'The moral power of representation: trust, rationality and urban conflict', in Farinelli, F., Olsson, G. and Reichert, D. (eds.), *The Limits of Representation*, Munich: Accedo, 155–74.

Soja, E. W., 1968, *The Geography of Modernization in Kenya*, Syracuse, NY: Syracuse University Press.

Soja, E., 1989, *Postmodern Geographies. The reassertion of space in critical social theory*, London: Verso.

Soja, E., 2000, *Postmetropolis. Critical studies of cities and regions*, Oxford: Blackwell.

Solov'ev, S. M., [1851–76] 1959–66, *Istoriia Rossii s drevenishikh vremen*, 29 vols., Moscow: Nauka.

Sopher, D., 1972, 'Place and location: notes on the spatial patterning of culture', *Social Science Quarterly*, vol. 53, 321–27.

Sorre, M., 1948a, 'La notion de genre de vie et sa valeur actuelle (premier article)', *Annales de géographie*, vol. 57, 97–108.

Sorre, M., 1948b, 'La notion de genre de vie et sa valeur actuelle (deuxième article)', *Annales de géographie*, vol. 57, 193–204.

Sorre, M., 1952, *Les Fondements de la géographie humaine*, vol. 3, Paris: Armand Colin.

Sorre, M., 1957, *Rencontres de la géographie et de la sociologie*, Paris: Librairie Marcel Rivière et Cie.

Sorre, M., 1961, *L'Homme sur la terre*, Paris: Hachette.

Sorre, M., [translated from 1953 French version] 1962, 'The role of historical explanation in human geography', in Wagner, P. L. and Mikesell, M. W. (eds.), *Readings in Cultural Geography*, Chicago, IL: University of Chicago Press, 44–7.

Soubeyran, O., 1997, *Imaginaire, science et discipline*, Paris: L'Harmattan.

Spate, O. H. K., 1942, 'Factors in the development of capital cities', *Geographical Review*, vol. 32, 622–31.

Spethmann, H., 1928, *Dynamische Länderkunde*, Breslau: Hirt.

Spethmann, H., 1936, *Das Ruhrgebiet im Wechselspiel von Land und Leuten, Wirtschaft, Technik und Politik*, Berlin: Schmit.

Spivak, G. C., 1988, 'Can the subaltern speak?', in Nelson, G. and Grossberg, L. (eds.), *Marxism and the Interpretation of Culture*, Urbana, IL: University of Illinois Press, 271–313.

Sprengel, R., 2000, 'Geopolitik und Nationalsozialismus: Ende einer deutschen Fehlentwicklung oder fehlgeleiteter Diskurs', in Diekmann, I., Krueger, P. and J. H. Schoeps (eds.), *Geopolitik. Grenzgaenge im Zeitgeist*, Potsdam: Verlag fuer Berlin-Brandenburg, 147–68.

Spykman, N. J., 1944, *The Geography of the Peace*, New York: Harcourt Brace.

Sraffa, P., 1960, *Production of Commodities by Means of Commodities*, Cambridge: Cambridge University Press.

Staeheli, L. A., Kodras, J. E. and Flint, C. 1997, *State Devolution in America*, Thousand Oaks, CA: Sage.

Staszak, J.-F., 1995, 'Geography before geography: pre-Hellenistic meteors and climates', in Benko, G. and Strohmayer, U. (eds.), *Geography, History and Social Science*, Dordrecht: Klüwer, 57–70.

Staszak, J.-F., 1999, 'Détruire Détroit. La Crise urbaine comme produit culturel', *Annales de géographie*, vol. 108, 277–99.

Steinmetz, S. R., 1920, *De nationaliteiten in Europa. Een sociographische en politische studie*, Amsterdam: van Looy.

Steinmetz, S. R., 1927, 'Die Nationalitaeten in Europa. Zeitschrift der Gesellschaft fuer Erdkunde zu Berlin', *Erganzungsheft*, vol. 2, 5–67.

Stoddart, D. R., 1986, *On Geography and its History*, Oxford: Blackwell.

Storper, M., 2001, 'The poverty of radical theory today: from the false promises of marxism to the mirage of the cultural turn', *International Journal of Urban and Regional Research*, 25, 155–79.

Storper, M. and Christopherson, S., 1987, 'Flexible specialization and regional industrial agglomerations: the case of the US motion-picture industry', *Annals of the Association of American Geographers*, 77, 260–82.

Storper, M. and Scott, A. J., 1989, 'The geographic foundations and social regulation of flexible production complexes', in Wolch, J. and Dear, M. (eds.), *The Power of Geography: how territory shapes social life*, Boston: Unwin Hyman, 21–40.

Strohmayer, U., 1993, 'Beyond theory. The cumbersome materiality of shock', in *Environment and Planning D: Society and Space*, vol. 11, no. 3, 323–47.

Strohmayer, U., 1996, 'Pictorial symbolism in the age of innocence: The 1937 World's Fair in Paris', *Ecumene*, vol. 3, no. 3, 282–304.

Strohmayer, U., 1997a, 'Technology, modernity and the restructuring of the present in historical geographies', *Geographiska Annaler*, vol. 79B, 155–69.

Strohmayer, U., 1997b, 'The displaced, deferred or was it abandoned middle: another look at the idiographic-nomothetic distinction in the German social sciences', *Revue of the Fernand Braudel Center*, vol. 10, nos. 3–4, 279–344.

Symanski, R. and Agnew, J., 1981, *Order and Skepticism: human geography and the dialectic of science*, Washington, D.C.: Association of American Geographers.

Takeuchi, K., 2000, *Modern Japanese Geography. An intellectual history*, Tokyo: Kokon Shoin.

Taylor, C., 1989, *Sources of the Self: the making of the modern identity*, Cambridge, MA: Harvard University Press.

Taylor, P. J., 1976, 'An interpretation of the quantification debate in British geography', *Transactions of the Institute of British Geographers*, vol. 1 (NS), 129–42.

Taylor, P. J., 1982, 'A materialist approach to political geography', *Transactions of the Institute of British Geographers*, vol. 7 (NS), 15–24.

Taylor, P. J., 1985a, 'The value of a geographic perspective', in Johnston, R. (ed.), *The Future of Geography*, London: Methuen, 92–110.

Taylor, P. J., 1985b, *Political Geography: world-economy, nation-state and locality*, London: Longman.

Taylor, P. J., 1985c, 'The value of a geographical perspective', in Johnston, R. J. (ed.), *The Future of Geography*, London: Methuen, 92–110.

Taylor, P. J. (ed.), 1993, *Political Geography of the Twentieth Century. A global analysis*, London: Belhaven.

Taylor, P. J., 1996, *The Way the Modern World Works: from world hegemony to world impasse*, New York: Wiley.

Taylor, P. J., 2000, 'World cities and territorial states under conditions of contemporary globalization' (Political Geography Plenary Lecture 1999 plus comments), *Political Geography*, vol. 19, 5–54.

Taylor, P. J. and Johnston, R. J., 1979, *Geography of Elections*, Harmondsworth: Penguin.

Taylor, P. J. and Flint, C., 2000, *Political Geography: world-economy, nation-state and locality*, 4th edn., Harlow: Pearson Education.

Terhorst, P. and Ven, J. van de, 1997, 'Fragmented Brussels and consolidated Amsterdam', *Netherlands Geographical Studies*, vol. 223, KNAG Amsterdam.

Thomale, E., 1972, *Sozialgeographie*, Marburg: Marburger Geographische Schriften, Heft 53.

Thrift, N., 1983, 'On the determination of social action in space and time', *Environment and Planning D: Society and Space*, vol. 1, 23–57.

Thrift, N., 1996, *Spatial Formations*, London: Sage.

Thrift, N., 1997, 'The still point: resistance, expressive embodiment and dance', in Pile, S. and Keith, M. (eds.), *Geographies of Resistance*, London: Routledge, 124–51.

Thrift, N., 1999a, 'Steps to an ecology of place', in Allen, J. and Massey, D. (eds.), *Human Geography Today*, Cambridge: Polity Press, 295–322.

Thrift, N., 1999b, 'Entanglements of power: shadows?', in Sharp, J. P., Routledge, P., Philo, C. and Paddison, R. (eds.), *Entanglements of Power: geographies of domination/resistance*, London: Routledge, 269–78.

Thrift, N., 2000a, 'Afterwords', *Environment and Planning D: Society and Space*, vol. 18, 213–55.

Thrift, N., 2000b, 'Pandora's box? Cultural geographies of economies', in Clark, G. L., Feldman, M. P. and Gertler, M. S. (eds.), *The Oxford Handbook of Economic Geography*, Oxford: Oxford University Press, 689–704.

Thrift, N. and Olds, K., 1996, 'Refiguring the economic in economic geography', *Progress in Human Geography*, 20, 311–37.

Thünen, H. von, 1826, *Der Isolierte Staat im Beziehung auf Landwirtschaft und Nationaloekonomie*, Jena: Fischer.

Tilly, C. H. (ed.), 1975, *The Formation of Nation States in Western Europe*, Princeton, NJ: Princeton University Press.

Tivers, J., 1978, 'How the other half lives: the geographical study of women', *Area*, vol. 10, 302–6.

Tivers, J., 1981, 'Perspective on feminism and geography I', in *Perspectives on Feminism and Geography*, London: Women and Geography Working Party, 4–7.

Tivers, J., 1985, *Women Attached: daily lives of women with young children*, London: Croom Helm.

Tivers, J., 1988, 'Women with young children: constraints on activities in the urban environment', in Little, J., Peake, L. and Richardson, P. (eds.), *Women in Cities: gender and the urban environment*, London: Macmillan, 84–97.

Tobler, W., 1962, 'Map Transformations of Geographic Space', Seattle, WA: University of Washington, Ph.D. dissertation.

Tobler, W., 1966, *Numerical Map Generalization and Notes on the Analysis of Geographical Distributions*, Ann Arbor, MI: The Michigan Inter-University Community of Mathematical Geographers.

Tobler, W., 1993, *Three Presentations on Geographic Analysis and Modeling*, Santa Barbara, CA: National Center for Geographic Information and Analysis.

Topalov, C., 1973, *Capital et propriété foncière*, Paris: Centre de Sociologie Urbaine.

Topalov, C., 1991, 'La ville "terre inconnue", l'enquête de Charles Booth et le peuple de Londres, 1886–1891', *Genèses*, vol. 5, 5–34.

Törnqvist, G., 1962, *Transport costs as a Location factor for Manufacturing Industry*, Lund Studies in Geography, Series B (Human Geography), N°23, Lund: C.W.K. Gleerup.

Törnqvist, G., 1970, *Contact systems and Regional Development*, Lund Studies in Geography, Series B (Human Geography), N°35, Lund: C.W.K. Gleerup.

Trochet, J.-R., 1998a, *Géographie historique. Hommes et territoires dans les sociétés traditionnelles*, Paris: Nathan.

Trochet, J.-R., 1998b, 'Les géographes, les historiens et les autres. A propos des origines et de l'épistméologie de la géographie humaine en France', *Géographie et cultures*, vol. 25, 3–16.

Tuan, Y.-F., 1974, *Topophilia: a study of environmental perception, attitudes, and values*, Englewood Cliffs, NJ: Prentice Hall.

Tuan, Y.-F., 1976, 'Humanistic geography', *Annals of the Association of American Geographers*, vol. 65, 266–76.

Tuan, Y.-F., 1977, *Space and Place: the perspective of experience*, London: Edward Arnold.

Tuan, Y.-F., 1980, *Landscapes of Fear*, Oxford: Blackwell.

Tuan, Y.-F., 1991, 'Language and the making of place: a narrative-descriptive approach', *Annals of the Association of American Geographers*, vol. 81, 684–96.

Tuan, Y.-F., 1998, *Escapism*, Baltimore, MD: Johns Hopkins University Press.

Tuan, Y.-F., 2002, 'A life of learning', in Gould, P. and Pitts, F. (eds.), *Geographical Voices*, Syracuse, NY: Syracuse University Press.

Turner, B. L., 1997, 'Spirals, bridges and tunnels: engaging human-environment perspectives in geography', *Ecumene*, vol. 4, 196–217.

Turner, M., 1981, 'Arable in England and Wales: estimates from the 1801 crop return', *Journal of Historical Geography*, vol. 7, 291–302.

Unstead, J. F., 1907, 'The meaning of geography', *Geographical Teacher*, vol. 4.

Unwin, T., 2000, 'A waste of space? Towards a critique of the social production of space', *Transactions of the Institute of British Geographers*, vol. 25, 11–30.

Urry, J., 1981, 'Localities, regions, and social class', *International Journal of Urban and Regional Research*, 5, 455–74.

Valentine, G., 1993, '(Hetero)sexing space: lesbian perceptions and experiences of everyday spaces', *Environment and Planning D: Society and Space*, vol. 11, 395–413.

Vallaux, C., 1908, *Géographie sociale: la mer*, Paris: O. Doin éditeur.

Vance, J. E., 1990, 'Democratic utopia and the American landscape', in Conzen, M. P. (ed.), *The Making of the American Landscape*, London: HarperCollins Academic, 204–20.

Vant, A., 1984, 'La géographie sociale face aux avatars de l'analyse urbaine', in Collectif français de géographie sociale et urbaine, *Sens et non-sens de l'espace*, Paris: Corlet, 249–62.

Vant, A. *et al.*, 1986, *Marginalité sociale, marginalité spatiale*, Paris: Editions du CNRS.

Vavilov, N., 1951, 'The origin, variation, immunity and breeding of cultivated plants', *Selected Writings, Chronica Botanica*, vol. 13, 1–361.

Veen, H. N. ter, 1931, *De geopolitiek als sociale wetenschap*, De Gids, vol. 95, 285–308, 348–369.

Vidal de la Blache, P., 1880, *Marco Polo, son temps, ses voyages*, Paris: Hachette.

Vidal de la Blache, P., 1902, 'Les conditions géographiques des faits sociaux', *Annales de géographie*, vol. 11, 13–23.

Vidal de la Blache, P., 1903, *Le Tableau de la géographie de la France*, Paris: Hachette.

Vidal de la Blache, P., 1913, 'Des caractères distinctifs de la géographie', *Annales de géographie*, vol. 22, 289–99.

Vidal de la Blache, P., 1917, *La France de l'Est (Lorraine-Alsace)*, Paris, Armand Colin.

Vidal de la Blache, P., 1921, *Principes de géographie humaine*, Paris: Armand Colin.

Vinogradoff, P., 1905, *The Growth of the Manor*, London.

Wagner, P., 1994, 'Forward: culture and geography: thirty years of advance', in Foote, K., Hugill, P., Mathewson, K. and Smith, J. (eds.), 1994, *Re-reading Cultural Geography*, Austin, TX: University of Texas Press, 3–8.

Wagner, P. and Mikesell, M. (eds.), 1962, *Readings in Cultural Geography*, Chicago, IL: University of Chicago Press.

Waibel, L., 1933, 'Probleme des Landswirtschaftsgeograpie', *Wirtschaftsgeographische Abhandlungen*, Breslau.

Wallerstein, I., 1974, 1980, 1988, *The Modern World-System*, 3 vols., New York: Academic Press.

Wallerstein, I., 1974, *The Modern World-System I: capitalist agriculture and the origins of the European world-economy in the sixteenth century*, San Diego, CA: Academic Press.

Wallerstein, I., 1979, *The Capitalist World-Economy*, Cambridge: Cambridge University Press.

Wallerstein, I., 1980, *The Modern World-System II: mercantilism and the consolidation of the European world-economy, 1600–1750*, San Diego, CA: Academic Press.

Wallerstein, I., 1989, *The Modern World System III: the second phase of great expansion of the capitalist world-economy 1730–1840*. San Diego, CA: Academic Press.

Wallerstein, I., 1991, '1968, revolution in the world-system', *Geopolitics and Geoculture*, Cambridge: Cambridge University Press, 65–83.

Walton, J. R., 1987, 'Agriculture and rural society', in Pacione, M. (ed.), *Historical Geography: progress and prospect*, London: Croom Helm, 123–57.

Warntz, W., 1957, 'Geography of prices and spatial interaction', *Papers and Proceedings of the Regional Science Association*, 3, 118–29.

Warntz, W., 1965, *Macrogeography and Income Fronts*, Philadelphia, PA: Regional Science Research Institute.

Warntz, W., 1984, 'Trajectories and co-ordinates', in Billinge, M., Gregory, D. and Martin, R. (eds.), *Recollections of a Revolution*, London: Macmillan, 134–49.

Waterman, S., 1998, '*Political Geography* as a mirror of political geography', *Political Geography*, vol. 17, 373–88.

Weber, A., 1909, *Über den Standort der Industrien*, Tubingen.

Webber, M. and Rigby, D., 1996, *The Golden Age Illusion: rethinking postwar capitalism*, New York: Guilford Press.

Weigmann, H., 1931, 'Ideen zu einer Theorie der Raumwirtschaft', *Weltwirtschaftliches Archiv*, 34.

Wells, E., 1708, *An Historical Geography of the New Testament*, London.

Werlen, B., 1986, 'Thesen zur handlungstheoretischen Neuorientierung sozialgeographischer Forschung', *Geographica Helvetica*, vol. 41, 67–76.

Werlen, B., 1993, *Society, Action and Space: an alternative human geography*, London: Routledge.

Werlen, B., 1995, 'Landschaft, Raum und Gesellschaft. Enstehungs- und Entwicklungsgeschichte wissenschaftlicher Sozialgeographie', *Geographishes Rundschau*, vol. 47, 513–22.

Werlen, B., 1997, *Sozialgeographie alltäglicher Regionalisierungen*, vol. 2, *Globalisierung, Region und Regionalisierung*, Stuttgart: Franz Steiner Verlag.

Werlen, B., 2000, *Sozialgeographie*, Bern: Verlag Paul Haupt.

Wesso, H., 1994, 'The colonization of geographic thought: the South African experience', in Godlewska, A. and Smith, N. (eds.), *Geography and Empire*, Oxford: Blackwell, 316–32.

West, R. C. (ed.), 1990, *Pioneers of Modern Geography*, Baton Rouge, LA: Louisiana State University.

Western, J., 1973, 'Social groups and activity patterns in Houma, Lousiana', *Geographical Review*, vol. 63, 301–21.

Whatmore, S., 1999, 'Hybrid geographies: rethinking the "human" in human geography', in Massey, D., Allen, J. and Sarre, P. (eds.), *Human Geography Today*, London: Macmillan, 22–39.

Wheatley, P., 1971, *The Pivot of the Four Quarters*, Chicago, IL: Aldine.

Whitehand, J. W. B. and Patten, J. H. C. (eds.), 1977, 'Change in the town', *Transactions of the Institute of British Geographers*, vol. 2, no. 3.

Whittlesey, D., 1929, 'Sequent occupance', *Annals of the Association of American Geographers*, vol. 19, 162–5.

Whittlesey, D., 1939, *The Earth and the State: a study in political geography*, New York: Holt.

Whittlesey, D., 1954, 'The regional concept and the regional method', in James, P. and Jones, C. (eds.), *American Geography. Inventory and practice*, Syracuse, NY: University of Syracuse Press, 19–68.

Wilbert, C., 1999, 'Anti-this – against-that: resistances along a human – non-human axis', in Sharp, J. P., Routledge, P., Philo, C. and Paddison, R. (eds.), *Entanglements of Power: geographies of domination/resistance*, London: Routledge, 238–55.

Willems-Braun, B., 1997a, 'Buried epistemologies: the politics of nature in (post)colonial British Columbia', *Annals of the Association of American Geographers*, vol. 87, 3–31.

Willems-Braun, B., 1997b, '"Reply": on cultural politics, Sauer, and the politics of citation', *Annals of the Association of American Geographers*, vol. 87, 703–8.

Williams, C. H., 1994, *Called unto Liberty! On language and nationalism*, Clevedon: Multilingual Matters.

Williams, R., 1983, *Keywords*, London: Fontana.

Wimmer, J., 1885, *Historische Landschaftskunde*, Innsbruck: Verlag der Wagner'schen Buchhandlung.

Wingo, L., 1961, 'An economic model of the utilization of urban land', *Papers and Proceedings of the Regional Science Association*, 191–205.

Withers, C., 1996, 'Place, memory, monument: memorializing the past in contemporary Highland Scotland', *Ecumene*, vol. 3, 325–44.

Wolpert, J., 1964, 'The decision making process in spatial context', *Annals of the Association of American Geographers*, vol. 54, 537–58.

Women and Geography Study Group, 1984, *Geography and Gender: an introduction to feminist geography*, London: Hutchinson.

Wood, D., 1993, *The Power of Maps*, London: Guilford Press.

Wooldridge, S. W., 1946, 'Geography and its components (correspondence)', *Geographical Journal*, vol. 108 (July–December), 275.

Wooldridge, S. W. and East, W. G., 1951, *The Spirit and Purpose of Geography*, London: Hutchinson.

Wreford Watson, J., 1951, 'The sociological aspects of geography', in Taylor, G. (ed.), *Geography in the Twentieth Century: a study of growth, fields, techniques, aims and trends*, London: Methuen, 463–99.

Wright, J. K., 1925, *The Geographical Lore of the Time of the Crusades: a study in the history of medieval science and tradition in Western Europe*, New York: American Geographical Society.

Wright, J. K., 1947, 'Terrae incognitae: the place of imagination in geography', *Annals of the Association of American Geographers*, vol. 37, 1–15.

Wusten, H. van der, 1991, 'Echoes of 1920: Steinmetz' views on the "nationalities question"', in Amersfoort, H. van and Knippenberg, H. (eds.), *States and Nations. The rebirth of the 'nationalities question' in Europe*, Netherlands Geographical Studies 137 KNAG, Amsterdam, 30–41.

Wyckoff, W. K., 1990, 'Landscapes of private power and wealth', in Conzen, M. P. (ed.), *The Making of the American Landscape*, London: HarperCollins Academic, 335–54.

Wynn, G., 1992, 'Ideology, identity, landscape, and society in the lower colonies of British North America, 1840–1860', in Baker, A. R. H. and Biger, G. (eds.), *Ideology and Landscape in Historical Perspective*, Cambridge: Cambridge University Press, 197–229.

Yang, B.-K., 2000, 'Traditional geography', in Yu, W.-I. and Son, I. (eds.), *Korean Geography and Geographers*, Seoul: Hanul Academy, 19–81.

Zanetto, G., 1989, *Les Langages des représentations géographiques: actes du colloque international, Venise*, Venice: Università degli studi di Venezia.

Zelinsky, W., 1972, 'In pursuit of historical geographers and other wild geese', *Historical Geography Newsletter*, vol. 3, 1–5.

Zelinsky, W., 1973, *The Cultural Geography of the United States*, Englewood Cliffs, NJ: Prentice Hall.

Zelinsky, W., 1984, 'Oh say can you see? Nationalistic emblems in the landscape', *Winterthur Portfolio*, vol. 19, 277–86.

Zelinsky, W., 1986, 'The changing face of nationalism in the American landscape', *Canadian Geographer*, vol. 30, 171–5.

Zelinsky, W., 1990, 'The imprint of central authority', in Conzen, M. P. (ed.), *The Making of the American Landscape*, London: Harper Collins Academic, 311–34.

Zipf, G. K., 1949, *Human Behavior and the Principle of Effort*, Cambridge, MA: Addison-Wesley.

INDEX